CareWise For Older Adults

Second Edition

Acamedica Press
A division of CareWise, Inc.
Seattle, Washington
1999

Reviewed for medical accuracy by a
panel of board certified physicians

CareWise For Older Adults: Self-Care For Lifelong Health
Second Edition

Published by
Acamedica Press
A division of
CareWise, Inc.
P O Box 34570
Seattle, Washington 98124-1570

Library of Congress Catalog Card Number 99-94497

ISBN 1-886444-04-8
05 04 03
10 9 8 7 6 5 4

Printed in the United States of America

The medical information in this book was reviewed for accuracy by a panel of board certified physicians and was found to be consistent with generally accepted medical practices at the time of review.

CareWise For Older Adults, intended to provide general information on common medical topics, is not a comprehensive medical text and does not include all the potential medical conditions that could be represented by certain symptoms. In addition, medical practices may change periodically; therefore, this guide cannot and should not be relied upon as a substitute for seeing an appropriate health care professional.

Know What To Do charts © 1999 Acamedica Press and Reliance Medical Information, Inc. (RMI)

Acamedica Press has made every effort to print trademarked product names within this book in initial capital letters to indicate trademark and/or registered trademark designation.

CareWise ®

Where to find what you need

A COMPLETE TABLE OF CONTENTS BEGINS ON PAGE XI

Turn to the first page of each section for specific topics and their page numbers. See the index, pages 365 to 398, for terminology and references as well as specific topics.

IMPORTANT PHONE NUMBERS

Emergencies 11 - 34

When to seek emergency care and what to do until you get help

Injuries 37 - 68

The most-asked-about injuries, from everyday scrapes to emergency conditions

Chief concerns 71 - 294

Close to 200 head-to-toe concerns described in terms of symptoms, prevention, what you can do and when to call a doctor

Medications 297 - 307

How and when to use medications to get the best results

Prevention 309 - 333

A variety of lifestyle and safety tips for getting and staying healthy

Managing illness 335 - 346

Steps for taking charge of your health, whether you are dealing with a temporary illness or a chronic condition

Planning for the future 349 - 357

Ways to plan for the years ahead in terms of lifestyle, care and independence

Helping You Make Wise Health Care Decisions

ACKNOWLEDGMENTS

We wish to acknowledge the many medical and communications professionals who contributed to the publication of *CareWise For Older Adults* including:

Editorial Staff
Diane Volk Young, managing editor
Peg Carver
Randi Holland, RN
Robynn Rockstad
Sherry Stoll, MSN, RN, CNA
Douglas Weiss

Research and Review Staff
Jan Anderson, RN; Katie MacFarlane; Shelby Platt

Outside Support
Contributing writers
Lynn Griffes; Jennie Krull Gulian; George Hein; Dick Malloy;
Marion Brinkley Mohler; Kip Richards, MN, RN; Ginny Smith

Text design, illustration and production/Peter Frazier
Text original design/Digital Ink Corporation
Text illustration/Woodcox Advertising and Communications
Cover design/Michael O'Sullivan
Cover illustration/Deborah Hanley
Biomedical copyediting services/Anne C. Bannister, ELS
Format consulting/Community Services for the Blind and Partially Sighted
Gerontology consulting/Marty Richards, MSW, ACSW
Proofreading services/The Write Stuff, Inc.

Special thanks to our many readers who are helping us continually improve our quality and who are taking the initiative for their own health.

TO HELP YOU WORK IN PARTNERSHIP WITH YOUR DOCTOR

CareWise For Older Adults is not intended to take the place of your doctor or other health care professionals. It is a resource to help you make the best decisions and get the *most* from the medical services available to you.

Contents

SECTION 3: CHIEF CONCERNS 71

Preface

Managing your own health and that of your loved ones is undoubtedly one of your primary concerns. So it should be especially comforting to know that — through this guide — you have convenient access to the health care information you need to help you make the best possible decisions.

CareWise For Older Adults: Self-Care For Lifelong Health is written especially for men and women approaching and in their later years. It gives you the best available health care information to help you decide when to apply self-care, when to seek professional medical care, how to work more effectively with your doctor and, most importantly, how to manage your health.

Health care decisions are personal and important, and they can have a tremendous impact on your overall well-being. Think of this resource as a tool you can use to take charge of your own health and medical care decisions. For many of you, taking charge may be a new concept. In our era of "managed care" you may be required to take greater control of your medical conditions and assume more responsibility for your health than ever before. And that can often leave you with questions and feelings of uncertainty about treatment methods and your best options for care. But it doesn't have to be this way. It is important for you, as a health care consumer, to take an active role in your health care — and this guide can help.

The guide's focus is on self-care and prevention — making healthy lifestyle decisions, understanding your symptoms and medical concerns, participating with your doctor in shared decision making, and effectively managing your medical conditions. Self-care doesn't mean you'll never get sick. Rather, it improves how you use the medical system and handle illness and injury when they do occur. It's never too late to make important lifestyle behavior changes, and doing so can dramatically improve the quality of your life.

We have taken our extensive health education experience, combined it with leading sources of health and medical information, and presented the material in an easy-to-understand format. With *CareWise For Older Adults*, you become the beneficiary of these years of experience — combined with information developed by physicians, nurses and health educators. In addition, the entire guide has been reviewed for accuracy by panel of board certified physicians.

Our goal is to help you become a wise health care consumer, which means getting in the habit of weighing the benefits, risks and costs when it comes to your specific medical concerns. As you do, you will experience better health, greater satisfaction when you seek medical care and — ultimately — the highest quality of care.

Introduction

What is aging?

From the moment of birth, the body begins to age. Physiological and mental changes occur as the years pass. "Aging" is a natural progression driven by the body's changes; however, "growing old" is a state of mind.

There are a number of myths about aging, including the idea that retirement signals the beginning of the end. In fact, the government-selected retirement age of 65 is the result of politics and not the realities of the body or mind.

Your lifestyle may change with retirement; your health doesn't have to. Today nearly eight out of 10 Americans will live beyond age 65 — and life expectancies are at their highest level in history.

Retirees of today may have 10, 15, 20 or more years ahead of them — time to spend on hobbies, start another career and enjoy the fruits of their labors. Quality of life during these years depends on choices you make about your health and lifestyle — choices that can be made with the information found in this guide.

WHAT DOES AGING MEAN TO MY HEALTH?

Getting older doesn't have to mean getting sicker. Most older adults are not seriously ill, and very few (5%) of Americans over 65 are in an institution for long-term health or mental care. The average age of admission is 80.[*]

The key to improving and maintaining your health is prevention, regardless of your age. According to research by the National Institute on Aging, many of the problems of old age are not due to aging at all, but to improper care of the body over a lifetime. In addition, figures indicate that the vast majority of health problems in older Americans are preventable or postponable. For instance, some can be prevented by periodic health screenings (such as mammograms), and by avoiding health risks (such as smoking). Prevention is just as important now as in your earlier years — in some cases more so, because of the increased risk older adults face for chronic illness (see *Prevention*, p. 309; *Managing Your Illness*, p. 336).

[*]Ken Dychtwald, Ph.D., and Joe Flower, *AgeWave: How the Most Important Trend of Our Time Will Change Your Future* (New York: Bantam Books, 1990).

Finding ways to cope with the effects of aging and manage long-term illness is crucial, too. Prevention will help you avoid some acute illnesses and injuries — and delay the onset of chronic illness. Once you have a long-term illness, your challenge is to learn self-management skills. This means moving into a new stage of prevention — one that slows a disease's progression, lessens its impact or helps prevent other illnesses from occurring.

The goal of *CareWise For Older Adults* is to help you prevent illness and manage your health as you get older, as well as to give you the information and self-confidence you need to make wise health care decisions.

A self-care approach

When centenarians are asked about their "secrets for long life," a consistent theme arises: the importance of possessing a positive attitude. In fact, an optimistic outlook on life and the feeling of being in control are essential for *healthy* aging. Helping you learn how to take charge of your health is one of the primary reasons for this book.

There is a common misconception that healthy living is hard work. In truth, an effective self-care approach is much easier and more rewarding than falling into poor health and having to work your way back to good health, or allowing a chronic illness to progress more rapidly than necessary.

A successful self-care strategy has three key ingredients: **prevention**, **participation** and **education**.

PREVENTION

Making healthy lifestyle and prevention decisions can have an enormous impact on reducing your risk of disease. The best place to start is with the behaviors that can make the biggest difference.

Taking steps to exercise regularly, eat a healthy diet, kick the habit if you smoke, reduce your alcohol consumption and use of drugs, and control your weight are essential to successful prevention. In addition to your lifestyle choices, immunizations and screening tests can help you prevent health risks, and identify and manage the onset of disease.

Of course, no amount of prevention can eliminate all disease, which is why your participation in the medical decision-making process is so important.

> Also see *Prevention*, p. 309, to learn more about prevention and recommended immunizations and screenings.

Becoming partners with your doctor

PARTICIPATION

Unfortunately, our use of medical services is based on the hope that modern medicine will provide a treatment and cure for all our bad habits. The result is that we often overuse medical services for situations we can better handle at home. (According to current findings, approximately 80% of all medical concerns can be effectively treated at home.) Also, our expectations for medical care often go unmet because we don't fully understand the importance of our own active participation in the process.

Participation means understanding when medical care is appropriate, and then becoming a partner with your doctor or other health professionals.

Whether your doctor suggests putting you on medication, running a few tests, or scheduling a minor procedure or major surgery — it *always* pays to find out what's going on and participate in making decisions about your health care.

Yes, your doctor has years of training and offers invaluable medical advice. But only you can really decide if the benefits outweigh the risks for your particular situation, and if the treatment plan is something you can live with and incorporate into your lifestyle.

Taking an active role in treatment decisions

- At the doctor's office, begin the conversation with the topics you are *most* worried about — not your minor complaints — and be as honest and direct as possible about your feelings and concerns. Keep it short and to the point, but take the time you need to describe your problem.

- Ask your doctor to explain the various treatment options — along with the benefits, risks and costs of each — before going ahead with *anything*. Questions to ask include: "What is the official name of the test/procedure/ medication?" "Why do I need it?" "What will the procedure involve?" "What are the risks and benefits?" "How much will it cost?" and "What are the alternatives?" Take notes if it helps, and keep all your notes. You may want to refer back to them from time to time.

- If you don't understand your doctor's explanations, be persistent and ask again: "Could you go over that part again?" "Do you have any material I can read at home?" "Can you show me on paper what will happen?"

- If a prescription drug is suggested, ask about the side effects, and the possibility of using a less expensive but effective generic substitute.

- If a major test or surgery is recommended, ask if there are other treatment options that are equally effective, or if you can watch and wait for a while without putting your health at risk.

- Ask if there will be any restrictions on activity and, if so, how long the restrictions will be necessary. If some treatment is suggested that you know you just can't or won't be able to handle, speak up. Chances are you and your doctor can work out a suitable alternative.

- Find out if there is anything else you can do for yourself — besides or in addition to a prescription or treatment — to help the problem or speed your recovery.

Sorting through your options

- If it's a nonemergency, don't rush into anything! Remember that very few medical procedures are actually emergencies. There is usually time to think about the options and select the one that seems best for you.

- If you find you have more questions for your doctor, or need additional information, call your doctor's office or professional telephone nurse counseling service and ask.

Once treatment is decided . . .

- Make sure you understand all the treatment instructions. If not, ask more questions!

- **Carefully follow your treatment plan.** For example, write down your medication schedule and keep a record of each time you take medications. Always fully comply with all instructions, and always talk to your doctor before altering your treatment or medication program (see *Personal Medications Record*, p. 364).

- Keep track of any side effects and call your doctor if you are worried, have any questions or think something doesn't seem right (see *Using Medications*, p. 298).

EDUCATION

When it comes to the health of you and your family, ignorance is not bliss. Learning what your self-care options are — when it is safe to treat health problems at home and when to see a doctor — saves everyone time and money. Being educated means sidestepping unnecessary treatment and testing, avoiding extra medical charges, and requesting generic drugs when they are less expensive but just as effective as name brands.

Additionally, working to improve your health and decrease your need for medical services is critical to solving our national concern over the cost of health care. You can improve the quality of care you receive by combining it with a self-care approach — becoming part of the solution rather than part of the problem.

Using *CareWise For Older Adults*

Let's say it's 1:00 a.m. and your throat is raw and sore. Or it's Sunday afternoon and you've pulled a muscle gardening. You're wondering whether to call your doctor or just wait. The problem is, you need help — now!

Open *CareWise For Older Adults*, a book that's designed to serve as your around-the-clock health care guide.

CareWise For Older Adults covers close to 300 topics, ranging from migraines to menopause, from appendicitis to varicose veins. We suggest you take a few moments, now, to browse through the book and familiarize yourself with its format and contents. We think you'll discover that it's filled with helpful information about all kinds of common, day-to-day health concerns — like what to do if you have a funny-looking mole, suddenly hurt your back or sprain your ankle.

Most topics include general information about the medical problem, as well as tips for:

- Prevention
- Treating the problem at home
- When to seek professional medical care
- Managing the condition

Where to find what you need

- **Emergencies and injuries** are covered at the beginning of the book — where they are readily accessible. **In case of an emergency, call 911 or your local emergency services number.**

- **Chief concerns** come next, and are organized in a head-to-toe fashion — beginning with neurological problems and working all the way through the body, right down to foot and toe pain. (In addition to the table of contents, see the reference chart on page v to quickly find various topics.) The detailed index in the back of the book is designed to help you look up specific words and references and direct you to related topics.

- **Other important sections** include *Medications, Prevention, Managing Illness, Planning For The Future* and an appendix that lists a variety of resources for further information and support.

- *Know What To Do* **sections**, which accompany most topics, are designed to help you decide when self-care is appropriate, when to call a doctor, and when to apply emergency first aid and seek emergency care. Read on for details on how to use the *Know What To Do* sections.

Using the *Know What To Do* sections

- First, read all the general information about the topic. It will help you better understand *Know What To Do*.

- Next, work your way through *Know What To Do.* Don't skip from point to point; each point is based on the assumption that you have answered yes or no to the previous one. Follow the arrows that apply to each of your answers.

- Take action based on the yes arrow that most appropriately applies to your health concern. Or, if *Know What To Do* refers you to another topic in the book, you can turn to that page for additional information. For example, *Know What To Do* for nausea and vomiting tells you to "see *Dehydration,* p. 192 " for details on that particular side effect of nausea and vomiting.

What does each step mean?

Begin emergency first aid **immediately**.

Get professional medical help **immediately**.

Call your doctor's office **now** and alert the doctor — or a nurse — to the problem. Ask them what you should do next. This is a situation that needs prompt, professional attention, but is not necessarily an emergency.

Phone your doctor's office today and talk to the doctor or a nurse about the problem. Make an appointment if it is decided that it's necessary.

Follow the directions for self-care (listed in the *What You Can Do* section) carefully. If you become worried about your condition, call your doctor, health care provider or professional telephone nurse counseling service.

Need more details?

After reading the section(s) covering your medical concern, you may have questions and want additional information. Ask your health care provider for additional medical information to help you evaluate options for care.

> *CareWise For Older Adults* is not intended to take the place of your doctor or other health care professionals. Instead, it is a resource to help you make the best decisions and get the *most* from the medical services available to you.

Emergencies 1

READER'S NOTE:

For medical concerns covered in *CareWise For Older Adults*, you'll find information that will help you determine whether you have an emergency. Look for this symbol.

SEEK EMERGENCY CARE

EMERGENCIES

The time to prepare for a medical emergency is now — not at the scene of a car accident or in the presence of someone who is having a heart attack.

An emergency by definition is an unexpected occurrence that demands immediate action. Staying calm — rather than panicking — is the key, and knowing what to do ahead of time is your best defense against panic.

Being prepared

These steps can help you begin your emergency planning, now:

- Write down the phone numbers of the nearest emergency facility, Poison Control Center and rescue squad in the front of this book and your telephone book.

- Know the best way to reach the emergency room by car, in case you need to drive yourself or someone else there.

- Take first-aid and CPR classes. Make both of them family affairs.

- Wear a medical-alert bracelet or necklace, or carry emergency medical information in your wallet, if you have a condition such as diabetes, epilepsy or serious allergic reactions. This information could save your life if you are unable to speak.

- Make a list of more detailed emergency information. Give a copy of this list to a close family member or trusted friend who can access the information on your behalf, if needed. Include the names and telephone numbers of all doctors (both primary care and specialists); names and dosages of all medications being taken (see *Personal Medications Records*, p. 364); hospital preference; the location of legal and financial documents including your will, insurance policies, Living Will and Durable Power of Attorney for Health Care (see *Planning For The Future*, p. 349); and the name and number of your personal attorney.

- A *personal emergency response system* can help if you live alone and are concerned about your ability to summon help in the case of an accident, illness or threat to your safety. This small, wireless device can be worn around your neck or wrist and can activate a telephone in your home to signal a hospital emergency room. Check with your local hospitals regarding the availability and reliability of this service in your area.

> For suggestions on a variety of safety precautions see *Safety*, p. 328.

IDENTIFYING AN EMERGENCY

It is sometimes difficult to decide whether a situation is an emergency. However, if you think symptoms seem critical or life-threatening, it's probably appropriate to seek emergency care.

These symptoms usually indicate an emergency situation:

- A serious wound (see *Wounds*, p. 38) or a broken bone (see *Broken Bones*, p. 59)
- No pulse or breathing (see *CPR*, p. 14)
- Unconsciousness (see *Unconsciousness*, p. 31)
- Active bleeding (see *To Control Severe Bleeding*, p. 39)
- Signs of a heart attack (see *Chest Pain*, p. 162)
- Disorientation in someone who has previously been alert (see *Shock*, p. 33; *Stroke/TIA*, p. 82)

If possible, call ahead to the emergency room to allow emergency personnel to prepare for your arrival. Explain the nature of the person's problem and provide the name and phone number of the person's doctor.

WHEN TO CALL AN AMBULANCE

Although it is always important to err on the side of safety, make sure you have a true emergency before calling an ambulance or aid car. It is expensive, and the medical assistance may be needed more somewhere else.

Generally, an aid car with paramedics is needed if the person has:

- Symptoms of a heart attack (severe chest pain — crushing, squeezing or increasing pressure in chest — shortness of breath, sweating)
- Severe breathing problems
- Possible spinal, neck or head injury (**do not attempt to move the person yourself**)
- Severe bleeding

Cardiopulmonary resuscitation (CPR)

CPR is an emergency first-aid technique for treating a person who is not breathing and has no heartbeat.

This is a skill that is most often used by friends and family members on each other. That is why it is a good idea to encourage each member of your household to learn the techniques.

When it's needed, the person who has the most experience and training in CPR should be the one to perform the procedure at the scene of an emergency.

THINK ABC — AIRWAY, BREATHING AND CIRCULATION

In basic life support, remember ABC:

- **A**irway — Establish an open airway.
- **B**reathing — Reestablish breathing.
- **C**irculation — Begin external compressions if the heart has stopped.

Step one — Check for consciousness/Call for help

- Find out if the person is conscious. Shout, "Are you OK?"

- Move the person only if necessary. Gently roll them over onto their back, keeping the head, neck and shoulders together as a unit. If you suspect a spinal injury, be careful not to move the person's neck.

- If the person doesn't respond, call 911 or your local emergency services number. Then begin CPR, if necessary.

- For children and infants, do one minute of CPR, if needed, before calling 911 or your local emergency services number.

Step two — Check for breathing/Open airway

If no air is passing through the person's lips (put your cheek next to their mouth to check) and the person's chest and abdomen are not moving, they are not breathing and you will need to open the airway (see Figure 1).

- If there is vomit or liquid in the mouth, clean it out with your fingers (cover fingers with a clean cloth if you have one).

> **Cardiopulmonary resuscitation (CPR) is a complex first-aid procedure. Although we describe all the steps for CPR, this section is not intended to replace a course that allows you to have actual hands-on experience with the procedures. To learn CPR, contact the American Red Cross, American Heart Association or other civic groups in your community for classes.**

Figure 1

- Push down and back on the forehead and lift up the chin by placing your fingers under the jaw bone.
- With an infant, be careful not to extend the head back too far since that can shut off the airway.
- Check the mouth, chest and abdomen again for movement. Sometimes opening the airway is enough to get the person to start breathing again.
- If the person does not begin breathing immediately, begin rescue breathing (step three).

Step three — Begin rescue breathing

Figure 2

- Pinch the person's nostrils shut with the same hand that you have on the person's forehead (see Figure 1).
- Place your mouth over the person's mouth, making a tight seal.
- Place your mouth over both the mouth and nose of an infant (see Figure 2). Be careful not to blow too hard into the infant since excess air can go into the stomach and cause vomiting or compression of the lungs. Either one will make delivering air more difficult.
- Slowly blow in air until the person's chest rises. Remove your mouth between breaths and allow time for the person to exhale passively before the next breath.

Step four — Check for pulse

Figure 3

- Locate the main (*carotid*) artery in the neck by placing the tips of your index and middle fingers on the Adam's apple and sliding them toward your own body into the groove between the *trachea* (windpipe) and the muscles at the side of the neck (see Figure 3).
- With an infant, check for the *brachial pulse* on the inside of the upper arm (see Figure 4).
- Hold your fingers in place for five to 10 seconds.

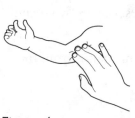

Figure 4

IF THERE IS A PULSE

Continue rescue breathing. **DO NOT do chest compressions on a person who has a pulse.** CPR performed on a person whose heart is beating can cause serious injury. Instead:

• Blow air into the lungs 12 times per minute (once every five seconds) for an adult and 15 times per minute for a small child (once every four seconds). Breathe 20 times per minute (once every three seconds) for an infant.

• Check the pulse once per minute to make sure the heart is still beating. Continue breathing as long as necessary. A person who seems to have recovered needs to be seen by a doctor, since shock is a common occurrence after breathing has stopped (see *Shock*, p. 33).

IF THERE IS NO PULSE

Step five — Begin chest compressions

Figure 5

• Find the lower rib cage and move your fingers up the rib cage to the notch where the ribs meet the lower breastbone in the center of the lower part of the chest (see Figure 5).

• Place the heel of one hand down on the breastbone and your other hand on top of the one that is in position (see Figure 6). In children 1 to 8 years old, use the heel of one hand rather than both hands.

• Do not compress the chest with your fingers. This can damage the ribs.

• Lock your elbows into position with your arms straight. Place your shoulders directly over your hands so the thrust of each compression goes straight down on the chest.

• Push down with a steady, firm thrust, compressing the chest one to two inches for an adult.

• Lift your weight from the person and repeat. Do not lift your hands from the person's chest between thrusts.

• Do 15 chest compressions in about 10 seconds.

Figure 6

• After 15 compressions, quickly tilt the head and lift the chin of the person (as previously instructed), pinch the nose and breathe two slow breaths to fill the lungs. The chest must deflate after each breath.

• Continue this cycle (15 compressions and two breaths) at the rate of 80 to 100 compressions per minute. Check the person's pulse after one minute. **Continue the compressions and breathing until help arrives if there is still no pulse.**

- For children 1 to 8 years old, compress the chest one to one and one-half inches and give five chest compressions to one breath.

Extra care must be taken when performing CPR on an infant

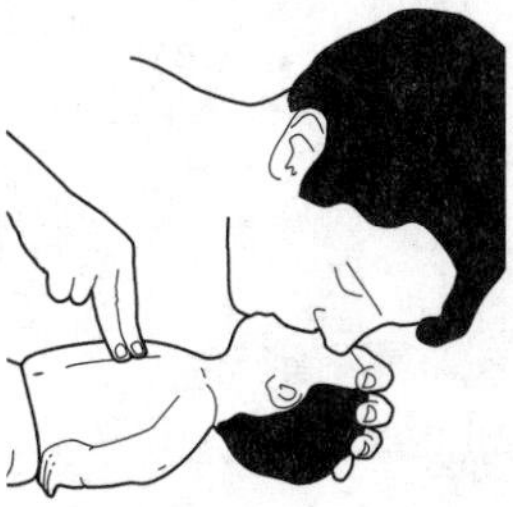

Figure 7

- If chest compressions are necessary, position your index and middle fingers on the infant's breastbone (see Figure 7).

- Gently compress the chest no more than one inch. Count out loud as you pump in a rapid rhythm — roughly one and one-half times a second or about 100 times a minute.

- Gently give one breath (with your mouth covering the infant's mouth and nose) after every fifth compression.

1

Choking

Thousands of Americans needlessly choke to death every year. People of any age can choke on pieces of food, vomit and small objects.

Prevention

FOR YOURSELF

- Take small bites and chew food thoroughly. Cut meat into small pieces.
- Don't eat too fast, or eat and talk or laugh at the same time.
- Don't drink too much alcohol before eating.
- If you smoke, wait until after you've finished eating to light up.

IF YOU'RE RESPONSIBLE FOR A SMALL CHILD

- Keep small objects that children might choke on out of reach.
- Do not let children run or jump with food or any other object in their mouth.
- Inspect all toys for small, removable parts that can cause choking. (Follow label guidelines that indicate "appropriate ages.")

What you can do

IF SOMEONE IS CHOKING

You may have only four to eight minutes to save a choking person's life, so it's important to know how to administer the Heimlich maneuver (see below) and CPR (see *CPR*, p. 14).

A conscious child or adult who is choking will breathe in an exaggerated way. They will be unable to talk or cough, and will probably nod in the affirmative to the question, "Are you choking?" They may grasp their throat. People who can cough or speak are still getting some air into their lungs, and should be encouraged to cough vigorously. The Heimlich maneuver should not be administered in these cases.

CHOKING RESCUE (HEIMLICH MANEUVER) FOR A CONSCIOUS PERSON

- Establish whether the person can speak or cough by asking, "Are you choking?"
- Stand behind the person.

Figure 8

- Wrap your arms around the person's waist.
- Grasp one of your fists with the other hand and place the thumb side of the fist just above the navel but below the rib cage (see Figure 8).
- Thrust your fist upward in five quick, sharp jabs.
- Repeat until the object is dislodged or the person becomes unconscious.

CHOKING RESCUE FOR AN UNCONSCIOUS PERSON

- Call 911 or your local emergency services number.

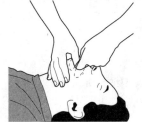

Figure 9

- Check for object in the mouth by sweeping deeply with a hooked finger to remove the object. Use tongue-jaw lift (see Figure 9) and sweep finger to remove object.
- Open airway (push down and back on the forehead and lift up the chin by placing your fingers on the jaw bone). Attempt rescue breathing by pinching the nostrils shut, placing your mouth over the person's mouth, and giving two breaths. If needed, open the airway and try again.
- If object is still obstructing airway, kneel down and straddle either the person's hips or legs.

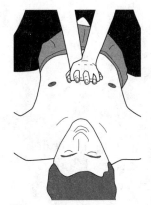

- Place the heel of one of your hands against the person's abdomen just above the navel but well below the rib cage, then place your second hand on top of the first (see Figure 10).
- Press into the person's abdomen with quick upward thrusts. Do this five times.
- Repeat sequence of finger sweep, rescue breathing attempt and abdominal thrusts until successful or help arrives.

Figure 10

OBSTRUCTED AIRWAY IN CHILDREN 1 TO 8 YEARS OLD

Use same procedure already covered with two important exceptions:

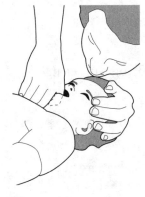

- Look into the airway and use your finger to sweep the object out **ONLY** if you can see it. **DO NOT** perform a blind finger sweep. Instead, perform a tongue-jaw lift (see Figure 11).
- If obstruction is not relieved after one minute, call 911 or your local emergency services number. Of course, if someone else is available, have that person call for help immediately. Continue sequence until successful or help arrives.

Figure 11

OBSTRUCTED AIRWAY IN INFANT LESS THAN I YEAR OF AGE

The following steps are appropriate if there is complete airway obstruction due to a witnessed or strongly suspected obstruction by an object. **DO NOT perform these maneuvers to clear an airway that is obstructed due to swelling caused by infection. SEEK EMERGENCY CARE IMMEDIATELY.**

Infant is conscious

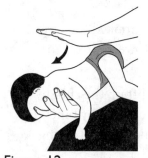

Figure 12

- Hold the infant face down along your forearm, supporting the head and neck with one hand.

- Give five back blows forcefully between the shoulder blades with the heel of your hand (see Figure 12).

- Turn the infant face up. Keeping the head supported and lower than the rest of the body, position your index and middle fingers on the infant's breastbone and give five thrusts with two fingers (see Figure 13).

- Do chest thrusts slower than you would for CPR (see *CPR*, p. 14).

- Repeat until the object is dislodged or the infant becomes unconscious.

Infant is unconscious

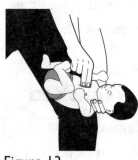

Figure 13

- Place the infant on their back on a firm surface.

- Open the airway (push down and back on the forehead and lift up the chin by placing your fingers under the jaw bone). With an infant, be careful not to extend the head back too far since that can shut off the airway.

- If the infant is not breathing, try to give rescue breaths by covering their mouth and nose with your mouth.

- If unable to give breaths, reposition the head and try again.

- Turn the infant face down and deliver five back blows (see Figure 12).

- Deliver five chest thrusts (see Figure 13).

- Do tongue-jaw lift (see Figure 11). Remove object **ONLY** if you can see it.

- Try again to do rescue breathing.

- Repeat back blows, chest thrusts, tongue-jaw lift and rescue breathing attempts until successful.

- After one minute of emergency first aid, call 911 or your local emergency services number. Of course, if someone else is available, have that person call for help immediately. Continue sequence until successful or help arrives.

Figure 14

IF YOU ARE CHOKING AND CAN'T GET HELP

- Try not to panic.
- Cough vigorously.
- If unsuccessful, stand behind a chair or over some other object that puts pressure on your abdomen just above your navel (but below your rib cage).
- Thrust yourself upon the object using strong, sharp thrusts (see Figure 14).
- Repeat until item is dislodged.

FOR A PREGNANT OR OBESE PERSON

- Stand behind the person and place your arms under their armpits.
- Place fist on the middle of breastbone in the chest, but not over the ribs.
- Place other hand on top of it.
- Give five quick, forceful movements. Do not squeeze with arms, but use your fist.

Final notes

Call your local hospital or American Red Cross chapter for more information and instruction on these procedures. **Those who have just had the choking rescue performed on them should see a doctor. The maneuver can cause trauma to the chest or abdomen, and the object may have damaged the throat.**

Burns

The skin is the body's largest organ, protecting us against infection and helping to regulate the balance of water and temperature. Burns — whether caused by fire, hot objects or fluids, electricity, chemicals, radiation or other sources — threaten these vital functions. For older adults, the very young or those with certain medical conditions, burns can be even more serious.

Burns are classified based on their depth of penetration of the skin.

- **First-degree** burns involve only the tough, outer layer of skin. The skin turns bright red and becomes sensitive and painful. It may be dry, but it does not blister.

- **Second-degree** burns are deeper than first-degree burns and are very painful, red and mottled. The burned area may blister and/or be swollen and puffy.

- **Third-degree** burns are deeper still and can involve muscle, internal organs and bone. The skin will look charred and dry and may break open. Underlying muscle or tendons may be visible. Pain may be severe. If nerves have been damaged, however, there may be no pain except around edges of the burn.

First- and second-degree burns are also called "partial thickness" burns, and third-degree burns are called "full thickness" burns.

What you can do

IF SOMEONE IS ON FIRE

- Try not to panic.

- Help the person drop down and roll in a blanket, rug, coat or some type of covering to smother the flames. Do not let the person run — this will cause the fire to burn more.

- Completely extinguish the fire and stop skin and clothes from smoldering by soaking with water. Do not remove burned clothing.

- Cover the burn with a cool, damp, sterile dressing or a clean, non-fibrous cloth such as a sheet.

- **Seek emergency care.**

What you can do

FOR SEVERE BURNS OF ANY KIND

Make sure:

- Person is breathing. If not, **call 911 or your local emergency services number for emergency medical assistance and start CPR immediately** (see *CPR*, p. 14).

- Bleeding is controlled (see *To Control Severe Bleeding*, p. 39).

- There are no signs of shock: altered consciousness, faintness, paleness, rapid and shallow breathing, rapid and weak pulse, cool and clammy skin (see *Shock*, p. 33).

- There are no signs of charring in the mouth or of nasal hairs. Check for sooty residue on the face, shortness of breath, a cough or hoarseness. If present, these signs indicate an emergency; the respiratory tract may be damaged. **Seek emergency care.**

FOR OTHER BURNS

Electrical burns

- Turn off power before touching someone who is in contact with an electrical wire or appliance. Assume a downed power line is live.

- Try not to move the person.

- If a power line has fallen across a car, passengers remain safest if they stay inside. If they have to leave because of fire or some other reason, they should jump clear of the car.

An electrical burn can appear minor even when it has caused major injuries. There will be wounds at the places of entry and exit of the electrical current that should be evaluated by a doctor.

Chemical burns

- Flush the skin with large amounts of cool, running water for 20 minutes or until the burning pain has stopped. If the chemical is a dry solid, brush it off first.

- If an eye has been burned, flush it immediately with lukewarm water. Angle the head so the contaminant does not flow into the other eye. After flushing, close the eye and cover with a loose, moist dressing or clean cloth, and **seek emergency care.**

- Remove any contaminated clothing, jewelry and other items.

Also see *What You Can Do* on the following page for information on first-, second- and third-degree burns.

What you can do

First-degree burns

- Run cool water over the area or soak it in a cool-water bath for two to five minutes. If this is not possible, apply cold compresses. (If the burn has occurred in a cold environment, **do not** apply water.)

- Cover the area with a cool, moist dressing or clean cloth.

 - Pain relievers — such as aspirin, ibuprofen and acetaminophen (Tylenol) — may help reduce pain and swelling. **NEVER give aspirin to children/teenagers. It can cause Reye's syndrome, a rare but often fatal condition.**

- Sunburn pain may be relieved with oatmeal baths or by adding baking soda to the bath water: one-half cup into cool or lukewarm water (see *Sunburn*, p. 93).

- A broken aloe vera leaf applied to the burned area may soothe the pain.

- While caring for your burn at home, be aware of signs of infection that can develop in 24 to 48 hours (see *Infected Wounds*, p. 42).

Second-degree burns

- Treat like first-degree burns if no bigger than two to three inches in diameter and not on face, hands, feet, groin, buttocks, a major joint, or completely encircling a digit or extremity — in which case you should **seek emergency care.**

Third-degree burns

- Cover the burned area with a cool, moist, sterile dressing or clean cloth and **seek emergency care immediately.**

Prevention

FOR ADULTS AND CHILDREN

- Conduct fire drills at home and work. Know the location of fire escapes when sleeping away from home.

- Install smoke detectors in every bedroom and on every floor and test them periodically.

- Keep emergency numbers by the telephone.

- Place a fire extinguisher in the kitchen and check the expiration date on a routine basis.

- Keep a large box of baking soda within easy reach of the stove.

- Keep a potted aloe vera plant in the kitchen (where most burns occur) and use the fresh jelly found in its leaves for treating minor burns.

 If you have a chronic illness or routinely take prescribed or over-the-counter (OTC) drugs, talk to your doctor or pharmacist before taking any other medications.

- Never put lighter fluid on lit charcoal briquettes.
- Only use kerosene or other space heaters that have the UL (Underwriter's Laboratory) seal of approval.
- Always follow safety instructions when using chemicals, and note any warnings or precautions on the container.
- Learn how to deal with an overheated engine, car fire or live wire on a car.
- Never touch a downed electrical wire.
- Know where all electrical wiring is located before starting construction or renovation. This also applies to any kind of outdoor digging.
- Check with your utility company if you are unsure about the location of power lines in your area.

FOR CHILDREN

- Never leave a young child at home alone.
- Keep matches and chemicals out of reach.
- Turn pot handles toward the back of the stove while cooking.
- Never drink hot beverages with a child on your lap.
- Never place hot beverages or liquids near a table edge.
- Don't use mats or tablecloths that can be pulled easily off a table.
- Make sure pajamas are flame-retardant.
- Cover electrical outlets when not in use.
- Set water heater thermostats no higher than 120° F to 125° F.

> Also see *Fires, Safety*, p. 330.

Final notes

FOR ALL TYPES AND DEGREES OF BURNS

- **NEVER** apply ointments, such as Vaseline, sprays, butter, oils or creams. They may slow healing and increase risk of infection. Use cool water instead.
- **NEVER** cover a burn with materials such as blankets, towels or tissue since fibers may become stuck to the wound. Use a clean sheet or sterile dressing.
- **NEVER** break blisters. Blisters protect the burn from infection and should only be ruptured if swelling constricts circulation.

Heat exhaustion

With age, sweat glands diminish in size, number and activity. This causes a decline in the efficiency of the body's cooling mechanism. *Heat exhaustion* occurs when the body is not able to cool off and maintain a comfortable temperature. Hot weather, dehydration and excessive exercise can cause you to overheat. Older adults, small children and those who are frail, obese or have a chronic illness are at greatest risk, as well as those in poor physical condition who overexert themselves.

Note your symptoms

- Headache
- Weakness
- Fatigue
- Dizziness
- Nausea
- Shallow breathing
- Muscle cramps
- Profuse sweating, cool, clammy skin, or body temperature slightly elevated or lower than normal.

What you can do

If you are overheating:

- Move to a cooler place and remain quiet.
- Loosen clothing.
- With dizziness, lie down with head lower than feet.
- Drink small amounts of liquid frequently.
- Place cool, wet cloth on forehead.
- Watch for signs of shock and heat stroke (see *Shock*, p. 33).
- Do not consume alcohol or apply it to the skin.

Seek emergency help

Heat stroke is the critical stage of heat exhaustion and is a medical emergency. All of the body's cooling systems are overloaded when the body temperature reaches 104° F and continues to rise. Symptoms of heat stroke are:

- Hot, dry skin
- Bright red or flushed skin
- Body temperature of 105° F or greater
- Person becomes delirious, disoriented or unconscious

While waiting for help, sponge the person's body with cool water or apply cool, wet sheets and monitor the person's temperature every 10 minutes. Stop cooling if temperature drops suddenly or signs of shock develop, such as cool, clammy skin and weak, rapid pulse (see *Shock*, p. 33).

Seek immediate care

If symptoms are severe, become worse with self-care or last longer than one hour, **quickly seek professional medical care.**

Prevention

- Unless your fluid intake has been limited by your doctor, drink more than 10 eight-ounce glasses of water a day if exercising or working in hot weather.
- Stay in the shade or in air-conditioned areas. Avoid sudden changes of temperature.
- Wear loose-fitting, light-colored clothing of natural fibers such as cotton or linen.
- Limit your activity and exercise during the hottest time of the day.
- Never leave an infant or child alone in a closed auto in hot weather.

Hypothermia and frostbite

As the body ages, the amount of *subcutaneous fat* — the body's insulation — decreases. This is why older adults often are bothered by feeling cold (see *PVD*, p. 161), and why hypothermia and frostbite can develop so quickly in this age group. In *hypothermia* your body temperature drops below normal when body heat is lost faster than it can be produced. *Frostbite* is the freezing of the skin or tissue near the skin surface. Hypothermia and frostbite can occur even when the temperature is above freezing but the weather is windy or wet.

Note your symptoms

HYPOTHERMIA

This condition can develop quickly and become a serious problem with little warning. Early symptoms include severe shivering, slurred speech, apathy, impaired judgment and cold, pale skin. As the body temperature continues to drop, shivering may stop; the abdomen and chest become cold, and there is slowing of the pulse and breathing. Weakness, drowsiness and confusion may quickly lead to unconsciousness.

FROSTBITE

Initially the skin feels soft to the touch but numb and tingly. It may turn white and, as the skin freezes and becomes hard, blisters may develop. In third-degree frostbite the skin may look blue or blotchy and the underlying tissue is hard and very cold.

What you can do

Treat for hypothermia before treating frostbite.

HYPOTHERMIA

- Get to warm, dry shelter.
- Rewarm slowly. Keep person awake.
- Replace wet clothing with dry clothes, sleeping bag or blankets, and apply body heat from another person, if possible.
- Give warm liquids and high-calorie food. **Do not give alcohol.**

What you can do

FROSTBITE

- Rewarm only if refreezing will not occur.
- Rewarm as quickly as possible.
- Warm small areas with breath or by placing them inside clothing and next to bare skin.
- Immerse body parts in warm (not hot) water of 104° F to 108° F for 15 to 20 minutes.
- Elevate and protect warmed part.
- Do not rub or massage frozen area — rubbing may cause further damage.
- Protect blisters. Do not break them.

- Aspirin or acetaminophen (Tylenol) may ease pain. **NEVER give aspirin to children/teenagers. It can cause Reye's syndrome, a rare but often fatal condition.**
- Watch for signs of infection (see *Infected Wounds*, p. 42).

Prevention

- Dress warmly in layers with wool and polypropylene for insulation and an outer layer that is windproof and waterproof.
- Wear a warm hat with ear protection. Wear mittens rather than gloves.
- Pace activities. Do not become exhausted or sweaty.
- Never touch cold metal with bare skin.
- Avoid alcohol and smoking before spending time in the cold.
- Eat well and carry extra food and water.
- Plan ahead and carry provisions in case of emergency or sudden weather changes.

SEE *Know What To Do, p. 30*

 If you have a chronic illness or routinely take prescribed or over-the-counter (OTC) drugs, talk to your doctor or pharmacist before taking any other medications.

Hypothermia and frostbite
DO THESE APPLY:

• Unconsciousness

• Slowing in pulse and breathing

• Weakness, drowsiness or confusion

• Shivering stops and warming has not begun

▶Until help arrives:

see *What You Can Do, Hypothermia,* p. 28

• Person is a small child, an older adult or frail

• You suspect frostbite
   - Skin is hard, cold, white and blotchy or blue
   - Blisters develop

• Signs of infection 24 to 48 hours after frostbite
   - Redness around the area or red streaks leading away
   - Swelling
   - Warmth or tenderness
   - Pus
   - Fever
   - Tender or swollen lymph nodes

▶Until seen by doctor:

see *What You Can Do, Frostbite,* p. 29

Unconsciousness

When a person is unconscious, they are completely unaware of themselves and their surroundings. They have no control over body functions or movement. Usually they are not able to recall or remember any of the time spent in an unconscious state.

There are many causes of unconsciousness, including stroke, epilepsy, diabetic coma, head injury, alcohol intoxication, poisoning, heart attack, bleeding, electrocution and shock.

IF SOMEONE IS UNCONSCIOUS

What you can do

- Check for breathing. If necessary, open the airway and begin rescue breathing (see *CPR*, p. 14; *Choking*, p. 18).

- Check pulse (feel for the pulse of the person's heartbeat on wrist or side of neck with the tips of your index and middle fingers, as shown on page 15, Figure 3). If no pulse, begin CPR.

- Call 911 or your local emergency services number for emergency medical assistance.

- Keep the person warm unless you suspect heat stroke (see *Heat Exhaustion,* p. 26).

- Lay the person down face up, with their head below their heart level. Move them as little as possible and only to provide life support or safety. **DO NOT move person if you suspect a head or neck injury** (see *Head/Spinal Injury,* p. 51).

- If there is vomit in the mouth, turn the person on their side to allow fluids to drain out.

- Look for medical identification or possible cause of unconsciousness.

- Do not give the person anything to eat or drink.

SEE > *Know What To Do, p. 32*

know
WHAT
TO DO

Unconsciousness
DO THESE APPLY:

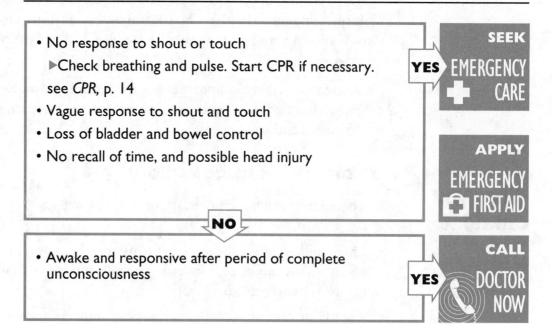

- No response to shout or touch
  ▶ Check breathing and pulse. Start CPR if necessary.
  see *CPR*, p. 14

  YES → SEEK **EMERGENCY CARE**

- Vague response to shout and touch
- Loss of bladder and bowel control
- No recall of time, and possible head injury

  APPLY **EMERGENCY FIRST AID**

NO

- Awake and responsive after period of complete
  unconsciousness

  YES → CALL **DOCTOR NOW**

Shock

If your vital organs are unable to get the blood and oxygen they need, your body can go into shock. Many conditions can cause this urgent situation, including an injury, bleeding, pain, poisoning, extremely high or low body temperature, allergic reaction or a severe illness.

Shock is always an emergency and requires professional medical help immediately.

PREPARING FOR AN EMERGENCY

- Learn your local emergency services phone numbers. Post them somewhere handy.
- Wear identification to alert medical help if you have any allergies or chronic medical conditions.

WHEN YOU SEE SIGNS OF SHOCK

What you can do

- Act immediately when you see any signs of shock. Do not wait to see if the person improves on their own.
- Call 911 or your local emergency services number. Then, while you wait for help to arrive:
  - Have the person lie down and elevate legs higher than heart, with support. **If head or neck injury is a possibility, keep person flat and do not move them** (see *Head/Spinal Injury*, p. 51).
  - If person vomits, roll them onto their side to allow fluid to drain out.
  - Control bleeding by applying direct pressure to wound (see *To Control Severe Bleeding*, p. 39).

SEE ▷ *Know What To Do, p. 34*

- Keep person warm unless cause of shock is heat stroke (see *Heat Exhaustion*, p. 26).

- Note the time. Take and record person's pulse rate every five minutes. (Feel for the pulse of the person's heartbeat on wrist or side of neck with the tips of your index and middle fingers, as shown on page 15, Figure 3. Count the number of beats in 15 seconds and multiply by four: 30 beats in 15 seconds x 4 = a pulse rate of 120 beats/minute.)

- Do not give the person anything to eat or drink.

- Comfort and reassure the person while waiting for medical assistance.

- Look for evidence of cause or medical-alert identification.

Shock
DO THESE APPLY:

• Cool, pale, clammy skin

• Weak, rapid pulse

• Shallow, rapid breathing

• Confusion, anxiety or restlessness

• Faintness, weakness, dizziness or loss of consciousness

• Dilated pupils

• Nausea, vomiting or thirst

see *What You Can Do*, p. 33

Injuries

2

INJURIES

As the body ages, the healing process begins to slow. Injuries that might once have been minor may now become more serious. Other common changes in eyesight, hearing and balance may interfere with your reaction time. This is important to know so you can become better prepared to avoid accidents, as well as handle them if they occur.

From a bump on the head (see *Head/Spinal Injury*, p. 51), to a strain or sprain (see *Strains And Sprains*, p. 55), to a hip fracture (see *Leg Pain*, p. 232), prompt and appropriate action helps minimize the effects of an injury. The key is knowing what to do.

Wounds

There are three kinds of wounds: cuts, abrasions and punctures. All of them — no matter how small — should be cared for promptly to promote healing, prevent infection and reduce scarring.

With every wound there is the potential for infection. Get a routine tetanus booster every 10 years and keep up-to-date immunization records (see *Immunization Schedule*, p. 327). If you have a dirty wound and have not had a tetanus booster within the last five years, or if you have not completed your primary series, your doctor will probably recommend a booster injection.

CUTS

There is rarely permanent damage from shallow, minor cuts (*lacerations*) in which the wound is limited to the skin and the fatty tissue beneath it, and they usually can be treated easily at home.

With most minor cuts, bleeding is slow and stops on its own after a few minutes. Slightly deeper cuts can reach the veins and cause steady blood flow that is slow and dark red. Pressure on the wound usually stops bleeding after a short period, unless you are taking aspirin or other *anticoagulants* (medicine that prevents or delays the blood from clotting). The most serious type of external bleeding, however, is from a cut that strikes an artery. Bleeding is profuse and can be difficult to control even with pressure on the wound. Blood will be bright red and come in spurts as the heart beats. A person with severe bleeding can slip into shock (see *Shock*, p. 33).

Because deep cuts can sever or damage major blood vessels, nerves or tendons, it is important to know the signs of a serious laceration. In general, be concerned more with cuts to the face, hands, chest, abdomen or back, which have the potential to be more critical than lacerations to other areas.

Stitches are usually not necessary if the edges of the cut can be pulled together with a bandage or sterile adhesive tape — except on the face, where scarring may be a problem. However, your doctor may *suture* (stitch) cuts in areas subject to frequent movement, such as a finger, or when a cut is more than one inch long, is deep and has jagged edges. Suturing should take place within eight hours of injury for best results. Call your doctor if you're not sure whether you need stitches.

What you can do

To control severe bleeding

- Call 911 or your local emergency services number.

- While waiting for help to arrive, have the injured person lie down with their head slightly lower than their body. Elevate their legs and the site of the bleeding.

- Keep the person warm to lessen the possibility of shock (see *Shock*, p. 33).

- Remove large pieces of dirt and debris from the wound, but only if it can be done easily. **DO NOT** remove any impaled objects or try to clean the wound (see *Punctures*, p. 41).

- Place a clean cloth over the wound and apply direct, steady pressure for 15 minutes. To avoid transmission of blood-borne infections, use your bare hands only if necessary.

- **DO NOT** apply direct pressure if there is an object in the wound or a bone is protruding or visible. Apply pressure around the wound instead.

- If the first cloth becomes soaked with blood, apply a fresh one over it while continuing to apply steady pressure. Do not remove used dressings.

- If bleeding does not slow or stop after 15 minutes, apply firm, continuous pressure on a *pressure point* between the wound and the heart to restrict blood flow through the major arteries. Pressure points are located on the inside upper arms and on the upper thighs in the groin area.

SEE *Know What To Do*, p. 43

To care for a minor wound

- Wash your hands with soap and water.

- Apply pressure on the wound for 10 or 15 minutes to stop bleeding, if necessary.

- Gently clean the cut with mild soap and water or 3% hydrogen peroxide immediately after injury occurs, using a clean cloth. Be sure to remove dirt, glass and other particles (if needed, use tweezers that have been disinfected with alcohol). Antiseptic creams are not necessary and will not lessen the risk of infection or speed healing.

- Keep the cut uncovered and exposed to air if possible.

- If the wound is slightly gaping, pull the edges of the wound together with a regular or butterfly bandage. If necessary, cover the wound with dry gauze and tape. Change gauze daily, but don't take the butterfly bandage off until the wound is knit together.

- If you must cover a cut that doesn't require a butterfly bandage, apply antibiotic ointment to a gauze pad and tape the pad over the wound. Change the dressing once a day, or whenever it gets wet.

- Watch for signs of infection (see *Infected Wounds*, p. 42).

ABRASIONS

An *abrasion* is a scrape that can scratch and tear the first few layers of skin. The injury is shallow but can be very painful because millions of nerve endings are exposed. The pain usually subsides within a few days as scabbing forms. These injuries can be very dirty and must be cleaned thoroughly to prevent infection.

What you can do

To care for an abrasion

- Wash your hands with soap and water.

- Clean the area with mild soap and warm water, making sure to remove all dirt and foreign particles.

- Leave skin flaps in place to act as a natural bandage. Dirty skin flaps can be cut away carefully with nail scissors. Stop cutting if it hurts.

- Place an ice pack over the wound for a few minutes to minimize the pain. For protection, place a washcloth between bare skin and ice.

 - Use a pain reliever such as aspirin, acetaminophen (Tylenol) or ibuprofen if pain persists. **NEVER give aspirin to children/teenagers. It can cause Reye's syndrome, a rare but often fatal condition.**

 If you have a chronic illness or routinely take prescribed or over-the-counter (OTC) drugs, talk to your doctor or pharmacist before taking any other medications.

- Large scrapes can be treated with antibiotic ointment and covered with a sterile, nonstick dressing. Put the ointment on the dressing, rather than rubbing it on the scrape.

- Watch for signs of infection (see *Infected Wounds*, p. 42).

PUNCTURES

A puncture wound is a penetrating injury with a sharp-pointed object such as a nail. Seemingly minor puncture wounds sometimes can cause considerable internal damage and — because they can be hard to clean — become easily infected.

What you can do

To care for a puncture wound

- **Seek emergency medical care if an object, such as a stick, projects from or is embedded in the skin.** Never try to pull the object out, since this could cause further injury. Very gently place a clean, damp cloth around the wound (for smaller objects, see *Splinters*, p. 67).

- Allow the wound to bleed freely to cleanse itself. Don't apply pressure unless blood is spurting out or bleeding is excessive (see *To Control Severe Bleeding*, p. 39).

- If the puncture wound isn't serious enough to need emergency medical attention, wash your hands with soap and water, then wash the wound thoroughly with mild soap and water or 3% hydrogen peroxide. Remove dirt carefully, using tweezers that have been disinfected with alcohol, to extract debris. Pat wound dry with clean cloth and stop bleeding. Small wounds should stop bleeding on their own. For others, you may need to apply pressure with a gauze pad or clean cloth and elevate the area above the level of the heart.

- Antiseptics, such as Mercurochrome and Merthiolate, aren't necessary and may cause tissue damage and pain. Nonprescription antibiotic ointments, such as Neosporin and bacitracin, may help prevent infection. Apply them to the side of the dressing that touches the wound, rather than to the wound itself.

- Cover the wound with a sterile dressing. Change the dressing at least once a day and keep the area clean and dry.

- Remove dressing and soak the area in warm water a few times a day for four or five days to promote healing.

- Watch for signs of infection (see *Infected Wounds*, p. 42).

SEE ▷ *Know What To Do*, p. 43

INFECTED WOUNDS

Anything that damages or changes the skin, from a rash to a major injury, has the potential to become infected — particularly if it has not been thoroughly cleaned. An infected wound will take longer to heal, is more likely to scar and can result in serious complications, including death. People with diabetes, organ transplants or cancer are at a higher risk of infection.

Symptoms of infection generally begin to appear about 24 to 48 hours after the injury, although the potential for infection continues until healing is complete. A wound that doesn't heal well within two weeks should be seen by a doctor.

Note your symptoms

Watch for signs of infection

- Redness around the wound or red streaks leading away from it toward the upper body
- Swelling
- Warmth or tenderness around the wound
- Pus
- A fever of any intensity (in older adults, even a low fever may indicate serious infection)
- Tender or swollen lymph nodes

What you can do

If an infection develops, consult your doctor and then:

- Expose wound to air unless it is necessary to bandage it.
- If bandaging is necessary, use a sterile dressing and change it daily or more often if it becomes wet.
- Remove dressing and soak wound in warm water several times a day.
- Apply an antibiotic ointment such as Neosporin or bacitracin.

Prevention

- Get a routine tetanus booster every 10 years. If you get a dirty wound and have not had a booster within five years, or if you have not completed your primary series, ask your doctor about a booster injection.
- See *What You Can Do, Cuts*, p. 39; *What You Can Do, Abrasions*, p. 40; *What You Can Do, Punctures*, p. 41.

know
WHAT
TO DO

Wounds
DO THESE APPLY:

- Bleeding is steady or profuse, or in rhythmic spurts

  see *What You Can Do, Cuts*, p. 39

- Wound continues to bleed through dressing even after 15 minutes of direct pressure and elevation

- Signs of shock are present: weakness; confusion; cold, pale, moist skin

  see *Shock*, p. 33

- Breathing is shallow and pulse is weak and rapid

- Wound involves head, chest, hand or abdomen, unless obviously minor

- Wound is deep and penetrates to muscle or bone

- An object, such as a stick, projects from or is embedded in wound

  see *What You Can Do, Punctures*, p. 41

see next page

DO THESE APPLY: see previous page

- You think the cut may have struck an artery or nerve
- There are signs of infection: redness around the area or red streaks leading away; swelling; warmth or tenderness; pus; fever; tender or swollen lymph nodes

  see *Infected Wounds*
- Edges of wound cannot be pulled together easily
- Wound is difficult to clean thoroughly
- Minor wound involves head, chest, hand or abdomen
- Bleeding persists despite applying pressure and elevating wound for 10 to 15 minutes
- You suspect the wound needs suturing or it involves the face
- Wound is severe and you have difficulty moving limb, finger or toe, or you have numbness or tingling near the injury
- Wound is extremely dirty and/or you are uncertain whether there is foreign material in it
- You think you need a tetanus booster

  see *Immunization Schedule*, p. 327

NO

YES

CALL DOCTOR NOW

- Wound has not healed within two weeks
- You have a serious chronic condition and have sustained a wound

YES

CALL DOCTOR

NO

see *What You Can Do, Cuts*, p. 39
see *What You Can Do, Abrasions*, p. 40
see *What You Can Do, Punctures*, p. 41
see *What You Can Do, Infected Wounds*, p. 42

APPLY SELF-CARE

Bites and stings

Most bites and stings are minor, and the reactions are localized. However, more serious problems may arise if you develop an infection or experience an allergic (*anaphylactic*) reaction (see *Allergic Reaction*, p. 107). If you have ever had an allergic reaction to any bite or sting, ask your doctor about wearing a medical-alert bracelet and getting a prescription for an anaphylactic kit.

ANIMAL/HUMAN BITES

The most common type of animal bites involves pets — usually dogs and cats. While only 5% of dog bites become infected, 30% to 50% of cat bites result in infections. Human bites are usually inflicted by children while playing or fighting, and rarely become infected because they are superficial. Adult human bites become infected in 15% to 20% of cases.

Bites that break the skin can cause several types of serious infections:

- *Rabies*, most commonly from bites by dogs, cats, skunks, bats, raccoons, opossums, foxes and other wild animals
- *Tetanus*, which can develop after any kind of bite if you have not been inoculated within the last five years or if you have not completed your primary series of tetanus shots
- *Pasteurella*, which is commonly caused by cat bites and can occur very quickly if not treated
- Other infections caused by various bacteria or microorganisms that enter the wound

What you can do

To care for an animal/human bite

- **Seek emergency care immediately if the bite seems serious, or affects the face or hands.**
- Rinse and clean the wound right away, after washing your hands with soap and water.
- Blood flow helps cleanse the wound. Control excessive bleeding by wrapping the wound with a dressing and applying direct pressure (see *To Control Severe Bleeding*, p. 39).

SEE > *Know What To Do, p. 48*

- Report all animal bites to the local health department, especially if the bite is from a wild or domestic animal whose rabies vaccination status is unknown. If a wild animal has symptoms of rabies (drooling, foaming at the mouth), it should be destroyed and tested. A domestic animal with uncertain rabies vaccination status should be observed for 15 days even if the animal appears healthy.

- Watch for signs of infection (see *Infected Wounds*, p. 42), which usually appear within 24 to 48 hours.

Prevention

- Treat all unfamiliar pets with caution.

- Don't try to touch any wild animal, especially if it appears sick.

- Obey "beware of dog" signs.

- Teach children not to touch or feed any animal they do not know — domestic or wild.

- Never leave an infant, young child or defenseless person unattended with a pet, especially a large dog.

INSECT BITES/STINGS

Often an insect injects a substance with its bite that causes a painful, stinging sensation. Or you may be bitten by a poisonous insect — such as a black widow or brown recluse spider — or experience an allergic reaction. Allergic reactions range from hives and intense itching (see *Hives*, p. 107) to *anaphylaxis*, a severe and life-threatening allergic reaction (see *Allergic Reaction*, p. 107; *Wheezing*, p. 148). **To find out whether you need emergency care, see *Know What To Do*, p. 48.**

> For details on tick bites, see *Tick Bites*, p. 49.

What you can do

If emergency care is required

- Call 911 or your local emergency services number.

- Administer an injection if an anaphylactic kit is prescribed by your doctor and is available.

- Apply ice or cold water to the bite for five minutes. For protection, place a washcloth between bare skin and ice.

- If the bite is on a hand or foot, keep the limb snugly bandaged above the bite for five minutes (but make sure there is still circulation to the limb). **DO NOT apply a tourniquet.**

- Keep the limb below the level of the heart.

When emergency care is not required

- Wash your hands with soap and water.

- Scrape out — with your fingernail — or flick out any stinger that may be left in the skin. Avoid squeezing the stinger.

- Use calamine lotion or over-the-counter (OTC) hydrocortisone cream to reduce itching and inflammation.

- Apply ice. For protection, place a washcloth between bare skin and ice.

Prevention

- Avoid wearing perfume if you'll be spending time outdoors. It attracts bees.

- Use insect repellent and extra caution when you are in areas that have insects you may be allergic to.

- Get reliable instructions before trying to remove a beehive or nest. Follow directions on commercial products.

- If you know you're allergic to bees, always carry an anaphylactic kit. You can get one with a prescription from your doctor.

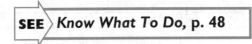

SEE *Know What To Do,* p. 48

Bites and stings
DO THESE APPLY:

- You experience signs of an allergic reaction following an insect bite: chest pain; palpitations or change in heart rate; difficulty breathing; violent coughing; loss of consciousness; fever; severe hives; tingling of mouth or throat; swelling of skin or lips; enlargement of stomach; intestinal spasms or cramping
- Severe pain or itching of wound, increased perspiration, weakness or listlessness, nausea, paralysis
- Bite by black widow or brown recluse spider, or other poisonous insect, marine animal or reptile
- Known sensitivity or allergy to insect that caused bite
- Any serious bite — especially if it affects the face or hand
- Signs of infection within several hours of a cat bite: redness around the area or red streaks leading away; swelling; warmth or tenderness; pus; fever; tender or swollen lymph nodes

see *What You Can Do, Animal/Human Bites*, p. 45

see *What You Can Do, Insect Bites/Stings*, p. 47

YES

 NO

- Signs of infection: redness around the area or red streaks leading away; swelling; warmth or tenderness; pus; fever; tender or swollen lymph nodes
- Human or animal bite and you have not had a tetanus shot in five or more years or you have not completed your primary series

YES

NO

- Any bite (especially a cat bite) that breaks the skin
- A dog or cat bite, and you're uncertain whether the animal has been vaccinated for rabies
- A wild animal bite

YES CALL DOCTOR

NO

see *What You Can Do, Animal/Human Bites*, p. 45; see *What You Can Do, Insect Bites/Stings*, p. 47; see *What You Can Do, Allergic Reaction*, p. 108; see *Immunization Schedule*, p. 327

Tick bites

Ticks are small parasites related to spiders that embed themselves in the skin of humans and other animals, including household pets. Although tick bites are rarely harmful, ticks may transmit serious diseases such as *Rocky Mountain spotted fever* and *Lyme disease.*

Ticks are common in all outdoor areas of the U.S. and may be passed to people by their pets. Ticks frequently lodge in the scalp, nape of the neck, ankles, genital area or skin folds. They should be removed promptly and completely from people and household pets.

Tick bites often go unnoticed. Although small, ticks embedded in the skin are usually visible. Tick bites are characterized by itching; a small, hard lump on the skin; and redness surrounding the bite.

Prevention

- Avoid tick-infested areas, such as thickly wooded brush, whenever possible.
- Use an insect repellent on your skin whenever you plan to be outdoors for any length of time, especially in the warm months of spring and summer.
- Wear light-colored clothing.
- Wear long-sleeved shirts and long pants. Make sure your shirt is tucked inside your pants, and tuck your pants inside your boots or socks.
- After being in a known tick-infested area, check your body thoroughly and remove any ticks you find.

What you can do

NEVER SCRATCH A TICK BITE

The body of the tick may break off, leaving the head embedded in the skin.

REMOVAL OF TICKS

Ticks should be removed carefully and promptly to help prevent the diseases they carry.

- With small tweezers, grip the tick as close to the surface of the skin as possible. Pull straight up and out using gentle, steady pressure. Do not squeeze the body of a tick, since this can increase the chance of getting a disease carried by ticks.

2

- Extract the tick slowly and firmly to ensure complete removal.
- Clean the area of the tick bite with soap and water, then apply antiseptic.

Final notes

Lyme disease is usually transmitted by small deer ticks, common in summer and early fall. Symptoms develop three to 32 days after a bite. Common regions for this disease are the Atlantic Coast, Wisconsin, Minnesota, California and Oregon. However, sporadic cases have been reported in 46 states.

Rocky Mountain spotted fever is usually transmitted by wood ticks in the West and by dog ticks and lone star ticks in the East and Southeast. This disease generally occurs in warm weather, and symptoms begin suddenly, two to 14 days after the bite.

know
WHAT
TO DO

Tick bites
DO THESE APPLY:

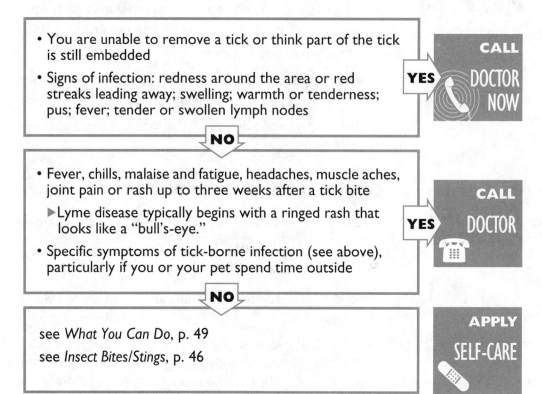

- You are unable to remove a tick or think part of the tick is still embedded
- Signs of infection: redness around the area or red streaks leading away; swelling; warmth or tenderness; pus; fever; tender or swollen lymph nodes

YES CALL **DOCTOR NOW**

NO

- Fever, chills, malaise and fatigue, headaches, muscle aches, joint pain or rash up to three weeks after a tick bite
  - ▶Lyme disease typically begins with a ringed rash that looks like a "bull's-eye."
- Specific symptoms of tick-borne infection (see above), particularly if you or your pet spend time outside

YES CALL **DOCTOR**

NO

see *What You Can Do*, p. 49
see *Insect Bites/Stings*, p. 46

APPLY **SELF-CARE**

Head/spinal injury

After any trauma involving the head, neck or back — even a bump on the head that may seem insignificant — it is important to watch for signs that may indicate damage to the delicate structures within the brain and spinal cord. An injury of this type can be serious and requires professional medical assistance immediately.

Fortunately, most injuries are limited to the surrounding protective tissues and can be treated with self-care. What's more, many injuries can be prevented (see *Safety*, p. 328). For details on injuries that may accompany head and spinal injuries, see specific topics.

What you can do

HEAD INJURY

- Make sure you are safe from additional injury.

- If there is external bleeding, apply pressure on the wound for 15 minutes or until bleeding stops completely. Use a clean cloth, and if the blood soaks through, apply additional cloths over the first one.

- Apply ice or cold packs to ease pain and reduce swelling (a "goose egg" may develop). For protection, place a washcloth between bare skin and ice.

- Immediately after injury, be alert for signs that bleeding may have occurred inside the skull. After that, monitor every two hours for the first 24 hours; every four hours for the next 24 hours; and every eight hours through the third day. Observation for 72 hours is important since bleeding inside the skull may be slow, and symptoms may develop gradually. Signs include:

  - **Changes in mental state** that may include unconsciousness, confusion, decrease in alertness, abnormally deep sleep or difficulty waking up

  - **Unequal size of pupils after the injury**; some people normally have a difference in pupil size, but a change after an injury can be a serious sign

  - **Severe, forceful vomiting** that is repeated or continues (one single episode of vomiting may be a reaction to the pain)

  - **Change or decrease in ability to move parts** of the body or a change in the ability to see, smell, hear, taste or touch

- Check for other injuries, especially to neck and back.

- Keep person sitting or lying down with head slightly elevated to decrease swelling.

- Avoid heavy exercise or exertion for at least 72 hours.
- Chronic headaches or changes in personality months after a head injury may be signs of very slow bleeding, which can cause pressure on the brain.

SPINAL INJURY

Injury to the spine can occur in any accident involving the neck or back. Strain from incorrect positions or movement, and damage from disease such as arthritis, can injure the spinal nerves. Self-care is directed toward preventing additional damage and permanent paralysis, decreasing symptoms and eliminating future injury.

What you can do

If you suspect an injury to the spine:

- **DO NOT move the person** unless there is an immediate threat to life, such as a fire.
- Call 911 or your local emergency services number for professional medical assistance to move the person. Keep the person still and warm. **DO NOT give anything to eat or drink.**
- If there is immediate danger and you must move the person, **immobilize the neck and back.** Slide a board or other firm surface under the person's head and back without moving the neck or back from the position it was in. Place soft, bulky material on each side of the head to prevent rotation.
- In a diving accident, **DO NOT pull the person from the water.** Float the person face up. The water will help support the neck and back.
- If there is much bleeding from the nose or mouth, roll the person onto their side (the entire body needs to roll in one, even movement) without twisting the neck or back. If the bleeding is minor, wipe out the mouth and nose without moving the person.

Prevention

- Wear your seat belt while in all motor vehicles and place children in proper car seats.
- Wear a helmet while biking, motorcycling, skating or horseback riding.
- Don't dive into shallow or unfamiliar water.
- Exercise to keep back, neck and abdominal muscles strong.

know
WHAT
TO DO

Head/spinal injury
DO THESE APPLY:

- Cessation of breathing or if no pulse; start CPR
  see *CPR*, p. 14
- Irregularity or slowing of breathing or heart rate
- Unconsciousness, confusion or any loss of memory
- Seizure or convulsions
- Bleeding from nose, ears, mouth or around eyes
- Clear fluid draining from nose
- Change in pupil size or sudden double vision
- Weakness, tingling or numbness in arms, legs or one side of body
- Loss of control of bladder or bowel
- ▶Do not move person. Do not give anything to eat or drink.
  see *What You Can Do, Head Injury*, p. 51
  see *What You Can Do, Spinal Injury*

YES ▶

SEEK
EMERGENCY CARE

APPLY
EMERGENCY FIRST AID

NO ▽

- Continued or repeated vomiting
- Severe pain or headache
- Person under influence of drugs or alcohol
- A cut that may need stitches
- ▶Do not give anything to eat or drink.
  see *What You Can Do, Head Injury*, p. 51
  see *What You Can Do, Spinal Injury*

YES ▶

CALL
DOCTOR NOW

NO ▽

- Minor injury and no immediate signs of brain or spinal injury
  see *What You Can Do, Head Injury*, p. 51
  see *What You Can Do, Spinal Injury*

YES ▶

APPLY
SELF-CARE

Bruises

Bruises (or *contusions*) usually result from a blow or fall. Small blood vessels rupture under the skin and cause blood to seep into the surrounding tissues. A black eye is a bruise to the area around the eye or to the eyeball itself.

As you become older, you are increasingly susceptible to bruising. This is because you lose thickness in the layer of fat that protects your skin and tissue, and your *capillaries* (small blood vessels connecting arteries and veins) are more fragile. People who regularly take *anticoagulants* (medicine that prevents or delays the blood from clotting), aspirin or other medications may bruise even more easily.

Bruises usually appear as red or purple areas, then change color — to green, yellow and brown — before disappearing. The process typically takes 10 to 14 days.

SOFT TISSUE INJURY

A soft tissue injury is similar to a bruise but involves damage to muscles and larger blood vessels, resulting in oozing of blood and swelling within the muscles or damaged tissues under the skin. Don't be misled into thinking these injuries can be ignored just because they may not result in discoloration like bruises. They can be serious and may require a doctor's care.

What you can do

- Apply an ice pack to the injured area for 10 to 15 minutes every hour for two hours, then leave ice off for two hours. Repeat this cycle for 48 hours or until the swelling is gone. For protection, place a washcloth between bare skin and ice. Do not apply heat as long as there is swelling. (Keep an ice pack handy for injuries by adding one cup of rubbing alcohol to two cups of water. Pour into a one-quart, resealable bag and store in the freezer.)

- Elevate the bruised area to reduce swelling and discomfort.

 - Take acetaminophen (Tylenol) to relieve pain. Avoid aspirin and ibuprofen, which interfere with blood clotting and may make the bruise worse.

- Apply a bandage only if the skin is broken.

 If you have a chronic illness or routinely take prescribed or over-the-counter (OTC) drugs, talk to your doctor or pharmacist before taking any other medications.

know
WHAT
TO DO

Bruises
DO THESE APPLY:

- Trauma to an eye causes bruising or swelling around the eye or to the eye itself
  - ▶ Begin self-care and call your doctor, who will be able to determine the extent of the injury.
- Bruised area shows signs of infection two to three days after injury
  - Redness around the area or red streaks leading away
  - Swelling
  - Warmth or tenderness
  - Pus
  - Fever
  - Tender or swollen lymph nodes

YES → **CALL DOCTOR NOW**

NO

- Bruises appear without any known trauma
- Bruises seem to develop after minor impacts

YES → **CALL DOCTOR**

NO

see *What You Can Do*

APPLY SELF-CARE

Strains and sprains

A *strain* is an injury to a muscle caused by over-stretching. Also called a "pulled muscle," the elastic fibers that make up the muscle are overextended and may tear, bleed and contract.

A *sprain* is an injury to a ligament and other soft tissue around a joint. *Ligaments* are bands of fiber that connect the bones at a joint. They can be stretched or torn when a joint is twisted, "jammed" or overextended. With a sprain, slight bleeding may produce skin discoloration that resolves slowly (see *Bruises*, p. 54).

What you can do

The basic treatment for strains and sprains is a two-part process: **RICE** (rest, ice, compression, elevation) to treat the immediate injury, and **MSA** (movement, strength, alternate activity) to help the injury heal and prevent further problems.

Begin the **RICE** process **immediately** following the injury:

- **Rest.** Do not put weight on injured joint or muscle, and limit movement in the area of the injury. Use crutches, splints or a sling as needed.

- **Ice.** Apply an ice pack for 10 to 15 minutes every hour for two hours, then leave ice off for two hours. For protection, place a washcloth between bare skin and ice. Repeat this cycle for 48 hours or until swelling is gone. Do not use heat as long as there is swelling.

- **Compress.** Wrap injured area in an elastic bandage for support and protection.

- **Elevate.** Place injured part on pillows while you apply ice and anytime you are seated or lying down. Raise injured area above the level of your heart whenever possible.

 Aspirin and ibuprofen may ease pain and inflammation. Acetaminophen (Tylenol) eases discomfort but does not decrease inflammation. Do not use other drugs to mask pain in order to continue using the injured part. **NEVER give aspirin to children/teenagers. It can cause Reye's syndrome, a rare but often fatal condition.**

 If you have a chronic illness or routinely take prescribed or over-the-counter (OTC) drugs, talk to your doctor or pharmacist before taking any other medications.

The **MSA** process can be started only if the initial swelling is gone:

- **Movement.** Begin gently moving the joint to resume full range of motion.

- **Strength.** After the swelling is gone and a full range of motion is reached, gradually begin to strengthen the injured part. Slow, gentle stretching during the healing process will make scar tissue flexible and prevent limited movement later.

- **Alternate activities.** Resume regular exercise through activities and sports that do not place a strain on the injured area. Go slowly and stop any activity that causes discomfort.

Any increase in pain or return of swelling is a sign to stop **MSA** and resume **RICE**.

Prevention

- Use correct form in all work and play activities.

- Adjust equipment and furniture to fit your needs.

- Go slowly when starting a new activity or sport.

- Use warm-up and cool-down exercises to help your body prepare and recover safely.

- Take frequent breaks when performing any continuous activity.

- Do not push beyond your strength or ability; advance your skill level gradually.

- Reduce the risk of falling (see *Falls*, p. 328).

SEE ▷ *Know What To Do, p. 58*

know
WHAT
TO DO

Strains and sprains
DO THESE APPLY:

After an injury there is:

• Excruciating pain

• Obvious deformity of an extremity or suspicion of a fracture

• Tearing or popping sensation in the knee

▶Splint or support injured area to keep it immobile (see *What You Can Do, Broken Bones,* p. 60). Do not attempt to straighten injured part. Apply ice pack immediately. For protection, place a washcloth between bare skin and ice.

see *Broken Bones,* p. 59

see *Knee Pain,* p. 236

YES

NO

• Injured area is greatly swollen, discolored, unstable

▶Splint or support injured area to keep it immobile (see *What You Can Do, Broken Bones,* p. 60). Do not attempt to straighten injured part. Apply ice pack immediately. For protection, place a washcloth between bare skin and ice.

YES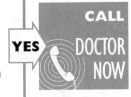

NO

• No decrease in pain or swelling after two or three days of self-care with RICE

see *What You Can Do,* p. 56

▶Continue RICE until appointment.

YES

NO

• Pain or swelling in joint or muscle following a related activity or movement

▶Start RICE immediately.

• Pain is decreasing and swelling is going away with RICE

▶Continue RICE until swelling is gone and then start MSA. Full healing may take four or more weeks.

see *What You Can Do,* p. 56

YES

Broken bones

Through the years your bones lose density, or thickness, which causes them to weaken and sometimes become brittle. They grow — and heal — more slowly. Fortunately, weight-bearing exercise and a calcium-rich diet can work wonders to maintain healthy bones.

Exaggerated loss of bone density is called *osteoporosis* (see *Osteoporosis*, p. 216). Even a minor injury or difficult movement can result in a broken bone, or *fracture* (for tips on preventing falls, see *Falls*, p. 328). Wrist and hip fractures are especially common (see *Leg Pain*, p. 232).

It is often difficult to tell if a bone has been fractured in an injury. Unless the fracture is obvious, an x-ray may be needed to be sure. The break may be a small crack such as a *stress fracture* caused by overuse, a *simple fracture* with the bone ends separated but in alignment, or a *compound fracture* where the soft tissue in the area is torn and the bone protrudes through the skin.

SUSPECT A FRACTURE IF

- Injured part is bent or deformed
- Bone is poking through the skin
- There is a bump or irregularity along the bone
- A cracking or snapping sound was heard at the time of injury
- There is rapid swelling or bruising immediately after the injury

What you can do

Until seen by a doctor:

- Assume there may be a fracture.

- Immobilize and support the injured area with a *splint.* To splint, attach a stiff object (such as a rolled-up magazine or newspaper, or a cane) to the injured limb with a rope or belt. Position the splint so the injured limb cannot bend.

- To immobilize and support a possible fractured toe, gently tape it to an adjacent toe.

- Do not attempt to move an abnormally bent or displaced bone back into place. Splint it as it is. Until medical help is available, apply an ice pack for 10 to 15 minutes every hour for two hours, then leave ice off for two hours. For protection, place a washcloth between bare skin and ice. Repeat this cycle for 48 hours or until swelling is gone. Do not use heat as long as there is swelling.

- Wrap the injury with an elastic bandage to immobilize and compress the area. Loosen the bandage if it becomes too tight.

- Elevate injured area.

- Avoid any unnecessary movement. Rest injury for at least 24 to 48 hours.

 Use aspirin or ibuprofen to ease pain and inflammation. **NEVER give aspirin to children/teenagers. It can cause Reye's syndrome, a rare but often fatal condition.**

 If you have a chronic illness or routinely take prescribed or over-the-counter (OTC) drugs, talk to your doctor or pharmacist before taking any other medications.

Broken bones
DO THESE APPLY:

- Limb is cold, blue or numb

- Injury is to pelvis, thigh or hip

- Signs of shock (cool, clammy, pale skin; dizziness or light-headedness; thirst)

  ▶ Keep person lying down and covered to stay warm. Do not give anything to eat or drink.

- Shortness of breath or difficulty breathing after chest injury

  ▶ Keep person quiet. Place in sitting position to assist breathing.

- Bone protruding through skin

- Suspect fracture near a joint

- Injured part is crooked or deformed

- Heavy bleeding or blood spurting out

  ▶ Cover open wound with clean, dry cloth. Apply direct pressure on bleeding wound with a sterile dressing or clean cloth. Apply only enough pressure to stop bleeding. If blood soaks through, apply another dressing. Do not remove first one. Do not apply tourniquet.

NO

- Injured part is unstable or unable to bear weight

- Large amount of swelling or bruising immediately after injury

see *What You Can Do*

NO

- Injured area does not improve after 48 hours of self-care

2

Smashed fingers

Fingers often get smashed, pinched or jammed during daily activities. Most finger injuries are not serious. Although they may be quite painful and inconvenient, these injuries heal well with self-care at home. Serious injuries with possible bone fractures, severe bleeding or severed parts require professional medical help.

What you can do

- Immediately apply an ice pack or insert finger into ice-cold water to decrease the pain and reduce swelling. For protection, place a washcloth between bare skin and ice.

- Apply ice pack for 10 to 15 minutes every hour for two hours, then leave ice off for two hours. Repeat this cycle for 48 hours or until swelling is gone. Do not use heat as long as there is swelling.

- Remove any jewelry if you can do so without causing additional pain.

- If skin is broken, gently wash with soap, then dry. Apply soft, clean dressing.

- Splint and support injured finger by taping it to a nearby healthy one.

- Rest and elevate hand for 24 to 48 hours. Immobilize hand in a sling or use hand as little as possible.

 - Take aspirin or ibuprofen to reduce swelling and pain. **NEVER give aspirin to children/teenagers. It can cause Reye's syndrome, a rare but often fatal condition.**

- When swelling is gone, apply warm compresses at intervals for comfort.

- Resume full range of motion as soon as swelling is gone. Gentle bending and movement will stretch the muscle tissue and prevent limited movement later.

- Stop any activity that causes pain to the finger.

DISLOCATED FINGERNAILS

- Trim the part of the nail that is still attached to avoid catching it on anything. It is not necessary to remove the nail.

- Keep area clean and watch for signs of infection (see *Infected Wounds*, p. 42).

- Protect the tip of the finger with soft cloth or dressing. A new nail will take one to two months to grow back.

 If you have a chronic illness or routinely take prescribed or over-the-counter (OTC) drugs, talk to your doctor or pharmacist before taking any other medications.

BLOOD UNDER A NAIL

- Apply ice as soon as possible. For protection, place a washcloth between bare skin and ice.

- Make a hole in the nail to relieve pressure and pain:
  - Straighten a paper clip and hold it with a pair of pliers in a flame until it is red hot.
  - Place the tip of the paper clip on the nail and let it melt through. You need not push. A thick nail may take several tries. As soon as the hole is complete, blood will escape and the pain and pressure will ease.

- If the blood and pressure build up again, repeat the procedure using the same hole.

- Soak the finger three times a day for 15 minutes in a solution of equal parts water and hydrogen peroxide.

know
WHAT
TO DO

Smashed fingers
DO THESE APPLY:

- Finger is severed
  - ▶ Apply direct pressure with sterile dressing to control bleeding. Wrap severed part in clean or sterile gauze and place in plastic bag. Place bag on ice but do not let the tissue freeze. Bring the severed part with the injured person.

- Severe bleeding or hemorrhage
  - ▶ Apply direct pressure with sterile dressing.

- Finger deformed or bent into abnormal shape or bone protruding through skin
  - ▶ Immobilize the hand. Avoid unnecessary movement. Do not move or reposition finger.

- Penetrating injury to finger
  - ▶ Do not attempt to remove object that is stuck in finger. Control bleeding and immobilize hand.

see *What You Can Do, Cuts*, p. 39

YES ▶ SEEK
EMERGENCY
CARE

APPLY
EMERGENCY
FIRST AID

NO ▼

see next page

DO THESE APPLY: see previous page

- Numbness or a sensation of pins and needles in finger or hand
- A sensation of tearing or popping with movement
- Signs of infection

  see *Infected Wounds*, p. 42
- Movement painful for 24 hours or more
- Unable to remove jewelry due to swelling
- Torn skin that is dirty and it has been five or more years since last tetanus shot or you have not completed your primary series

  see *Immunization Schedule*, p. 327

YES · CALL **DOCTOR NOW**

NO

- Torn skin that is clean, and it has been 10 or more years since last tetanus shot or you have not completed your primary series

  see *Immunization Schedule*, p. 327
- Pain and swelling do not ease with self-care

YES · CALL **DOCTOR**

NO

see *What You Can Do*, p. 62

APPLY SELF-CARE

Fishhooks

Fishhooks are designed with a barb to keep the fish hooked. Unfortunately, the barb works the same way on people once the skin is punctured. It is useful to know how to remove a fishhook for yourself or a companion, especially if you are any distance from medical help. If the injured person is a small child or unable to cooperate, a local anesthetic to numb the injured area may be needed.

What you can do

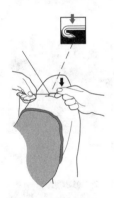

Figure 15

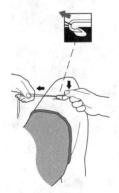

Figure 16

IF THE HOOK IS NEAR THE SKIN SURFACE

- **Step 1:** Apply ice or cold water to provide temporary numbing.
- **Step 2:** Loop a piece of fishing line through hook (see Figure 15). Make the line long enough to grasp securely with your hand.
- **Step 3:** Grasp eye or shaft of hook with one hand and press down about one-eighth inch to disengage barb.
- **Step 4:** While still pressing down on hook, jerk the line parallel to skin surface so hook shaft leads barb out of skin (see Figure 16).
- **Step 5:** Wash wound thoroughly with soap and water. Treat as you would a puncture wound (see *Punctures*, p. 41).

IF THE HOOK IS DEEPLY EMBEDDED

- **Step 1:** Apply ice or cold water to provide temporary numbing.
- **Step 2:** Push hook through the skin.
- **Step 3:** Cut off barb with wire cutters.
- **Step 4:** Pull hook back out.
- **Step 5:** Wash wound thoroughly with soap and water. Treat as you would a puncture wound (see *Punctures*, p. 41).

SEE ⟩ *Know What To Do, p. 66*

2

Fishhooks

DO THESE APPLY:

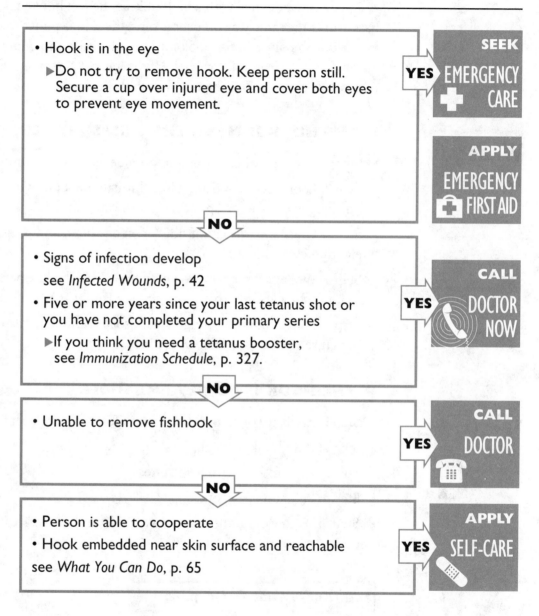

- Hook is in the eye
  ▶ Do not try to remove hook. Keep person still. Secure a cup over injured eye and cover both eyes to prevent eye movement.

YES → **SEEK EMERGENCY CARE**

APPLY EMERGENCY FIRST AID

NO

- Signs of infection develop
  see *Infected Wounds*, p. 42

- Five or more years since your last tetanus shot or you have not completed your primary series
  ▶ If you think you need a tetanus booster, see *Immunization Schedule*, p. 327.

YES → **CALL DOCTOR NOW**

NO

- Unable to remove fishhook

YES → **CALL DOCTOR**

NO

- Person is able to cooperate
- Hook embedded near skin surface and reachable
  see *What You Can Do*, p. 65

YES → **APPLY SELF-CARE**

Splinters

A sharp, slender piece of wood, metal or glass can easily pierce the skin and become lodged. This type of injury usually can be treated at home by removing the splinter, cleaning the area and watching for signs of infection. Be sure to wash your hands with soap and water before applying first aid.

What you can do

IF THE SPLINTER CAN BE REACHED

- Grasp end of splinter with tweezers and gently pull it out along the entry track.
- Cleanse the area with soap and water.
- Keep area clean and dry; apply dry bandage if necessary.
- Watch for signs of infection:
    - Redness around the area or red streaks leading away
    - Swelling
    - Warmth or tenderness
    - Pus
    - Fever
    - Tender or swollen lymph nodes

IF THE SPLINTER IS DEEPLY EMBEDDED

- Clean a needle by dipping it in alcohol or holding it in a match flame.
- Pick the skin over end of splinter and make a small hole.
- Lift splinter with the tip of needle until it can be grasped by tweezers. Withdraw along the entry track.

SEE ⟩ *Know What To Do, p. 68*

Splinters
DO THESE APPLY:

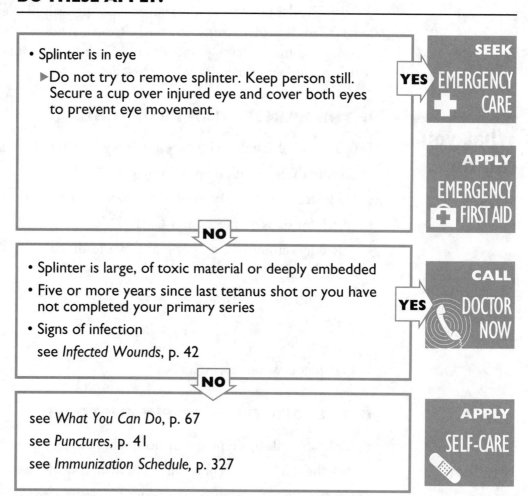

- Splinter is in eye
  ▶ Do not try to remove splinter. Keep person still. Secure a cup over injured eye and cover both eyes to prevent eye movement.

YES → **SEEK** EMERGENCY CARE

APPLY EMERGENCY FIRST AID

NO

- Splinter is large, of toxic material or deeply embedded
- Five or more years since last tetanus shot or you have not completed your primary series
- Signs of infection

  see *Infected Wounds*, p. 42

YES → **CALL** DOCTOR NOW

NO

see *What You Can Do*, p. 67

see *Punctures*, p. 41

see *Immunization Schedule*, p. 327

APPLY SELF-CARE

Chief concerns

3

NEUROLOGICAL

It is a fact that neurological functions of the body change over time. For example, blood flow to the brain may decrease.

Occasionally forgetting things is another common change in brain function that occurs with age. If you've ever forgotten a name or neglected to unplug the iron, don't automatically assume you're suffering from serious conditions like *dementia*, a significant, ongoing decline in intellectual capacity, or *Alzheimer's disease*, a type of dementia.

Although certain changes to the neurological system are a natural function of aging, some of the conditions in this chapter (even those involving disease) can be avoided — or at least well managed — through making healthy lifestyle choices related to diet, exercise and the decision to stop smoking.

Fever

As the body ages, its immune system also changes so that it doesn't fight inflammation or infection as efficiently as it once did. Fever may now become an inaccurate gauge of serious illness. You can be seriously ill and have no fever, or a very low fever.

Fever is a rise in body temperature above "normal." However, normal body temperatures can vary in individuals, and a person's body temperature varies throughout the day. A person is considered to have a fever if their oral temperature is higher than 99.5° F.

Fever can occur as a result of exercise, dehydration or injury to the *hypothalamus* (the temperature regulator in the brain); from a reaction to certain chemicals (such as caffeine); and as a symptom of the body's immune system fighting inflammation or infection.

Note your symptoms

Generally, fever is caused by viruses, bacterial infections, fungi or parasites. Fever can also result from inflammatory diseases (like lupus and rheumatoid arthritis) and from cancers (such as Hodgkin's disease and kidney cancer).

Other physical signs of fever include:

- Feeling hot or cold
- Shivering
- Headache
- Muscle aches
- Joint pains
- General malaise (feeling "lousy")

What you can do

- Take acetaminophen (Tylenol), aspirin or ibuprofen to lower temperature and minimize discomfort. **NEVER give aspirin to children/teenagers. It can cause Reye's syndrome, a rare but often fatal condition.**
- If medication is prescribed, follow your doctor's instructions and be sure to report any new symptoms.
- Good hygiene, particularly handwashing, is important in preventing infectious illnesses that cause fever.
- Warm (but never cold) baths or showers can also help to lower fever. Cool sponge baths may help in the case of a high fever.

SEE ⟩ *Know What To Do, p. 74*

 If you have a chronic illness or routinely take prescribed or over-the-counter (OTC) drugs, talk to your doctor or pharmacist before taking any other medications.

Fever

DO THESE APPLY:

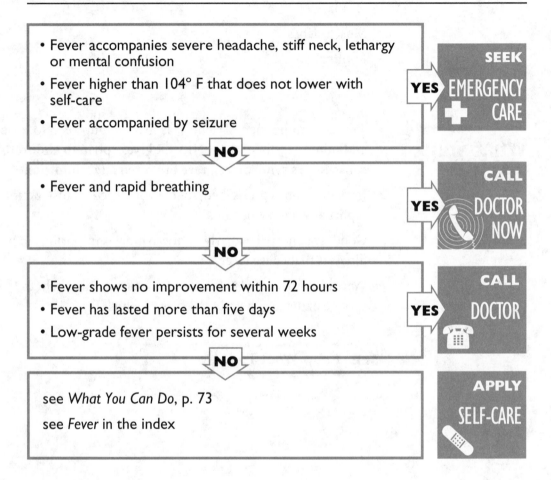

* Fever accompanies severe headache, stiff neck, lethargy or mental confusion
* Fever higher than 104° F that does not lower with self-care
* Fever accompanied by seizure

YES → SEEK EMERGENCY CARE

NO

* Fever and rapid breathing

YES → CALL DOCTOR NOW

NO

* Fever shows no improvement within 72 hours
* Fever has lasted more than five days
* Low-grade fever persists for several weeks

YES → CALL DOCTOR

NO

see *What You Can Do*, p. 73

see *Fever* in the index

APPLY SELF-CARE

Headaches

Almost everyone gets headaches — ranging from a dull ache to unbearable pain.

TENSION-TYPE HEADACHE

Tension-type headaches may be caused by reactions of the pain pathways in your head and may be triggered by a number of factors, including stress. The pain of a tension-type headache may feel like a band around your head, and is generally dull and continuous, with fluctuations in intensity.

Tension-type headaches are frequently triggered by emotional or physical factors. Figuring out the exact triggers of your particular headaches can help you reduce or avoid them in the future. Situations that make you grit your teeth, tighten your shoulders or clench your fist may trigger headaches.

MIGRAINE HEADACHE

Migraine headaches can cause excruciating pain and prevent sufferers from carrying out daily activities. Migraines account for 2% to 7% of all headaches, and affect more women than men. Some people experience fewer episodes of migraines as they grow older and may even enjoy a complete remission after age 50.

Migraines are believed to occur when pain pathways to the brain are triggered too easily, resulting in inflammation and blood vessel changes in the head. Researchers have found that *serotonin*, a chemical that transmits messages in the brain, is involved in migraines. Migraine medications can bind to serotonin sites, called receptors, and relieve headache symptoms. Migraine symptoms include: pain, sensitivity to light or noise, nausea, vomiting, or visual changes.

Factors that trigger migraines include glare from harsh light, stress, hunger, climatic changes, certain foods and beverages, oral contraceptives and medications, the menstrual cycle, physical or mental exhaustion, or too much or too little sleep.

What you can do

For tension-type headaches:

- Soak in a hot bath
- Get a massage
- Take a nap

For tension-type or migraine headaches:

- Aspirin, ibuprofen or acetaminophen (Tylenol) can blunt or eliminate pain. **NEVER give aspirin to children/teenagers. It can cause Reye's syndrome, a rare but often fatal condition.**
- Lie down in a darkened room with an ice bag on your forehead. For protection, place a washcloth between bare skin and ice.
- Exercise regularly and consider yoga, meditation or other muscle-relaxation techniques (for exercises see *Stress*, p. 284).

The key to managing migraines is to identify your triggers. Keeping a diary of your symptoms, possible triggers and which self-care techniques work and don't work provides helpful information for both you and your doctor.

Medication may be prescribed to reduce your migraine symptoms or help prevent chronic migraines. *Sumatriptin* is a relatively new drug that is proving helpful to many.

Avoid medication and food or beverages containing caffeine, which can cause a *rebound headache* (a new headache that is triggered before or as the previous one ends).

The good news is that with the right combination of self-care techniques and appropriate medication, you can make a significant difference in your ability to manage, and possibly eliminate, migraines.

 If you have a chronic illness or routinely take prescribed or over-the-counter (OTC) drugs, talk to your doctor or pharmacist before taking any other medications.

Headaches
DO THESE APPLY:

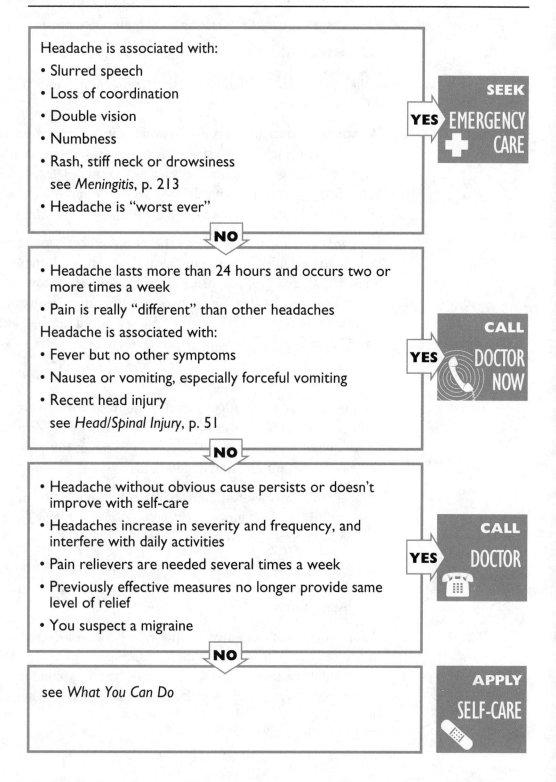

Headache is associated with:

• Slurred speech

• Loss of coordination

• Double vision

• Numbness

• Rash, stiff neck or drowsiness
see *Meningitis*, p. 213

• Headache is "worst ever"

YES → SEEK EMERGENCY CARE

NO

• Headache lasts more than 24 hours and occurs two or more times a week

• Pain is really "different" than other headaches

Headache is associated with:

• Fever but no other symptoms

• Nausea or vomiting, especially forceful vomiting

• Recent head injury
see *Head/Spinal Injury*, p. 51

YES → CALL DOCTOR NOW

NO

• Headache without obvious cause persists or doesn't improve with self-care

• Headaches increase in severity and frequency, and interfere with daily activities

• Pain relievers are needed several times a week

• Previously effective measures no longer provide same level of relief

• You suspect a migraine

YES → CALL DOCTOR

NO

see *What You Can Do*

APPLY SELF-CARE

Weakness/fatigue/dizziness/fainting

WEAKNESS/FATIGUE

Although they are often discussed together, weakness and fatigue are two distinctly different problems.

Weakness is a decrease in your physical ability or an increase in difficulty moving one or more muscles. It is usually the more serious symptom, especially when it involves a large group of muscles such as an arm or a leg, or one whole side of the body. Temporary or prolonged weakness in one part of the body may be a warning of injury to the nervous system or a stroke (see *Stroke/TIA*, p. 82).

Fatigue is a feeling of weariness, exhaustion or decrease in energy. Causes may include stress, sudden change in physical activity level, change in medication, limited or altered sleep, exposure to toxic chemicals, recovery from a major health or emotional event, depression, poor nutrition or excessive alcohol intake. In many cases, symptoms can be treated and relieved through self-care within several months.

Anemia

Prolonged or extreme fatigue that does not respond to self-care may be a sign of a more serious problem. Occasionally, fatigue can be the result of gastrointestinal bleeding (see *Peptic Ulcer*, p. 175; *Colon Cancer*, p. 199), resulting in *anemia*, a decrease in the number of red blood cells.

With anemia, adequate amounts of oxygen do not get to all of the tissues of the body. If the brain and heart receive less oxygen, you may feel tired or weary. Less oxygen to the muscles may cause weakness.

Anemia may be caused by an iron deficiency, a lack of certain nutrients, a serious illness or a disease of the bone marrow (such as leukemia or the spreading of breast or prostate cancer).

If your doctor suspects anemia, you will be given blood tests to help determine the cause and treatment. Treatment can range from taking iron or nutrient supplements to, in the most serious cases, having a blood transfusion. If the anemia results from a serious illness, your doctor will treat the illness rather than the anemia.

Prevention

Prevention and self-care are important in avoiding and coping with weakness and fatigue:

- Exercise regularly. Include exercises that strengthen and tone muscle and improve aerobic endurance (see *Staying Active*, p. 316).

- Eat a well-balanced diet that is high in fiber and low in fat (see *Eating Right*, p. 310).

- Improve your sleeping habits (see *Insomnia*, p. 293).

- Deal with any feelings of depression (see *Depression*, p. 289).

- Limit your use of alcohol, caffeine and tobacco products.

- Provide variety in your activities and interests.

- Avoid exhaustion by scheduling time for rest and relaxation.

What you can do

- Follow the prevention guidelines above.

- You can help your doctor diagnose the cause of your fatigue by keeping track of when the feeling starts, when it occurs or is most intense, anything that seems to make it worse or better, whether others in your home or work setting have similar problems, and any other changes or symptoms you notice.

- Listen to your body. Notice the effect medications, activities and stress have on you.

SEE *Know What To Do, p. 81*

DIZZINESS/FAINTING

Almost everyone has felt faint or dizzy at some time. There are many causes for these sensations — some minor and a few more serious. Most of these problems can be eased or eliminated with self-care.

Although many of these sensations seem similar, the differences in symptoms are important to help determine the cause and treatment. *Dizziness* is a sensation of spinning inside your head and can cause a loss of balance. Fainting (*syncope*) is the temporary decrease or loss of consciousness due to a momentarily inadequate supply of blood to your brain. *Light-headedness* is a very mild faint or "woozy" feeling.

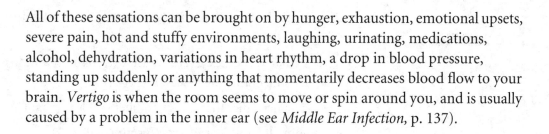

All of these sensations can be brought on by hunger, exhaustion, emotional upsets, severe pain, hot and stuffy environments, laughing, urinating, medications, alcohol, dehydration, variations in heart rhythm, a drop in blood pressure, standing up suddenly or anything that momentarily decreases blood flow to your brain. *Vertigo* is when the room seems to move or spin around you, and is usually caused by a problem in the inner ear (see *Middle Ear Infection*, p. 137).

Prevention

- Eat well-balanced meals at regular intervals and snacks between meals if you are hungry.

- Work and exercise in moderate amounts. Stop and rest at intervals to avoid becoming exhausted.

- Unless your fluid intake has been limited by your doctor, drink eight glasses of water daily. Drink more in hot conditions.

- Limit your alcohol intake, especially in warm weather.

- Read and learn about the side effects of all medications you are taking.

- Get up slowly after sitting or lying in one position for a long time.

 - Treat motion sickness with appropriate medications such as Dramamine or Bonine.

- Try to identify the cause of dizziness and avoid that activity in the future.

What you can do

- If you feel faint or dizzy, lie down and raise your legs above the level of your heart. If sitting, put your head down between your knees.

- Drink small amounts of liquid frequently if dehydrated (see *Dehydration*, p. 192).

- Move to a cool area if you're in a warm, stuffy environment.

- Check with your doctor about side effects of medication.

 If you have a chronic illness or routinely take prescribed or over-the-counter (OTC) drugs, talk to your doctor or pharmacist before taking any other medications.

know
WHAT
TO DO

Weakness/fatigue/dizziness/fainting
DO THESE APPLY:

- Complete loss of consciousness
  - ▶Lay person down in safe place. Check for breathing and pulse. Start CPR if needed (see *CPR*, p. 14).
- Weakness or dizziness accompanied by headache, loss of hearing, blurred vision, weakness or numbness in arms or legs, sudden weakness on one side of the body
  - ▶Have person lie down or sit in supported position. Check breathing and keep airway clear.
- Symptoms follow head injury

  see *Head/Spinal Injury*, p. 51

YES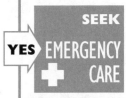

SEEK
EMERGENCY
CARE

APPLY
EMERGENCY
FIRST AID

 NO

- Fainting has occurred, but person is now awake and alert
- Irregular heartbeat with dizziness or light-headedness

  see *Palpitations*, p. 166

- ▶Don't drive yourself to doctor appointment.

YES

CALL
DOCTOR
NOW

 NO

- Dizziness not relieved with prevention or self-care
- Dizziness may be caused by prescribed medication
- Weakness or fatigue do not improve after two weeks of self-care

YES

CALL
DOCTOR

NO

---

see *What You Can Do, Weakness/Fatigue*, p. 79

see *What You Can Do, Dizziness/Fainting*

APPLY
SELF-CARE

Stroke/TIA

STROKE

A stroke, also called a *cerebrovascular accident* (CVA), occurs when an artery in the brain or neck is blocked or when a blood vessel in the brain ruptures. This interruption of blood flow to part of the brain results in death of brain tissue. Depending on the part of the brain affected, a stroke can impair memory, thinking, speech, comprehension, the senses and behavior. Most strokes diminish muscle control, causing weakness or paralysis — typically on one side of the body.

Most strokes are a by-product of *atherosclerosis*, the narrowing of arteries by fatty plaques and the formation of clots (see *Heart Disease*, p. 159). One of the most common causes of stroke occurs when an artery, narrowed by atherosclerosis, is blocked by a clot (*cerebral thrombosis*).

Other causes of stroke can include when a clot breaks off from another part of the body and blocks a small artery in the brain (*cerebral embolism*), and when a defective artery in the brain ruptures, allowing blood to leak into the brain (*cerebral hemorrhage*). Most cerebral hemorrhages are associated with high blood pressure, but some are the result of head injury.

Aphasia is a common complication of stroke. It is the inability to speak or write or to make sense of spoken and written language. It does not affect intelligence, however. Those with aphasia can be mentally alert even if speech is jumbled or incoherent.

Many stroke patients lose control of their emotions. They laugh or cry inappropriately or get very angry. Many also develop post-stroke depression, which is believed to be part of the brain's response to stroke injury as well as a psychological reaction.

TRANSIENT ISCHEMIC ATTACK (TIA)

A *transient ischemic attack* (TIA) occurs when the blood and oxygen supply to part of the brain is interrupted for a short time. A TIA may cause all of the symptoms of a stroke, but these symptoms are temporary. Brain cells generally do not die during a TIA; they malfunction for a short period of time.

A TIA is a warning sign that a stroke is likely. One-fourth of all strokes are preceded by a TIA. To reduce risk of stroke, a doctor may recommend aspirin therapy. Aspirin, besides lessening pain, can prevent cells in the blood from sticking together and blocking arteries.

Risk factors

Hypertension, or high blood pressure, is the single biggest risk factor for strokes caused by clots, emboli and hemorrhage. Other risk factors are diabetes, heart disease, age, gender (males are more susceptible), family history, prior stroke, TIA, high level of red blood cells, sickle cell disease, smoking (especially if you're a woman taking oral contraceptives), stress and being overweight.

Over the past three decades in the U.S., the number of people suffering from stroke has been cut in half. This is mostly due to better control of diabetes and high blood pressure. However, strokes are still the third leading cause of death of those 75 years of age or older.

Prevention

When brain cells die, they cannot be regenerated. That's why stroke prevention is so important. To lessen the risk of stroke:

- Control high blood pressure.

- Control diabetes.

- If you smoke, start taking steps to kick the habit. Quitting at any age reduces the risk of stroke.

- Improve cardiovascular fitness through a low-fat, low-cholesterol diet and exercise.

 If you have a chronic illness or routinely take prescribed or over-the-counter (OTC) drugs, talk to your doctor or pharmacist before taking any other medications.

What you can do

If you have had a stroke, or are a family member supporting a person who has had a stroke, it is important to know that stroke symptoms tend to improve with time. Even though dead brain tissue cannot function properly again, other parts of the brain can take over some or all of a lost function (such as speaking or walking).

To maximize recovery and to prevent muscles from deteriorating because of inactivity, rehabilitation and physical therapy should begin as soon as the person is out of danger. Health care professionals who can help include physical and occupational therapists, social workers, and speech and language specialists. People can relearn how to walk or sit, improve their balance and speak clearly.

Almost one-third of stroke survivors are able to resume their pre-stroke level of activity, and more than half can carry on daily activities with assistance.

The support and understanding of family and friends are essential to recovery. One of the most important tasks is helping the person tap into community resources.

Stroke clubs, sponsored by hospitals or local chapters of national health organizations, are a good source of information and encouragement for stroke survivors and their families. The American Heart Association offers brochures and a quarterly newsletter regarding strokes.

Also see *Resources*, p. 360, for more information.

Stroke/TIA

DO THESE APPLY:

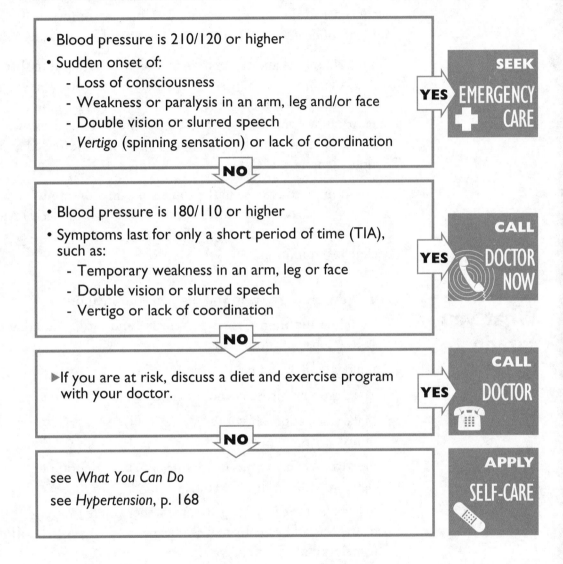

- Blood pressure is 210/120 or higher
- Sudden onset of:
  - Loss of consciousness
  - Weakness or paralysis in an arm, leg and/or face
  - Double vision or slurred speech
  - *Vertigo* (spinning sensation) or lack of coordination

YES → **SEEK EMERGENCY CARE**

NO

- Blood pressure is 180/110 or higher
- Symptoms last for only a short period of time (TIA), such as:
  - Temporary weakness in an arm, leg or face
  - Double vision or slurred speech
  - Vertigo or lack of coordination

YES → **CALL DOCTOR NOW**

NO

▶ If you are at risk, discuss a diet and exercise program with your doctor.

YES → **CALL DOCTOR**

NO

see *What You Can Do*
see *Hypertension*, p. 168

APPLY SELF-CARE

Memory loss

Growing older does not mean losing the ability to think, reason or remember. Many older adults worry when they feel confused or forgetful, concerned that these are signs of *dementia* or *senility*. Senility actually just means "old age."

Your brain selects and stores information or memory into three categories, each with its own purpose. *Short-term* memory is temporary. You look up a phone number and only remember it as long it takes to place the call. Long-term *recent* memory allows you to recollect events of the past few days. And long-term *remote* memory holds your distant memories and bulk of knowledge. You could call remote memory the "database" of your life.

As a common experience in the course of aging, the ability to recall long-term recent events may decline. Stress, depression and other factors can impact memory temporarily. Staying active and challenging your memory can help keep this decline to a minimum.

What you can do

Here are a few tips to help you sharpen your memory:

- Exercise your brain. Crossword puzzles and card games that require memory skills (Concentration, bridge) are good.

- Build your day around a routine.

- Make grocery, birthday and things-to-do lists.

- Make associations. If your wedding anniversary is October 10, think: "The minister was ten minutes late."

- Practice. When you meet a new person, pay attention to the name. Try to use it right away: "Nice to meet you, Hank!"

- Relax. Excessive worrying about whether you're losing your memory can be distracting and actually make your memory worse. Relaxation techniques may be helpful (see *Stress*, p. 284).

DEMENTIA

Dementia is a serious decline in memory. Those with dementia forget whole events, not just the minor details. In the early stages, symptoms may be subtle. Over time, loss of mental powers becomes obvious. Recognition of people, places or objects becomes difficult. Words and numbers can be hard or impossible to use.

Disorientation can occur. Personalities alter. Some causes of treatable dementia include poor nutrition, medications, brain tumors and certain other diseases such as Parkinson's disease.

Alzheimer's disease and *multi-infarct dementia* are responsible for two-thirds of all cases of dementia. Alzheimer's causes a slow, steady decline in mental powers and is the most common cause of dementia. Although it can occur at any age, it is more common in later years. There is no current cure for this ultimately fatal disease. Researchers, however, are learning more about the disease all the time. Multi-infarct dementia, on the other hand, is a result of small strokes (*infarcts*) that destroy brain tissue. The decline occurs in stages.

What you can do

Most people can be cared for at home in the early stages of dementia. You may want to follow these suggestions for creating a safe and orderly home environment:

- Lock away chemicals, drugs and other potentially harmful substances.
- Put bells on doors or door knobs.
- Provide the person with an ID bracelet to wear.
- Use signs to identify the bathroom, bedroom, etc.
- Provide healthy foods and plenty of fluids.
- Stimulate the senses with touch, songs, hugs and exercise.
- Review all medications and dosages with a doctor or pharmacist since some drugs can add to mental confusion (see *Using Medications*, p. 298).

If behavior problems arise, try to divert interest to something else — food, a colorful book, a loving pet. Always encourage the person to live life to their fullest potential. Daily routines, gatherings with friends and memory aids all help maintain personal dignity. It's equally important to remember that the caregiver has special needs and considerations as well (see *Care For The Caregiver*, p. 354).

Final notes

Memory loss is not necessarily serious. However, if you or someone you know is having increasing symptoms of dementia, which are interfering with the ability to carry on normal daily activities, talk with your doctor about an evaluation.

Parkinson's disease

Parkinson's disease is caused by a degeneration of part of the brain that produces a chemical called *dopamine,* a *neurotransmitter* that allows brain cells to communicate with one another. It is the deficiency in dopamine that accounts for the uncoordinated movements, tremor and stiffness commonly seen in Parkinson's.

Early in the disease, the facial muscles responsible for expression do not respond normally, giving a flat or expressionless look to the person. Often, this is mistaken for depression. The second noticeable effect is usually the change in the person's walk. Movement starts slowly, and the ability to change direction is often affected. The *tremor* (or bodily shaking) often associated with Parkinson's disease does not always occur, but when present usually occurs when the arm or leg is at rest. As the disease progresses, symptoms worsen and the muscles that coordinate swallowing are affected. This makes choking a likely possibility. Dementia also occurs in up to one-third of those with advanced Parkinson's.

What you can do

Although medical science has not been able to find what causes the disease, there are treatments for Parkinson's. The most commonly used medication (*L-dopa*) is a chemical that changes into dopamine within the brain. Physical and occupational therapy can be beneficial. In some cases, surgery is an option.

Caring for a person with Parkinson's disease takes careful monitoring of medications. It's important to emphasize self-reliance as much as possible when assistance with eating, personal hygiene and daily activities is provided. Support for the caregiver is also available and highly recommended. Many communities have associations to help the caregiver and family members better understand the disease (see *Care For The Caregiver,* p. 354; *Resources,* p. 360).

If you have a chronic illness or routinely take prescribed or over-the-counter (OTC) drugs, talk to your doctor or pharmacist before taking any other medications.

Shingles

Shingles is a blistering rash that usually occurs on one side of the body (most often on the torso) and is accompanied by sharp nerve pain.

It is caused by the same virus that causes chicken pox. Once you've had chicken pox, the virus takes up residence in a bundle of sensory nerve cells connected to the spinal cord. For most people, the virus remains dormant. However, in some cases, the virus is reactivated and travels down the nerve, infecting the surrounding skin with the rash.

No one knows for sure what reactivates the virus, but stress, trauma, some illnesses and a compromised immune system can be triggers.

Most people recover from shingles within one month with no complications. However, for some, pain may persist for months after the blisters have healed.

Shingles is most likely to affect older adults. Once the initial episode of shingles is over, the infection seldom recurs. If you have shingles, it is possible to pass chicken pox on to someone who has never had the disease, although the virus is not often spread this way.

A vaccine against chicken pox, *Varivax* (or VZV vaccination), is available.

Note the symptoms

Symptoms that precede an active outbreak of shingles include:

- Chills
- Fever
- Malaise (feeling "lousy")
- Upset stomach
- Pain and itching along the site of the future eruption

After four or five days, the characteristic symptoms appear:

- Pain (which can be severe) or a tingling sensation that travels down the nerve pathway along one side of the torso
- Itching (which may be intense)
- A rash of small, fluid-filled blisters, frequently occurring on one side of the body. The blisters begin to dry and scab in about five days.

What you can do

- Take analgesics, such as aspirin, acetaminophen (Tylenol) or ibuprofen, for pain relief. **NEVER give aspirin to children/teenagers. It can cause Reye's syndrome, a rare but often fatal condition.** If these aren't sufficient, your doctor may prescribe a stronger pain reliever.

- Wear soft cotton clothing over affected skin (clothing may stick to the skin as the blisters ooze), and avoid tight clothing.

- Apply cool compresses for temporary relief.

- Wash the affected area gently with mild, nonperfumed soap.

The drug *Acyclovir* (Zovirax) is often prescribed to accelerate healing and reduce pain after the sores heal.

know
WHAT
TO DO

Shingles
DO THESE APPLY:

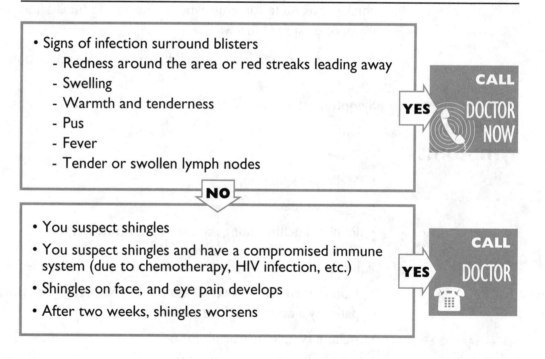

- Signs of infection surround blisters
  - Redness around the area or red streaks leading away
  - Swelling
  - Warmth and tenderness
  - Pus
  - Fever
  - Tender or swollen lymph nodes

YES → **CALL DOCTOR NOW**

NO

- You suspect shingles
- You suspect shingles and have a compromised immune system (due to chemotherapy, HIV infection, etc.)
- Shingles on face, and eye pain develops
- After two weeks, shingles worsens

YES → **CALL DOCTOR**

If you have a chronic illness or routinely take prescribed or over-the-counter (OTC) drugs, talk to your doctor or pharmacist before taking any other medications.

SKIN CONCERNS

As the body ages, many changes in the *integumentary system* (skin) can occur.

The loss of thickness in the layer of *subcutaneous fat* (a layer of fat under the skin) leaves the deeper layers of skin unable to support the top layer, forming folds — or wrinkles. This loss of fat also causes older adults to more readily become chilled.

The skin itself also becomes thinner, and the small blood vessels supply less nutrition to the skin. Bruises and cuts occur more easily and heal more slowly. The pressure of sitting or lying in one position for more than two hours at a time can kill skin by preventing blood flow to the area. Older adults who are not able to move frequently because of injury, disease or weakness may develop *bed sores,* or pressure ulcers, on their skin. All skin ulcers should be brought to the attention of a doctor.

With aging, some skin cells lose the ability to produce pigment (causing hair, which is part of the skin, to turn gray) while other cells produce too much pigment (causing *age spots*). The oil in older skin also decreases, causing dry skin and *xerosis* (itching, burning, cracking or scaling skin).

Repeated exposure to sun without sunscreen speeds the aging process of skin and increases the risk of skin cancer.

Age spots and dry skin

AGE SPOTS

Age spots are pigment changes in the skin that don't cause any medical problems. Some skin cells lose the ability to produce the pigment *melanin*, while other cells produce too much. Age spots or adult freckles are generally not raised above the skin's surface.

Seborrheic keratosis is a common skin growth that appears as grayish, raised or flat and scaly, and can be darker (but not black) than the surrounding skin. These generally require no treatment. However, any spot or growth that you can feel should be examined by your doctor (see *Skin Cancer*, p. 95).

DRY SKIN

As the body ages, skin produces less oil, causing dry skin to develop. Although it is water in skin cells that keeps skin moist, it is the natural oil in skin that keeps the water from evaporating. Very dry skin may itch, burn, crack or scale. This is called *xerosis*.

What you can do

To treat dry skin you must minimize the loss of oil and/or supplement the oil your body produces. If you have dry skin:

- Bathe or shower no more than once a day. Very hot water may irritate the skin.
- Use a natural sponge or soft washcloth. Avoid scrubbing with brushes or rough washcloths.
- Use a gentle soap with moisturizing oils — one free of harsh detergents.
- Pat skin dry with a soft towel rather than rubbing it.
- After bathing or showering, apply a moisturizer. Moisturizers containing *urea* are particularly helpful in treating dry skin. Ask your pharmacist for advice.

Serious xerosis may require medication, usually a cream containing steroids.

Sunburn

Sun — and more specifically, sunburn — is an enemy to skin, especially aging skin. Repeated sunburning and tanning increases exposure to damaging ultraviolet (UV) rays, speeding the development of wrinkles and increasing the risk of some cancers (see *Skin Cancer*, p. 95).

A sunburn is a true burn of the outer layer of your skin. It is usually a *first-degree* burn causing skin redness and moderate discomfort. Severe sunburns with blisters, pain and swelling are *second-degree* burns and involve the deeper skin layer (see *Burns*, p. 22).

Prevention

- Use sunscreen with a sun protection factor (SPF) of at least 15. Apply sunscreen 15 minutes before exposure and reapply every two hours. Use a sunscreen that protects against both UVA and UVB light. Ask your pharmacist for recommendations.

- Check with your doctor or pharmacist to find out if any of your medications increase your skin's sensitivity to sunlight. If they do, use *extra* caution in the sun.

- Wear long sleeves and a hat with a broad brim or visor while you are in the sun.

- Unless your fluid intake has been limited by your doctor, drink extra fluids on sunny days, even if the temperature is not hot.

- Avoid the sun between 11 a.m. and 1 p.m. when the sun's rays are the strongest. Cloudy conditions do not screen out the rays that can burn your skin.

- Take sunburn precautions at high altitudes, in tropical climates, and around snow or water.

What you can do

- Cool compresses or baths may ease the discomfort. Adding one cup of baking soda or finely ground oatmeal to the bath water may increase the soothing effects.

 - Take aspirin or ibuprofen to ease the pain and decrease inflammation. **NEVER give aspirin to children/teenagers. It can cause Reye's syndrome, a rare but often fatal condition.**

SEE Know What To Do, p. 94

 If you have a chronic illness or routinely take prescribed or over-the-counter (OTC) drugs, talk to your doctor or pharmacist before taking any other medications.

- Aloe vera gel or lotion may make your skin more comfortable.

- Avoid oil-based products, such as petroleum jelly, for the first 24 hours. They may actually retain the heat.

- Avoid products that contain anesthetic "caines" such as benzocaine. They may cause an allergic reaction in sensitive skin.

- Unless your fluid intake has been limited by your doctor, drink extra water and watch for signs of dehydration (see *Dehydration*, p. 192).

- Get extra rest and avoid exertion for 24 hours.

Sunburn
DO THESE APPLY:

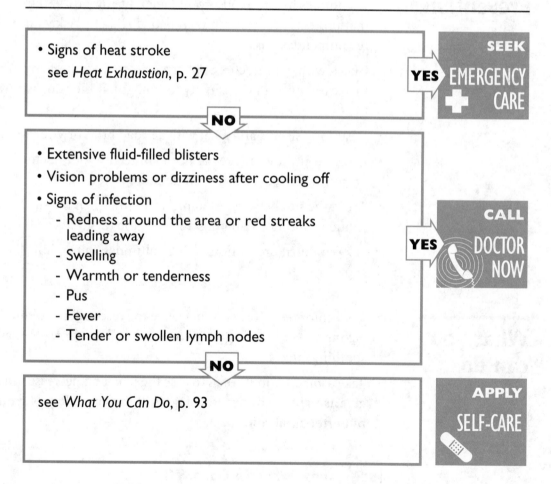

- Signs of heat stroke
  see *Heat Exhaustion*, p. 27

YES → SEEK EMERGENCY CARE

NO

- Extensive fluid-filled blisters
- Vision problems or dizziness after cooling off
- Signs of infection
  - Redness around the area or red streaks leading away
  - Swelling
  - Warmth or tenderness
  - Pus
  - Fever
  - Tender or swollen lymph nodes

YES → CALL DOCTOR NOW

NO

see *What You Can Do*, p. 93

APPLY SELF-CARE

Skin cancer

People who are aging often notice changes in the general appearance of their skin, including lumps and bumps that weren't always there. This can lead to worries about skin cancer.

On one hand, the worrying is understandable. The primary known cause of skin cancer is continued exposure to the sun's ultraviolet (UV) radiation. So, older adults who have spent a lot of unprotected time in the sun are at greater risk.

However, the vast majority of skin changes that develop with age are not skin cancers. More often they are *seborrheic keratoses* (grayish, raised, flat, scaly lesions), warts or noncancerous skin "tags," tiny flaps of skin called *papillomas*.

There are many types of skin cancer, but the three most common are:

Basal cell carcinoma: the most common type, which affects more women than men, and usually occurs over the age of 40. It first appears as small sores that do not heal. Over weeks to months the sores enlarge and may *metastasize* (spread) to other areas. It is a slow-growing cancer that forms in the basal cells of the outermost layer of the skin. If treated early, it is usually completely curable. If untreated, it can ultimately metastasize to bone and cartilage.

Squamous cell carcinoma: the second most frequent type, which is more common in men, and usually occurs after the age of 60. It first appears as small sores that do not heal. This cancer grows more quickly and may metastasize to other areas. Out of 2,500 deaths annually from nonmelanoma skin cancer, 75% are from squamous cell carcinoma.

Malignant melanoma: the third most common and the most deadly type of skin cancer. This is cancer of the *melanocyte*, the pigment cell of the skin. Unlike most other types of skin cancer, malignant melanoma can spread through the lymph system and the bloodstream. That's why it is very important that it be detected in the earliest possible stage. Over 70% of cases of early melanoma can be cured. However, the prognosis is not as favorable for cases that are treated in later stages. Other factors that influence the outcome of treatment include age and general health.

SOME CAUSES

People who live in sunny climates and those with fair skin, freckles, blond or red hair, or blue eyes are at greatest risk. However, people with dark skin also can develop skin cancer. Some people with many moles (*nevi*) that contain abnormal (*dysplastic*) cells have an increased risk of developing melanoma.

Other factors that increase the risk of skin cancer include exposure to artificial sources of UV radiation (such as commercial tanning devices and phototherapy for certain skin disorders), concurrent use of certain drugs or cosmetics, immunosuppressive treatment, AIDS, hereditary disorders, and exposure to x-rays, uranium and a variety of chemicals.

Note your symptoms

Skin cancer forms without causing any symptoms of illness. Therefore, it's extremely important to be aware of the signs, especially in people with known risk factors.

Check your skin once a month for any skin irregularities. If you have any suspicious growths on your skin, have them checked by your doctor. A skin *biopsy*, in which part or all of the tissue from a mole or suspicious growth is removed for analysis, may be required. Biopsy is the only definitive test.

MALIGNANT MELANOMA

The "hallmark" sign of melanoma is a change in the size or shape of a mole. "ABCD" is an abbreviation used to make it easy to remember the four basic signs of possible melanoma:

- **A**symmetry — The shape of one half of a mole doesn't match the other.
- **B**order — The edges are ragged, notched or blurred.
- **C**olor — The color is uneven and shades of black, brown or tan are present. Areas of white, red or blue may also be seen.
- **D**iameter — There is change in size. The mole may be raised or flat, round or oval.

Other signs include a mole that scales, oozes, bleeds or changes in the way it feels. Some moles will become hard, lumpy, itchy, swollen or tender. Melanoma may also appear as a new mole.

OTHER SKIN CANCERS

Watch for skin irregularities that:

- Have a smooth, shiny or waxy surface

- Are small in size

- Bleed or become crusty

- Are flat or lumpy, red or pale

Prevention

The best approach to skin cancer is preventing it in the first place:

- Stay out of sun as much as possible, especially if you have fair skin, a history of sunburns or a current diagnosis of skin cancer.

- If you can't avoid sun exposure, wear protective clothing (hats and long sleeves) and gradually build up exposure to sunlight.

- Avoid or limit sunlight exposure between 11 a.m. and 1 p.m., when the sun's rays are the most direct.

- Some medications can greatly increase the likelihood of sunburn. Check all prescription and over-the-counter (OTC) medications for precautions about sun exposure.

- **ALWAYS** use sun block, even on overcast, cloudy days. Sunscreens are rated by a sun protection factor (SPF); the higher the SPF number, the greater the protection.

- Avoid commercial tanning booths.

- Check your skin regularly.

Skin cancers
DO THESE APPLY:

- Any skin lesion or growth that concerns you
- A change in the size, shape or feel of a mole

YES ▶ CALL DOCTOR ☎

Eczema and psoriasis

ECZEMA

Eczema, also known as *dermatitis*, is characterized by dry, scaly and itchy skin common to the face, neck, hands, elbows, wrists and/or knees. It is caused by the inability of the skin to retain enough water. Causes range from contact with detergents or other harsh substances (also called *contact dermatitis*) to emotional stress. Often, the cause of eczema is unknown.

A common form of eczema is called *atopic dermatitis*. You're a likely candidate if you have a personal or family history of asthma, hay fever or some other allergy. Recent studies suggest that certain foods — such as citrus fruits, wheat, eggs and nuts — might also be responsible for some cases of eczema.

What you can do

- Avoid drying out the skin. Limit baths and showers and the use of soap. Use an unscented moisturizer.

- Use hypoallergenic makeup, or none at all. Wear rubber gloves for dishwashing and other household chores. Wear cotton clothing (wool and synthetic materials may be irritating). Sweat aggravates eczema, so wear lightweight, loose-fitting clothes, especially during exercise.

- Swimming in fresh or chlorinated pool water can aggravate eczema, but salt water is not harmful.

- Most complications result from scratching or rubbing. Trim nails to minimize the effects of scratching.

- Do not apply anesthetic lotions or antihistamine creams unless your doctor prescribes them; they can actually increase irritation. For the worst areas, try using a cool gauze dressing soaked in diluted Burrow's solution, which is available in most drugstores. Apply the dressing three times a day for about 15 minutes.

PSORIASIS

Eczema can be confused with other skin conditions, such as *psoriasis,* another chronic skin condition. Psoriasis appears as silvery skin patches, or *plaques,* which are often on the knees, elbows and scalp. Normally, skin cells mature and are shed once a month. With psoriasis this occurs at a much faster rate, every three to four days. Because the *dermis* (lower layer of skin cells) is dividing so rapidly, dead cells accumulate in thicker-than-normal patches on the *epidermis* (skin's outermost layer). The symptoms of this chronic disease typically come and go over weeks or months and then disappear altogether.

As many as 4 to 5 million Americans cope with psoriasis. Although there is no cure, the right therapy can help control symptoms. Care is individualized and based on the severity of symptoms. Treatment may consist of self-care, *phototherapy* (exposure to ultraviolet or infrared light) and a variety of medications to help relieve the scaling.

What you can do

- Bathe daily to help soak off the scales.
- Avoid hot water or harsh soap. Anything that is drying to your skin will worsen psoriasis.
- Use an unscented moisturizer that does not contain lanolin.
- Treat small patches with occasional use of hydrocortisone cream.
- Try medicated shampoos (such as Head & Shoulders, Selsun Blue and Capitrol) for scalp psoriasis.

If you think you have psoriasis, consult your doctor for a treatment plan that is best for your symptoms. If you've been diagnosed with psoriasis and your current treatment is no longer working, call your doctor. There are new products being developed that may help.

SEE ❯ *Know What To Do, p. 100*

know
WHAT
TO DO

Eczema and psoriasis
DO THESE APPLY:

- Signs of infection
  - Redness around the area or red streaks leading away
  - Swelling
  - Warmth or tenderness
  - Pus
  - Fever
  - Tender or swollen lymph nodes

YES → CALL **DOCTOR NOW**

NO ⬇

- You think you may have psoriasis
- Eczema sores become crusty or develop weepy discharge
- No improvement after one week of treatment, or symptoms worsen
- Itching makes sleeping difficult despite self-care
- Eczema or psoriasis interferes with daily functions or causes increased emotional stress
- Prescribed treatment is no longer working

YES → CALL **DOCTOR**

NO ⬇

see *What You Can Do, Eczema*, p. 98
see *What You Can Do, Psoriasis*, p. 99

APPLY **SELF-CARE**

DIFFERENT SYMPTOMS?

see *Skin Symptoms*, p. 111

Hair loss

Hair is constantly being lost and replaced by your body. By far the most common reason for hair loss, or *alopecia*, is male-pattern baldness, in which hair replacement fails to keep up with hair loss. Typically the hair loss starts with a receding hairline, continuing until only a horseshoe-shaped area of hair remains around the head. The scalp looks healthy. Both aging and genetics play a part in balding, with as many as 60% of men over age 50 affected. *Female-pattern baldness*, which is a general thinning of hair at the crown or hairline, is also genetic and influenced by hormonal changes during or after menopause.

Chemotherapy can cause complete or partial hair loss on the body, with hair almost always growing back when treatment ends. Some common medications that can cause significant hair loss include heparin, oral contraceptives, amphetamines and beta blockers.

Hair loss that develops over weeks, months or even years can be due to autoimmune diseases (such as *systemic lupus*), infectious diseases (such as *syphilis*) or endocrine disorders (such as problems affecting the thyroid).

Hair loss that is accompanied by an inflamed or scaly scalp may be caused by *psoriasis* (see *Psoriasis*, p. 99) or *dandruff*. The hair usually thins because of the intense scratching or applied treatment. If hair loss leaves bald spots with a gray-green scale, *ringworm* (a fungal infection) should be suspected (see *Fungal Infections*, p. 105).

What you can do

Male- and female-pattern baldness can't be prevented, but the over-the-counter (OTC) drug *minoxidil* (Rogaine) has been used with mixed results. When rubbed on the scalp, this expensive cream has sometimes slowed hair loss and generated new hair growth, but many have been disappointed with the results.

Another alternative is hair transplantation, but successful cosmetic results are not always achieved, and the procedure is painful, time-consuming and expensive. If you are bald or balding, you are at an increased risk of sunburn or skin cancer. Wear a hat or a sunscreen with a sun protection factor (SPF) of 15 or higher for protection.

SEE ⟩ *Know What To Do*, p. 102

Hair loss

DO THESE APPLY:

- Bald areas have gray-green scales
  see *Fungal Infections*, pp. 106, 112
- Sudden or dramatic hair loss
- New hair fails to grow normally
- Bald spots are patchy, don't follow the normal progression of male/female-pattern baldness
- Hair loss causes persistent or severe anxiety or depression
- Skin does not appear normal in area of hair loss

YES ▶ **CALL DOCTOR**

NO

see *What You Can Do*, p. 101

APPLY SELF-CARE

Boils

A *boil* is a red, swollen, painful bump that looks like a large pimple. It is usually caused by an infected hair follicle in an area of your body that is under pressure or chafed.

Common sites for boils are the buttocks, groin, waistline, armpits, neck and face. Bacteria, most often *staphylococcus*, get blocked in the follicle and develop an abscess. The tissue around the follicle becomes tender and inflamed as it tries to wall off the infection. This forces the abscess outward until it ruptures on the skin surface and drains. If the wound is left open and clean, it can heal; if it closes off too soon, the pus pocket can form again.

Prevention

- For areas that are prone to boils, wash well with antibacterial soap and dry thoroughly.

- Avoid clothing that is too tight. Eliminate chafing and ease pressure against your skin whenever possible.

- Keep clothes and personal linen of someone with a boil separate from the rest of the household to prevent spreading the infection.

What you can do

- Bathe with antibacterial soap to prevent boils from spreading.

- Apply warm, moist compresses to the boil for 20 to 30 minutes, four times a day. The moist heat will help bring the boil to a head and soften the skin to ease the rupture. This may take up to a week of compress treatments.

- **DO NOT squeeze, scratch, cut or force the boil to drain.** Any pressure or forced opening can push the bacteria deeper into the skin and spread the infection.

- Once the boil begins to drain, keep the wound open and clean, and:
  - Continue applying compresses at least three times a day.
  - Wash the area thoroughly with soap and water two times a day or as needed.
  - If you must cover the boil, apply antibacterial ointment and a sterile dressing after each compress treatment or whenever the old dressing becomes moist.

SEE ▷ *Know What To Do, p. 104*

• Take aspirin or ibuprofen to ease pain and inflammation (follow the directions on the package). **NEVER give aspirin to children/teenagers. It can cause Reye's syndrome, a rare but often fatal condition.**

• Watch for signs of infection: redness around the area or red streaks leading away; swelling; warmth or tenderness; pus; fever; tender or swollen lymph nodes.

Boils

DO THESE APPLY:

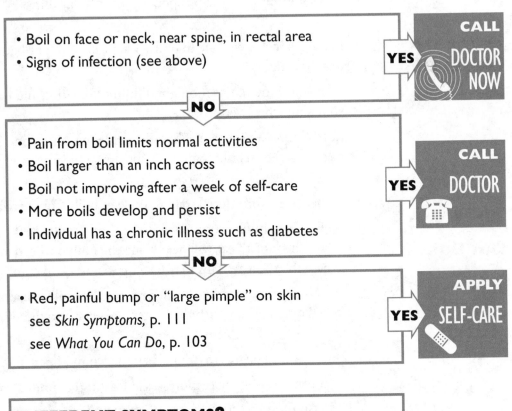

• Boil on face or neck, near spine, in rectal area

• Signs of infection (see above)

YES → CALL DOCTOR NOW

NO

• Pain from boil limits normal activities

• Boil larger than an inch across

• Boil not improving after a week of self-care

• More boils develop and persist

• Individual has a chronic illness such as diabetes

YES → CALL DOCTOR

NO

• Red, painful bump or "large pimple" on skin

see *Skin Symptoms,* p. 111

see *What You Can Do,* p. 103

YES → APPLY SELF-CARE

DIFFERENT SYMPTOMS?

see *Skin Symptoms,* p. 111

If you have a chronic illness or routinely take prescribed or over-the-counter (OTC) drugs, talk to your doctor or pharmacist before taking any other medications.

Fungal infections

Fungus requires moisture to grow. That's why common fungal infections develop in the folds of skin that trap moisture. They tend to spread from person to person in public areas such as showers and swimming pools.

Ringworm, an infection of the nails, skin or scalp, has nothing to do with worms, but gets its name from its characteristic red rings.

Athlete's foot, a form of ringworm, causes feet to be red, itchy and irritated.

Jock itch affects boys and men. Symptoms include minor to intense itching in the groin area and, in more serious cases, patches of redness, scaling and raised areas that ooze. The penis and *scrotum* (the skin "sac" that holds the testes) are usually not involved.

Prevention

- Always use your own towels.
- Wear sandals in public showers, pools or locker rooms.
- Wear cotton socks to absorb moisture and change them every day.
- Have all pets checked for ringworm before bringing them into your home. Avoid touching stray dogs or cats.
- Launder secondhand clothing.

What you can do

Keep the infected area clean and dry. Wear loose, cotton clothing and clean all clothes in hot water and detergent. Avoid damp public areas, such as shower rooms.

Many over-the-counter (OTC) anti-fungal medications applied to the skin are effective treatments for these infections. Follow all directions on the container.

SEE ⟩ *Know What To Do, p. 106*

know WHAT TO DO

Fungal infections
DO THESE APPLY:

- Any signs of infection, such as:
  - Redness around the area or red streaks leading away
  - Swelling
  - Warmth and tenderness
  - Pus
  - Fever
  - Tender or swollen lymph nodes

YES → **CALL DOCTOR NOW**

 NO

- Symptoms of athlete's foot or other foot problems and you are diabetic and/or have peripheral vascular disease
- Thickened, distorted, yellowish, crumbly toenails (possible fungal infection of nails)
- Symptoms of ringworm on scalp or on large areas of chest or abdomen
- Jock itch seems to spread to anal area
- Symptoms of any fungal problems persist or worsen after self-care
- Ringworm is not completely gone after four weeks of treatment

YES → **CALL DOCTOR**

 NO

- Rash begins as small, round, pink patches
- Patches turn red and grow into ring shape
- Center of ring clears as it enlarges

see *What You Can Do*, p. 105

YES → **APPLY SELF-CARE**

Allergic reaction

Allergic reactions result from a complex process that releases chemical substances in the body in response to a specific irritant, or *antigen.*

Allergens (antigens that cause an allergic response in a hypersensitive person) can be medications (such as penicillin and other antibiotics and anesthetics), vaccines (especially those containing horse serum), foods (such as seafood, milk, eggs, wheat, chocolate, nuts), insect venom (such as in bee or wasp stings, or mosquito bites — see *Insect Bites/Stings*, p. 46) or in the dye used for certain diagnostic x-ray exams.

Inhalent allergens (such as pollen, molds and animal dander) cause what is commonly called *hay fever* (see *Hay Fever*, p. 124). *Asthma* is a disease that constricts the airways and can be an allergic reaction to antigens inside or outside of the body (see *Asthma*, p. 151).

No one knows for sure why certain individuals have allergies or why reactions vary from person to person. As part of the body's immune system, *histamine* and other proteins are released, causing many allergic symptoms and the wide range in the severity of those symptoms.

HIVES

Hives are red, itchy, raised welts on the skin that may vary in size from less than a quarter-inch to more than an inch. Hives may appear immediately or a few days after exposure and may last a few minutes or several days, or come and go for weeks. You may react on the first exposure or after many contacts with the antigen.

Hives also can occur as a reaction to cold, heat, sunshine or stress. It is often difficult to determine the cause, and mild cases are treated only to relieve symptoms. Allergy testing is done if the symptoms become severe and interfere with your normal activities.

ANAPHYLAXIS

Anaphylaxis is a severe and life-threatening allergic reaction. The response generally begins minutes or seconds after exposure to the antigen. A mild allergic reaction may amount to hives and intense itching. A severe reaction usually results in constriction of the airway and throat, accompanied by *shock*, a sudden drop in blood pressure and vascular collapse. This can lead to death if not immediately treated.

The standard treatment for anaphylaxis is an adrenaline (or *epinephrine*) injection. Those with a known risk of anaphylaxis should carry an anaphylactic kit (called an ani- or epi-kit) obtained through a prescription. A medical-alert bracelet can inform others of your allergy if you are unconscious.

Prevention

- Avoid foods, medications or contacts that may have caused hives or other allergic reactions in the past.
- Use insect repellent and extra caution when you are in areas that have insects you may be allergic to.
- Inform all your doctors and dentists of your allergies.
- Learn stress management techniques if stress appears to be a trigger for your hives (see *Stress*, p. 284).

What you can do

- Relieve itching skin areas by applying cool, wet compresses soaked in ice water or Burrow's solution (available in most drugstores).
- Bathing in lukewarm water containing one-half to one cup of Aveeno powder, one cup of baking soda or finely ground oatmeal may ease itching in large areas.
 - To relieve hay fever symptoms or itching, try over-the-counter (OTC) oral antihistamines such as Benadryl or Chlor-Trimeton. Read the precautions on the label regarding drowsiness.
- Apply a very thin layer of over-the-counter (OTC) hydrocortisone cream to ease itching on small areas. **DO NOT** use near your eyes, mouth or genitals.
- To reduce further irritation from hives, cut nails short or wear cotton gloves at night to prevent harmful effects of scratching.
- Avoid the cause of your hives.

 If you have a chronic illness or routinely take prescribed or over-the-counter (OTC) drugs, talk to your doctor or pharmacist before taking any other medications.

Allergic reaction
DO THESE APPLY:

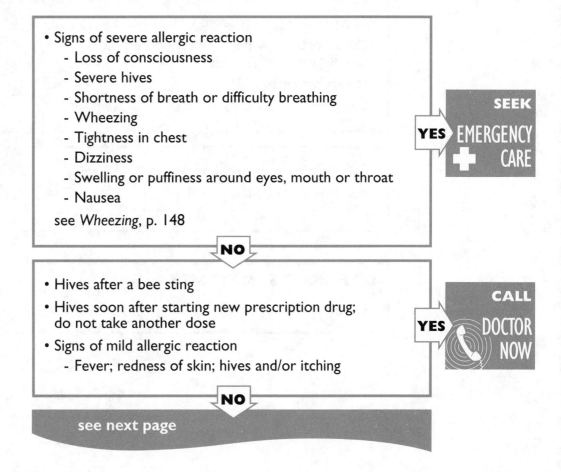

- Signs of severe allergic reaction
  - Loss of consciousness
  - Severe hives
  - Shortness of breath or difficulty breathing
  - Wheezing
  - Tightness in chest
  - Dizziness
  - Swelling or puffiness around eyes, mouth or throat
  - Nausea

see *Wheezing*, p. 148

YES **SEEK EMERGENCY CARE**

NO

- Hives after a bee sting
- Hives soon after starting new prescription drug; do not take another dose
- Signs of mild allergic reaction
  - Fever; redness of skin; hives and/or itching

YES **CALL DOCTOR NOW**

NO

see next page

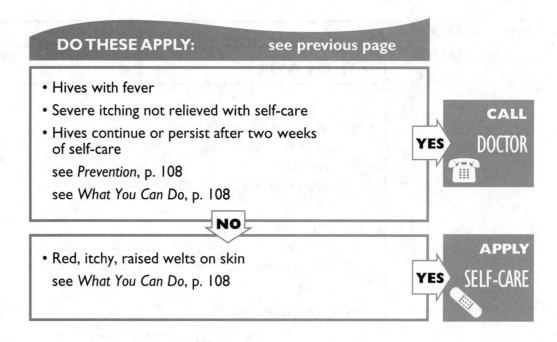

DO THESE APPLY: see previous page

- Hives with fever
- Severe itching not relieved with self-care
- Hives continue or persist after two weeks of self-care

  see *Prevention*, p. 108

  see *What You Can Do*, p. 108

YES → CALL DOCTOR

NO

- Red, itchy, raised welts on skin

  see *What You Can Do*, p. 108

YES → APPLY SELF-CARE

DIFFERENT SYMPTOMS?

see *Skin Symptoms*, p. 111

SKIN SYMPTOMS

Rash	Appearance/ Location	Itching	Fever	Other Symptoms/ Comments
General Skin Conditions				
Boil p. 103	Red, swollen, painful bump (like a large pimple); common on buttocks, groin, waist, armpits, neck, face	No	No	Occurs in infected hair follicles that are under pressure or chafed
Dandruff p. 101	White to yellow to red, some crusting: on scalp, eyebrows, groin	Occasional	No	Fine, oily scales and flaking
Eczema p. 98	Red; cracking and thickening of dry areas: on elbows, wrists, knees, cheeks	Moderate to intense	No	Moist, oozing, water-filled blisters
Psoriasis p. 99	Thick, silvery skin patches: often on knees, elbows, scalp	Moderate to intense	No	Symptoms come and go over weeks to months
Shingles p. 89	Small, fluid-filled blisters: usually on one side of body (most often the torso), accompanied by sharp nerve pain	Intense	Maybe	Blisters rupture, forming yellow, crusty scabs
Skin Cancer p. 95	Change in size or shape of mole	Occasional	No	Skin irregularity that is smooth, shiny or waxy; mole that scales, oozes or bleeds
Warts p. 243	Raised, grainy, lump anywhere on the body	No	No	If in area of pressure, like soles of feet, can be flat

Continued on next page

SKIN SYMPTOMS

Rash	Appearance/ Location	Itching	Fever	Other Symptoms/ Comments
Fungal Rashes				
Athlete's Foot p. 105	Colorless to red: between toes	Mild to intense	No	Cracks, scaling, oozing blisters
Jock Itch p. 105	Patches of redness, scaling and raised areas that ooze: on groin	Mild to intense	No	Penis and scrotum usually not involved
Ringworm p. 105	Red, slightly raised rings: located anywhere, including nails, scalp	Occasional	No	Fungus can cause hair loss and patchy bald spots
Allergic Reactions				
Hives p. 107	Welt-like elevations, surrounded by redness: located anywhere	Intense	No	Reaction to an allergen; many possible causes
Poison Ivy/Poison Oak	Red, elevated blisters: on any exposed area; oozing; some swelling; rash begins 12 - 48 hrs. after contact with plant and may persist for up to two weeks	Intense	No	Also spread by pets, contaminated clothing, smoke from burning plants; to treat, clean affected skin area with soap and water, bathe with Aveeno powder; an OTC product, Ivy Block, can be used for prevention
Rashes caused by chemicals	Red, possibly blisters: on any exposed area	Moderate to intense	No	Oozing and/or swelling

EYE CONCERNS

After about age 40, the lens and functions of the eye become less flexible. This is called *presbyopia*, which makes focusing on close objects difficult.

It is also common for eyes to adjust less easily to changes in light, and for eyelids to droop as skin around the eyes becomes less elastic. Drooping may even obstruct vision. In addition, your eyes tear less, making them feel dry and sometimes itchy. Other more serious changes require prompt medical attention.

Glaucoma/cataracts/ macular degeneration

Eyesight is precious — something you want to protect with proper care and regular checkups. When changes in vision occur, it's not unusual to delay taking action or pretend the problems don't exist. However, many eye conditions are very treatable. Three of the most common eye problems affecting older adults are *glaucoma*, *cataracts* and *macular degeneration*. (For information on *diabetic retinopathy*, see *Diabetes*, p. 201).

GLAUCOMA

Glaucoma, the leading cause of blindness, affects more than 2 million people in the U.S. It causes pressure inside the eye to increase, gradually destroying nerve fibers in the eye's *retina*, the light-sensitive area at the back of the eyeball that receives and transmits images to the brain. Glaucoma can cause tunnel vision and eventual blindness.

There is no pain with glaucoma, and there are no early symptoms, so regular checkups are important. Testing for glaucoma is easy and painless. Treatment involves either medication or surgery to reduce the pressure inside the eye.

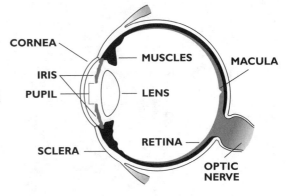

Figure 17

Depending on your medical condition, your doctor will probably recommend a type of eye drops. Many over-the-counter (OTC) and prescription medications should not be taken if you have glaucoma — check with your doctor or pharmacist (see *Medications That Can Cause Problems . . .*, p. 302).

Depending on the type of glaucoma, outpatient laser surgery may be appropriate.

CATARACTS

Opaque or cloudy areas in the eye lens, known as *cataracts*, cause vision to gradually become dull and fuzzy, make glare uncomfortable and may eventually make it impossible to read. Cataracts occur in more than 50% of people over 75. Cataracts can occur in anyone at any age, but are most common in individuals with diabetes (see *Diabetes*, p. 201) or who have years of unprotected exposure to sunlight, and those who have taken long-term steroids.

If the cataract is not yet mature (ready for surgery), reducing the glare both indoors and while outside will lessen how much the cataract affects your vision. Use indirect lighting (light that bounces off walls and ceilings) in the home, and wear sunglasses outdoors.

Once the cataract begins to severely affect your vision, surgical removal should be considered. Cataracts can be removed in a relatively simple surgical procedure that does not require an overnight stay in a clinic or hospital.

MACULAR DEGENERATION

The *macula* is the central area of your retina and contains the largest portion of light-sensitive nerves (see Figure 17, p. 113). With age, some degeneration of the macula is normal, causing a blurring of central vision, but *peripheral vision* (vision on the far left or right while looking straight ahead) is not affected. The macula is difficult to examine and may require an evaluation by an *ophthalmologist*, a doctor specializing in diseases of the eye.

Good glasses, strong lighting and magnifying lenses can help you cope with the condition.

What you can do

- Be alert for changes in your vision such as:
  - Blurring
  - Inability to focus on small or faraway objects or printed type
  - Loss of peripheral vision, leading to "tunnel vision"
  - Dull or fuzzy vision
  - Inability to tolerate bright sunshine
- See your eye doctor for a checkup if any of the above symptoms are present.
- Wear sunglasses to protect your eyes from the harmful rays of the sun.

Conjunctivitis and styes

Eye discomfort ranges from simple itching, which can be caused by a common cold or an allergic reaction, to pain, which can be a symptom of much more serious eye disease.

CONJUNCTIVITIS

Conjunctivitis (pinkeye) is an inflammation of the *conjunctiva* — the outermost membrane covering the eye and inner part of the eyelid — and is the most common eye disease. Pinkeye can be caused by bacteria, viruses, allergies, pollution or other irritants such as cigarette smoke. The most common symptoms are redness of the whites of the eyes, scratchy or itchy eyes, tearing, swelling, sensitivity to light and a yellow discharge that becomes crusty at night.

Prevention

There are some preventive measures that can reduce your risk of eye problems:

- Don't share towels.
- Never use anyone else's makeup.
- Discard your mascara after a couple of months.
- Wear goggles to protect your eyes against chlorinated swimming pools or airborne irritants such as chemicals or smoke.
- Air conditioning in your home and/or car can reduce *allergens* (irritants) that cause eye discomfort.

What you can do

- Avoid rubbing or touching your eyes. This can aggravate the symptoms and spread the infection.
- Wash your hands every time you touch your eyes. If you're around a child who has pinkeye, remember to wash your hands frequently with soap and water.
- Don't share washcloths or towels while infected with pinkeye.
- Change bed linens and pillowcases daily.
- Apply warm or cool compresses.
- If you wear contact lenses, remove them until the infection goes away.
- Over-the-counter (OTC) eye drops or boric-acid washes can relieve itchiness.

- Antihistamines may help relieve allergic eye discomfort.

If you have a chronic illness or routinely take prescribed or over-the-counter (OTC) drugs, talk to your doctor or pharmacist before taking any other medications.

STYES

Styes are caused by a bacterial infection of the tiny glands near the base of the eyelashes. They almost never result in damage to the eye or sight and soon disappear when properly treated.

Note your symptoms

A stye typically starts out looking like a pimple on the eyelid — a small, red, tender and swollen bump — and grows to full size over a day or so. The stye then fills with pus and ruptures within a few days. If the bacteria spread, more than one stye may occur. Styes can also form inside the eyelid, but this is less common.

Styes are common enough that many people can identify them on their own. Occasionally, they are confused with a *chalazion*, a swelling caused by a blocked gland within the eyelid. Unlike a stye, a chalazion is painless and is usually not helped by self-care.

What you can do

Wring out a clean cloth soaked in warm or hot water. Place it directly on the affected (closed) eye. For best results, do this three or four times a day for about 10 minutes each time. The stye will then rupture and drain, which usually occurs after about two days. Sometimes a stye may fade away without ever coming to a head and draining.

Since styes can be spread from one eye to another, and from one person to another through close contact, wash your hands frequently. Never pinch the stye to remove the pus, since this may spread the infection.

A doctor may prescribe an antibiotic solution applied directly to the eyelid. Oral antibiotics are usually reserved for styes that do not respond to other treatment, are very large, or are located inside the eyelid. A particularly stubborn stye may need to be lanced and drained by a surgeon. Never try to do this on your own.

Final notes

Styes and conjunctivitis are two common sources of eye pain. Other causes of eye pain can be injury, infection or some other disease. Pain in both eyes when exposed to bright light is common with viral infections such as flu, and will disappear when the infection clears up. Injury to the eye by a foreign object can cause considerable pain. This type of eye pain should be treated by your doctor (see *Foreign Object In Eye*, p. 119).

SEE > *Know What To Do*, p. 118

Conjunctivitis and styes
DO THESE APPLY:

• Eye pain or worsening symptoms

• Change in vision

• Severe light sensitivity

• Swelling or redness spreading over the eye or tear duct (when stye is suspected)

• Pupils are different sizes

YES → **CALL DOCTOR NOW**

NO

You suspect conjunctivitis and:

• Have watery drainage that contains pus

• Symptoms spread from one eye to the other

• Symptoms don't improve after three to five days of self-care, or after a few days of prescribed treatment

• Symptoms begin to improve, then worsen

• Symptoms disappear completely for a short time but reappear in the same or other eye

You suspect a stye and:

• The stye keeps recurring, is under the eyelid or is still there after two days of self-care

• There is crusty, yellow discharge on eyelid

YES → **CALL DOCTOR**

NO

see *What You Can Do, Conjunctivitis*, p. 116

see *What You Can Do, Styes*, p. 117

APPLY SELF-CARE

Foreign object in eye

Tears and blinking are your natural defenses against sand, dust and other particles that enter the eye. But when something larger injures the eye, other steps are necessary to protect your vision and speed recovery.

Prevention

Nearly all eye injuries reported each year could be prevented by wearing goggles or safety glasses during sports activities or while using tools (drills, hammers, grinders and saws) and heavy machinery. Other injuries could be avoided simply by using common sense when handling potential hazards.

What you can do

REMOVE ONLY THOSE OBJECTS FLOATING ON THE EYE'S SURFACE

Never rub the injured eye. Ask someone to help you remove the object from your eye, or use a mirror to locate it yourself. Sit in a well-lit room, and use clean hands to pull the lower eyelid gently down while you look up. If you do not see the object, gently pull the upper lid out as you look down. Only attempt to remove foreign material if it is "floating." **DO NOT try to remove anything embedded in the eye. Instead, seek emergency care.**

If you cannot readily see the object, grasp the lashes of your upper lid and pull down. Blink several times. This will sometimes remove small particles.

- Flush the eye with clean water by pressing the rim of a small glass against the eye socket and tilting your head back. Open and close the eye.

- If flushing with water is unsuccessful, moisten a cotton swab and gently lift off the object. Flush with water afterward.

- Do not use ointments or anesthetic drops on the eye.

HANDLING POSSIBLE COMPLICATIONS

- If a trip to the doctor is necessary (see next page, *Know What To Do*), cover the eye with a sterile dressing or clean cloth and keep it still. Close both eyes to prevent involuntary movement.

- If you can't close your eye, tape a paper cup over it.

SEE *Know What To Do*, p. 120

Final notes

An object in the eye can scratch the *cornea* (the covering of the eye), and may cause significant vision loss (see Figure 17, p. 113). Your recovery will depend on how deeply the object penetrates the eye, how quickly the injury is treated and whether an infection develops.

Foreign object in eye
DO THESE APPLY:

- Eye pain is severe
- Object is embedded, or on pupil or *iris* (colored part of eye)
- Object can't be located, but you felt something hit your eye
- Object can't be easily extracted

see *Handling Possible Complications*, p. 119

- Pain and irritation continue for more than 24 hours, even if object was supposedly removed

YES → **CALL DOCTOR NOW**

NO ↓

see *What You Can Do*, p. 119

APPLY SELF-CARE

EAR/NOSE/THROAT

As with other body systems, the *sensory system* (such as sight, hearing, taste, smell) changes from the effects of time. (For more on sight, see *Eye Concerns*, p. 113.) The number of taste buds decrease, for example, dulling the ability to perceive salty and sweet flavors. Foods naturally begin to take on a different flavor (see *Mouth Concerns*, p. 142). The sense of smell — connected to taste — also begins to fade a bit.

The ability to hear high-frequency tones decreases, making the range of spoken words harder to understand.

Because the *immune system* responds more slowly, you are less able to fight off common infections, such as cold or flu, that affect the ears, nose and/or throat. The good news is that with a healthy diet and exercise, you can fight back against many common complaints.

The common cold

A *cold* is a viral illness that can cause a sore throat, runny nose and other symptoms. Most colds are caused by *rhinoviruses* ("rhino" refers to the nose), which are transmitted through sneezes, coughs or handling virus-contaminated objects.

Prevention

Since there's no cure, avoiding the cold virus is the best way to beat the bug.

- Wash your hands frequently.
- Avoid touching your eyes, nose or mouth after touching objects that could be contaminated with the cold virus, such as doorknobs or stair railings.

Note your symptoms

 Cold symptoms develop suddenly within two to six days of exposure. A runny nose is a very common symptom. However, runny noses are also caused by hay fever or *allergic rhinitis* (see *Hay Fever*, p. 124), or by prolonged use of nose drops. Never use over-the-counter (OTC) nose drops for more than three consecutive days.

 If you have a chronic illness or routinely take prescribed or over-the-counter (OTC) drugs, talk to your doctor or pharmacist before taking any other medications.

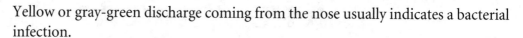

Yellow or gray-green discharge coming from the nose usually indicates a bacterial infection.

The excess mucus produced by a runny nose can cause postnasal drip, which triggers a nighttime cough and can cause a sore throat. Ear or sinus infections may develop if mucus plugs up the *eustachian tube* between the nose and ear or the sinuses (see *Sinusitis,* p. 126; *Ear Pain,* p. 137).

Other cold symptoms include:

- Scratchy or sore throat
- Sneezing
- Watery eyes
- Headache
- Swollen glands
- Cough that fails to bring up *sputum* (material such as mucus, blood or pus from the respiratory tract; also known as *phlegm*)
- Fever (see *Fever,* p. 72)

A cold usually runs its course in five to seven days.

What you can do

SIMPLE STEPS TO RELIEF

- Get plenty of rest.
- Unless your fluid intake has been limited by your doctor, drink lots of fluids.
- Use a cool-mist vaporizer to relieve congestion. Change the water daily and rinse the vaporizer with a weak bleach-and-water solution.

MEDICATION CONSIDERATIONS

 Over-the-counter (OTC) medications will not shorten the course of a cold, but they may offer temporary relief from some symptoms. All have side effects (see *Using Medications,* p. 298; *Home Pharmacy,* p. 303).

- Nose drops or nasal sprays are effective decongestants, but they can increase stuffiness if used for more than three consecutive days. Instead, substitute a homemade saline solution of one-quarter teaspoon of salt to a pint of water.

 - Oral decongestants may act as stimulants and make you restless or unable to sleep. Often they are combined with antihistamines to lessen this side effect.

 If you have a chronic illness or routinely take prescribed or over-the-counter (OTC) drugs, talk to your doctor or pharmacist before taking any other medications.

• Antihistamines appear to be more effective against allergy symptoms than cold-related complaints. They cause drowsiness, which can help you sleep. Never use antihistamines while driving or operating heavy machinery because of their tendency to cause drowsiness or dizziness.

 • Pain relievers, such as aspirin, ibuprofen and acetaminophen (Tylenol), can lessen aches, pains and fevers. **NEVER give aspirin to children/teenagers. It can cause Reye's syndrome, a rare but often fatal condition.**

Final notes

In some cases, the common cold can lead to ear or sinus infections, laryngitis, bronchitis or pneumonia. Other conditions — such as strep throat and allergies — produce symptoms that mimic a cold.

The common cold
DO THESE APPLY:

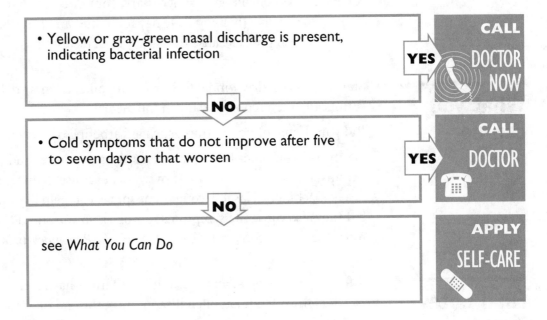

• Yellow or gray-green nasal discharge is present, indicating bacterial infection — **YES** — CALL DOCTOR NOW

NO

• Cold symptoms that do not improve after five to seven days or that worsen — **YES** — CALL DOCTOR

NO

see *What You Can Do* — APPLY SELF-CARE

 If you have a chronic illness or routinely take prescribed or over-the-counter (OTC) drugs, talk to your doctor or pharmacist before taking any other medications.

Hay fever

Hay fever sufferers can blame pollen for the sneezing, watery eyes and runny nose that mark this common allergy. Some form of pollen is almost always in the air, whether from trees in the spring, summer grass or fall ragweed. The severity of your symptoms can depend on the time of year and the amount of airborne pollen on a particular day.

Note your symptoms

Hay fever occurs when your body's antibodies react to pollen and prompt the release of *histamine*. Histamine inflames the lining of nasal passages and causes sneezing, itching and watery eyes. Headaches, irritability and insomnia are possible, too.

Hay fever can be confused with the common cold, but you can suspect you have allergies if your symptoms last for long periods of time and return during the same season each year. If hay fever runs in your family, chances are your sneezes are based on allergies. If necessary, your doctor can test your nasal secretions to confirm that you have hay fever, and an *allergist* can conduct tests to identify which pollens cause the most problems for you.

What you can do

- Stay indoors on dry, windy days or when pollen counts are high. Pollen counts are often reported daily in the media.
- Rid your home of pollen traps, such as carpeting or dirty air filters.

- Try over-the-counter (OTC) antihistamines to relieve mild symptoms. Antihistamines can make you drowsy, so never use them when driving or using heavy machinery. Nasal decongestant sprays will help dry up your runny nose, but they also cause the symptoms to worsen so you should never use them for more than three consecutive days (see *Home Pharmacy*, p. 303).

Final notes

Hay fever can develop at any age. While irritating, hay fever symptoms will go away when the offending pollen disappears at the end of the season.

 If you have a chronic illness or routinely take prescribed or over-the-counter (OTC) drugs, talk to your doctor or pharmacist before taking any other medications.

know
WHAT
TO DO

Hay fever
DO THESE APPLY:

- Symptoms interfere with daily routine
- Symptoms are not relieved with over-the-counter (OTC) medications
- You have hay fever and develop symptoms of sinusitis
- You have hay fever and develop symptoms of an ear infection

YES ▶

CALL
DOCTOR

NO

see *What You Can Do*
see *The Common Cold*, p. 121
see *Sinusitis*, p. 126
see *Middle Ear Infection*, p. 137
see *Home Pharmacy*, p. 303

APPLY
SELF-CARE

Sinusitis

Sinusitis is an inflammation of the *sinuses*, the four pairs of empty chambers in the facial bones around the nose and eyes. These chambers are located near the cheekbones, above the eyebrows, behind or between the eyes and near the temples. Inflammation can be caused by a viral, bacterial or fungal infection, or by allergies.

The condition is usually brought on by an upper respiratory tract infection, hay fever (see *Hay Fever*, p. 124) or a *deviated septum* (a deformity in the structure between the nostrils that divides the inside of the nose into right and left sides). About 25% of chronic sinusitis in the area near the cheekbones is related to dental infections (see *Dental Care*, p. 142).

Note your symptoms

- Tenderness and swelling over the area involved
- Pain around the eyes or cheeks
- Difficulty breathing through the nose
- Inside of nose is red and swollen
- Yellow or gray-green nasal discharge
- General feeling of illness
- Fever may or may not be present

What you can do

- Inhaling steam helps promote drainage. Try sitting in a steamy bathroom.
- Stay indoors and keep rooms at an even temperature.
- Unless your fluid intake has been limited by your doctor, drink plenty of fluids (a glass of water or juice every one to two hours).
- Nasal sprays such as *phenylephrine* 0.25% may be effective, but they should not be used for more than three consecutive days.
- Over-the-counter (OTC) decongestants may help open the nasal passages and cause drainage of the sinuses.
- Hot and cold compresses applied to the forehead and cheeks (apply them alternately, one minute each, for 10 minutes) may aid sinus drainage.
- Increasing home humidity with a cool-mist vaporizer may help.

 If you have a chronic illness or routinely take prescribed or over-the-counter (OTC) drugs, talk to your doctor or pharmacist before taking any other medications.

Anyone with a history of recurring sinusitis should use self-care treatment at the first sign of a cold or other respiratory tract infection or when they experience an allergic reaction.

A doctor may prescribe antibiotics to treat chronic sinusitis or sinusitis caused by a bacterial infection. On rare occasions, surgical repair of the sinuses may be necessary.

know
WHAT
TO DO

Sinusitis
DO THESE APPLY:

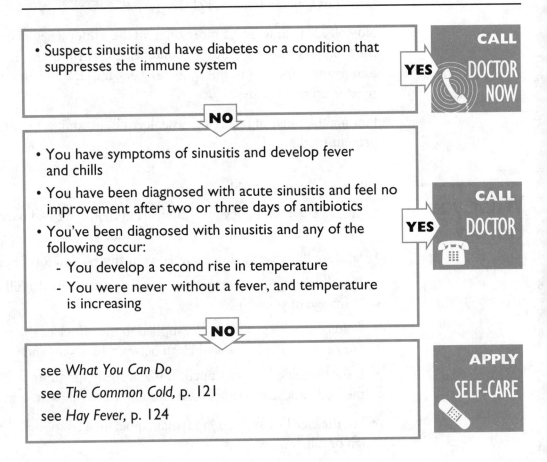

- Suspect sinusitis and have diabetes or a condition that suppresses the immune system

YES ▶ **CALL DOCTOR NOW**

NO

- You have symptoms of sinusitis and develop fever and chills
- You have been diagnosed with acute sinusitis and feel no improvement after two or three days of antibiotics
- You've been diagnosed with sinusitis and any of the following occur:
    - You develop a second rise in temperature
    - You were never without a fever, and temperature is increasing

YES ▶ **CALL DOCTOR**

NO

see *What You Can Do*
see *The Common Cold*, p. 121
see *Hay Fever*, p. 124

APPLY SELF-CARE

Nosebleeds

Nosebleeds are usually messier and more embarrassing than they are serious, and can almost always be stopped with self-care. Nosebleeds are usually caused by trauma to the nose or by anything that irritates normal tissue integrity, such as dry air, low humidity, allergies, picking the nose or blowing the nose during a cold.

Prevention

Frequently, nosebleeds are related to the common cold — the blood vessels in the nose are irritated by either a virus or constant nose blowing. If this is the case, treating cold symptoms reduces the probability of having more nosebleeds (see *The Common Cold*, p. 121).

Nosebleeds tend to occur more often in the winter when people spend more time indoors where the air is dry and heated. Turning the heat down and using a cool-mist vaporizer to put moisture back into the air sometimes brings relief from nosebleeds.

Finding the cause of recurring nosebleeds is, of course, the first step in preventing them.

What you can do

When you have a nosebleed:

- Sit in a chair, keeping your head level rather than tilted back. This prevents the blood from running down your throat.
- Squeeze the nostrils shut between your thumb and forefinger.
- Breathe through your mouth and apply pressure for 10 full minutes without letting go of your nose.
- Cold compresses or ice packs applied to the bridge of the nose may also help. For protection, place a washcloth between bare skin and ice.
- If the bleeding hasn't stopped, apply pressure for another 10 minutes. This method almost always works if enough time is allowed for the bleeding to stop.

When the bleeding stops, try to remain quiet for a few hours. Don't blow your nose, laugh or talk loudly.

Nosebleeds
DO THESE APPLY:

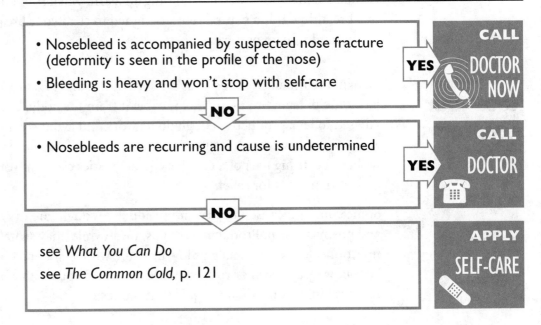

- Nosebleed is accompanied by suspected nose fracture (deformity is seen in the profile of the nose)
- Bleeding is heavy and won't stop with self-care

YES → CALL DOCTOR NOW

NO

- Nosebleeds are recurring and cause is undetermined

YES → CALL DOCTOR

NO

see *What You Can Do*
see *The Common Cold,* p. 121

APPLY SELF-CARE

Coughs

A cough is the body's way of sounding an alarm when something interferes with free breathing. It is a natural reflex designed to clear your breathing tubes of mucus and foreign particles.

Note your symptoms

Coughs are usually referred to as *productive* or *nonproductive*. A productive cough jars loose phlegm or pus and helps expel it from the body. You'll probably be advised to let a productive cough do its work and avoid cough suppressants. A nonproductive cough is dry or hacking, and you may need to take steps to quiet it. Learning to spot a cough's characteristics can help you pinpoint the appropriate steps for relief.

Some common causes for dry, nonproductive coughs are dry air, smoking and postnasal drip. Productive coughs, meanwhile, may signal viral or bacterial infections. Mucus is usually yellow or white with a viral infection, but it can be yellow, gray-green or rust-colored and contain pus with a bacterial infection. Bacterial infections usually require antibiotics.

What you can do

- Unless your fluid intake has been limited by your doctor, drink lots of water to loosen phlegm and soothe your irritated throat.
- Use a cool-mist vaporizer to increase humidity.
- Use throat lozenges or hard candies to relieve the "tickle" and throat irritation.
- If postnasal drip is causing the dry, hacking cough, try an over-the-counter (OTC) decongestant. Avoid medications with antihistamines, which will thicken the secretions you are trying to dislodge.
- Ask about trying a nonprescription cough medication containing *guaifenesin*, which can thin secretions. Over-the-counter (OTC) cough suppressants with *dextromethorphan* (or "DM" in their name) may help quiet the cough at night so you can get some rest (see Home Pharmacy, p. 303).
- Use pillows to elevate your head at night.
- If you smoke, see *Smoking Cessation*, p. 319, for ways to kick the habit.

 If you have a chronic illness or routinely take prescribed or over-the-counter (OTC) drugs, talk to your doctor or pharmacist before taking any other medications.

Coughs
DO THESE APPLY:

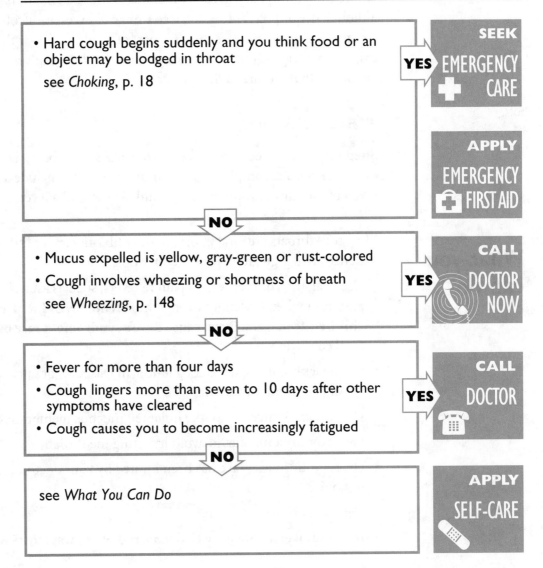

• Hard cough begins suddenly and you think food or an object may be lodged in throat

see *Choking*, p. 18

YES ▶ SEEK **EMERGENCY CARE**

APPLY **EMERGENCY FIRST AID**

NO

• Mucus expelled is yellow, gray-green or rust-colored
• Cough involves wheezing or shortness of breath

see *Wheezing*, p. 148

YES ▶ CALL **DOCTOR NOW**

NO

• Fever for more than four days
• Cough lingers more than seven to 10 days after other symptoms have cleared
• Cough causes you to become increasingly fatigued

YES ▶ CALL **DOCTOR**

NO

see *What You Can Do*

APPLY **SELF-CARE**

Sore throat and laryngitis

A sore throat, or *pharyngitis,* is often the result of a viral or bacterial infection, although dry or polluted air, tobacco smoke or excessive alcohol use can also cause irritation. Typically, a sore throat is part of a cold or flu, or the result of postnasal drip from allergies, but in some cases it can be the symptom of a more serious condition that requires a doctor's care.

STREP THROAT

Strep throat is caused by an infection of *streptococcal* bacteria, and if left untreated can cause serious complications. Symptoms usually include a bright red and severely sore throat, swollen tonsils and glands, and a fever.

What you can do

Most sore throats are viral in origin, so antibiotics are of little help. Time and patience are the greatest healers. Other tips:

- Use over-the-counter (OTC) pain relievers, such as aspirin, ibuprofen and acetaminophen (Tylenol), to ease the soreness. **NEVER give aspirin to children/teenagers. It can cause Reye's syndrome, a rare but often fatal condition.**

- Gargle with warm salt water (one-fourth teaspoon of salt added to eight ounces of water) several times a day.

- Use throat lozenges to soothe inflamed mucous membranes.

- Eat a soft or liquid diet to avoid irritating the throat.

- Unless your fluid intake has been limited by your doctor, drink plenty of liquids.

- Get plenty of rest.

- If you smoke, see *Smoking Cessation,* p. 319, for ways to kick the habit.

 If you have a chronic illness or routinely take prescribed or over-the-counter (OTC) drugs, talk to your doctor or pharmacist before taking any other medications.

LARYNGITIS

Laryngitis is an inflammation of the *larynx* (voice box), which is located at the top of the windpipe. When the vocal cords, which are part of the larynx, become inflamed, they swell and cause hoarseness and distortion of the voice.

Laryngitis may be caused by illnesses such as the common cold, bronchitis or the flu, or by:

- Excessive talking, singing or shouting
- Allergies
- Inhaling irritating chemicals
- Excessive alcohol intake (see *Use Of Alcohol*, p. 322)
- Heavy smoking (see *Smoking Cessation*, p. 319)

Note your symptoms

Laryngitis is usually identified by its primary symptom, hoarseness. Other symptoms can include loss of voice, tickling, rawness or pain in the throat, or a constant need to clear your throat.

What you can do

There is no specific medical treatment for laryngitis, but you may be able to relieve symptoms by:

- Resting your voice
- Inhaling steam (sit in the bathroom with the shower turned on hot to make steam)
- Drinking lots of liquids, especially warm, soothing ones, unless your fluid intake has been limited by your doctor
- Not smoking
- Gargling with warm salt water (one-fourth teaspoon of salt added to eight ounces of water) to soothe the throat
 - Taking antihistamines to relieve symptoms caused by allergy

If laryngitis is caused by exposure to irritants or alcoholism, the cause must be dealt with directly before the symptoms can be eliminated.

SEE ⟩ *Know What To Do, p. 134*

 If you have a chronic illness or routinely take prescribed or over-the-counter (OTC) drugs, talk to your doctor or pharmacist before taking any other medications.

3

know
WHAT
TO DO

Sore throat and laryngitis
DO THESE APPLY:

- Laryngitis or a sore throat with severe difficulty breathing

  see *CPR*, p. 14, if person stops breathing

- Symptoms of laryngitis begin suddenly, and you think food or an object may be lodged in throat

  see *Choking*, p. 18

YES ▶
SEEK
EMERGENCY CARE

APPLY
EMERGENCY FIRST AID

NO ▽

- Beginning to develop severe difficulty breathing
- Severe pain when swallowing

YES ▶
CALL
DOCTOR NOW

NO ▽

- Swollen glands in neck and fever lasting more than a few days
- Sore throat and a fever of 101°F or higher, a rash or a strawberry red tongue or throat, or pus visible at the back of the throat
- Sore throat persists or worsens after a few days
- You have been exposed to strep throat
- Symptoms of laryngitis accompanied by fever that don't improve in two to three days
- Chronic laryngitis or symptoms have lasted for two weeks or more

YES ▶
CALL
DOCTOR

NO ▽

see *What You Can Do, Strep Throat*, p. 132

see *What You Can Do, Laryngitis*, p. 133

APPLY
SELF-CARE

Swollen glands

Lymph glands swell to help the body fight infection. Frequently, swollen glands mean there's an infection in the area of the body where the glands are located. For example, swollen neck glands often accompany sore throats and earaches. Lymph glands in the groin area sometimes swell when there is an infection in the feet, legs or genital region. Swollen glands behind the ears can be a sign of a scalp infection.

Glands become painful as a result of their rapid enlargement when they first begin to fight an infection. The pain usually goes away in a couple of days, but the lymph glands may stay enlarged for quite a while, sometimes several weeks.

On rare occasions, glands that have been enlarging over several weeks are a symptom of a serious underlying cause.

What you can do

Most swollen glands don't require any treatment because they are fighting an infection somewhere else in the body. An exception to this is if the gland itself develops a bacterial infection, making it red and tender. Sometimes a doctor will prescribe antibiotics to get rid of the bacteria causing the infection.

> If you have swollen glands and a sore throat, see *Sore Throat And Laryngitis*, p. 132.

SEE ❯ *Know What To Do*, p. 136

know
WHAT
TO DO

Swollen glands
DO THESE APPLY:

• Swollen glands and signs of infection
 - Redness around the area or red streaks leading away
 - Swelling
 - Warmth or tenderness
 - Pus
 - Fever
 - Tender or swollen lymph nodes

YES ▶ **CALL**
DOCTOR
NOW

NO

• Swollen glands for more than two or three days, fever and a sore throat (with or without painful swallowing)

• Swollen glands persist or have increased in size for two to three weeks

• Swollen glands and rash

• Swollen glands and fever for two to three days

YES ▶ **CALL**
DOCTOR

NO

see *What You Can Do*, p. 135

APPLY
SELF-CARE

DIFFERENT SYMPTOMS?

see *Sore Throat And Laryngitis*, p. 132

Ear pain

When fluid accumulates in the *middle ear* (that part of the ear behind the eardrum) pressure builds up and causes pain.

MIDDLE EAR INFECTION

Middle ear infections (*otitis media*) usually occur as a complication of an upper respiratory infection (see index for specific topics), when the tubes between the ear and the throat (*eustachian tubes*) swell and close. Fluid and mucus gather in the middle ear, and bacteria breed.

The hallmark symptom of otitis media — persistent ear pain — may be accompanied by decreased hearing, a sense of fullness or ringing in the ear (see *Tinnitus*, p. 141), fever, headache, runny nose and dizziness.

Vertigo is the dizzy feeling of being off balance. More specifically, it's the sensation that the room or objects are moving around you. A middle ear infection can cause vertigo, as can toxic substances in the body or other types of infection.

What you can do

Otitis media requires a visit to your doctor, who will probably prescribe antibiotic treatment and possibly a decongestant.

After the visit, self-care may include:

- Getting plenty of rest
- Increasing the amount of clear fluids you drink, unless your fluid intake has been limited by your doctor
- Placing a warm washcloth, water bottle or heating pad (set on low) directly on the affected ear (see *Heating Pad, First-Aid Supplies*, p. 307)
- Blowing your nose gently, with your mouth open
- Using a cool-mist vaporizer to moisturize the air and help control levels of mucus

- Taking acetaminophen (Tylenol), ibuprofen or aspirin to relieve discomfort; antihistamines, decongestants or nose drops may help decrease the amount of nasal secretion and shrink mucous membranes. **NEVER give aspirin to children/teenagers. It can cause Reye's syndrome, a rare but often fatal condition.**

Note: **DO NOT** insert **any** type of object in the ear to relieve itching or pain.

For symptoms of vertigo:

- Lie quietly in a darkened room.
- Avoid sudden movements.
- Focus on one object or keep eyes closed to help ease spinning sensation.

FLUID IN MIDDLE EAR

Serous otitis media results when fluid collects in the middle ear, either from a previous infection or ongoing irritations such as allergies. An infection is not necessarily associated with this condition but can occur if bacteria build up. Symptoms may include temporary hearing loss and a feeling of stuffiness or sensitivity in the ear.

What you can do

Most cases of serous otitis media clear up in about a week. Chewing gum or swallowing may help open the eustachian tube, and taking decongestants or pain relievers may provide additional relief.

If the problem does not clear up with self-care, a doctor may prescribe a higher dose of decongestant or use a device to force air into the eustachian tube and middle ear. If a bacterial infection is involved, antibiotics may be prescribed.

RUPTURED EARDRUM

If you've recently had a cold with ear pain and congestion, and then notice white to yellow ear discharge (even on your pillow), contact your doctor. Infections, blows to the head or inserting sharp objects into the ear can rupture the eardrum.

If you have a chronic illness or routinely take prescribed or over-the-counter (OTC) drugs, talk to your doctor or pharmacist before taking any other medications.

know
WHAT
TO DO

Ear pain
DO THESE APPLY:

• Ear pain accompanied by headache, fever and stiff neck
see *Meningitis*, p. 213

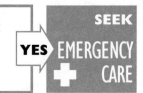

YES SEEK EMERGENCY CARE

NO

• White, yellow, bloody or foul-smelling ear discharge
• Sudden loss of hearing
• Ear infection is suspected
• Acute ear pain lasts more than an hour
• Any earache lasting longer than 12 to 24 hours
• You suspect ruptured eardrum
• Vertigo increases or recurs
• Symptoms increase — or fail to improve — after
two or three days of antibiotic treatment
• Stuffy ears or hearing loss persists, without other
symptoms, more than 10 days after cold clears up

YES CALL DOCTOR

NO

see *What You Can Do, Middle Ear Infection*, p. 137
see *What You Can Do, Fluid In Middle Ear*, p. 136
see *Hearing Loss*, p. 140

APPLY SELF-CARE

Hearing loss

Twenty-five percent of people over age 65 experience some degree of hearing loss. It can affect a person's thinking and memory. Fortunately, there are steps you can take to prevent hearing loss or improve the situation if it already exists.

PRESBYCUSIS

The most common form of age-related hearing loss is *presbycusis*, the gradual loss of the ability to hear high-pitched sounds. People with presbycusis continue to hear midrange or lower-pitched tones, but have difficulty discriminating spoken words, which are usually composed of high-frequency tones. While it's progressive, presbycusis doesn't usually lead to deafness. Fortunately, it's the kind of hearing loss that can most easily be helped by a hearing aid.

What you can do

- Be alert to changes in your hearing, particularly the inability to hear high-pitched sounds.
- Those around you will be the first to notice your hearing loss. Notice their reactions — are you missing parts of conversations? Do they claim you're shouting? Are you avoiding social situations that may call attention to your hearing loss?
- If so, see your doctor and arrange for a hearing evaluation.

HEARING AIDS

A hearing aid amplifies those frequencies you hear least well. It consists of a small microphone, a battery-powered amplifier to make the sound louder, a volume control and a small speaker that transmits the amplified sound into your eardrum. An *audiologist* can help you determine what kind of hearing aid will be best for you, fit the device to your ear and show you how to operate it.

EAR WAX

The purpose of ear wax is to protect the ear and keep it clean. The wax is normally in a liquid form and will drain by itself. Ear wax almost never causes problems unless you try to "clean" your ears using a cotton swab or some other instrument, which can pack the ear wax down tightly. If the ear wax builds up, it can become crusty and black, sometimes causing a stuffy feeling and hearing loss.

Ear wax usually will not cause pain or a fever. If you experience these symptoms, suspect an ear infection (see *Ear Pain*, p. 137).

In most cases, taking warm showers or washing the outside of the ears with a washcloth and warm water provides enough vapor to prevent the buildup of wax.

What you can do

Normally, packed-down ear wax can be removed by gently flushing the ear with warm water using a syringe (available at drugstores). Always use water that is as close to body temperature as possible. Using cold water can result in dizziness and vomiting.

Wax softeners such as olive oil, Debrox or Cerumenex also can be used. Follow instructions carefully for commercial softening products.

Never put anything into the ear if you think the eardrum might be ruptured (see *Ruptured Eardrum*, p. 138). Call your doctor if you are unsuccessful at removing ear wax.

TINNITUS

 Tinnitus is the persistent sensation of noise (ringing, buzzing, roaring, whistling or hissing) in the ear. It can be the symptom of almost any ear disorder as well as many diseases. Some common treatable causes include excess ear wax, ear infections, dental problems and certain medications (antibiotics and large amounts of aspirin).

Tinnitus can also be caused by prolonged exposure to loud noise that damages the hair cells of the *cochlea* (the winding, cone-shaped tube that forms part of the inner ear).

What you can do

To protect your hearing, limit your exposure to loud noises such as power tools, industrial machinery and loud music (wear ear plugs when needed). If tinnitus persists, talk to your doctor to figure out the possible causes. If the cause is unclear, your treatment will probably involve ways to mask or reduce the sensation. You may find your symptoms are helped by reducing the amount of *sodium* (salt), caffeine and alcohol in your diet (see *Eating Right*, p. 310). Learning ways to eliminate and cope with stress may also make a difference (see *Stress*, p. 284).

 If you have a chronic illness or routinely take prescribed or over-the-counter (OTC) drugs, talk to your doctor or pharmacist before taking any other medications.

MOUTH CONCERNS

Your mouth is critical to your enjoyment of life — for speaking, eating, smiling — so it pays to take care of it over the years and preserve your oral health.

The aging process results in some subtle changes within the mouth. Taste buds on the tongue decrease, so some foods may seem blander than they used to. However, the ability to sense bitter tastes does not decrease, and the combination of bland and bitter may result in an unpleasant, metallic taste in the mouth.

As taste becomes a little "duller," many people resort to using more and more salt and sugar to enhance the flavor of foods. A healthier alternative is to add flavor with herbs and spices such as garlic, onion, rosemary, oregano, thyme, cinnamon and nutmeg (see *Salt*, p. 314).

Dry mouth is a common occurrence among older adults. Mouth tissues become thinner and hold less moisture, and certain medications may reduce the amount of saliva the glands produce. Dehydration caused by hot weather, drinking inadequate amounts of water, or using *diuretics* (medication known as "water pills" that increases fluid loss) can also contribute to a dry mouth (see *Dehydration*, p. 192).

A severely dry mouth (*xerostomia*) can affect chewing, swallowing and digestion. Sucking on lozenges or hard candy or taking frequent sips of water can help minimize symptoms. Talk to your doctor or dentist if symptoms persist.

Dental care

Prevention is an important part of good dental care. Bacteria that are not removed from the teeth by brushing or flossing become a sticky, colorless film called *plaque*. Food particles, especially sugar, stick to plaque and produce acid, which damages tooth enamel. When this damage, or decay, spreads down the root canal to the nerve, it causes pain and inflammation — a toothache.

Another problem caused by an accumulation of plaque is gum disease, or *gingivitis*. It's an inflammation of the gums that can cause redness, discomfort, swelling, watery discharge and bleeding when you brush or chew. Gingivitis also causes the gums to become deformed, with the crevice between the gums and teeth deepening and forming pockets. In severe cases, this can result in tooth loss.

Badly fitting dentures can cause problems — difficulty in chewing, pain, mouth sores and *leukoplakia*, damaged tissue that can develop into mouth cancer.

Prevention

Most dental problems can be prevented by good self-care and regular visits to the dentist. If you wear dentures, take good care of them. Clean them regularly so you'll look your best and avoid bad breath. If your dentures don't fit well, ask your dentist to adjust them or ask about newer kinds of artificial teeth.

REGULAR CHECKUPS

Have teeth professionally checked and cleaned every six to 12 months.

BRUSHING

Brush teeth thoroughly twice a day, especially after eating. Try to remove plaque from all teeth surfaces. Use a soft-bristled toothbrush with rounded tips and replace it every three to four months.

Waterpiks and electric toothbrushes may help clean hard-to-reach areas. Check with your dentist about what's best for you.

The formation of *tartar*, mineral deposits that get trapped on the teeth by plaque, can be slowed by tartar-control toothpastes.

FLOSSING

Daily flossing is the best way to prevent gum disease between the teeth. Curve the floss around the tooth being cleaned and slide it under the gumline. With both fingers holding the floss against the tooth, move the floss up and down several times to scrape off the plaque.

What you can do

If you have a toothache, aspirin, ibuprofen or acetaminophen (Tylenol) may lessen the pain until you see a dentist. **NEVER give aspirin to children/teenagers. It can cause Reye's syndrome, a rare but often fatal condition.**

Final notes

If you have tooth or gum pain, see your dentist or call your doctor.

If you have a chronic illness or routinely take prescribed or over-the-counter (OTC) drugs, talk to your doctor or pharmacist before taking any other medications.

Mouth sores

COLD SORES

Oral herpes, which causes cold sores and fever blisters, is a common viral infection characterized by small, fluid-filled sores on the skin and mucous membranes of the mouth. This herpes simplex type 1 virus is not the same as — but is related to — herpes simplex type 2, which causes *genital herpes.*

About 90% of Americans are infected with oral herpes by the age of 5. Following the initial infection, the virus remains dormant with new episodes recurring at different frequencies for different people. New outbreaks can be triggered by a variety of factors including dental treatment, sunburn, food allergies, anxiety, menstruation, fever-producing illness or a suppressed immune system.

Prevention

The virus is very contagious and can be transmitted through personal contact or contact with contaminated objects such as kitchen utensils, razors or towels. If you have an active infection, avoid close physical contact with others and do not share personal items.

What you can do

- Salves can relieve pain, but are not effective in all cases. Try various methods, such as over-the-counter (OTC) oral and topical analgesics. Use what works best for you.
- *Acyclovir* (Zovirax) is an antiviral agent that may speed healing if applied during the initial outbreak. Oral acyclovir is sometimes prescribed for frequent or severe outbreaks.

Attacks of oral herpes usually go away, with or without treatment, within seven days and have no lasting complications.

CANKER SORES

The canker sore (*aphthous stomatitis*) is a painful ulcer that develops on the gums, tongue or inside the mouth. The cause is unknown but any of the following increase the likelihood of getting one: viruses; allergies; gastrointestinal disease; immune reactions; deficiencies of iron, B_{12} or folic acid; and stress and trauma to the inside of the mouth.

What you can do

There's no known way to prevent canker sores, but nonprescription topical anesthetic gels or rinses (such as 2% lidocaine) will lessen the pain. A dental protective paste, such as Orabase, prevents irritation of the sores.

know
WHAT
TO DO

Mouth sores
DO THESE APPLY:

- An undiagnosed mouth sore persists for two weeks
- Suspect medication may be causing mouth sores
- Outbreak of sores on gums, tongue or inside of mouth, especially with large or multiple sores
- Frequent or severe cold sores

YES

CALL
DOCTOR

 NO

see *What You Can Do, Cold Sores*
see *What You Can Do, Canker Sores*

APPLY
SELF-CARE

RESPIRATORY CONCERNS

Changes in the respiratory system occur gradually in older adults. Lungs become restricted by ribs that don't move quite as freely. As *vertebrae* (the bones in the spine) compress with age, lung volume may diminish.

These changes typically don't cause problems in healthy adults — especially if you're getting regular exercise to strengthen and expand your chest muscles. However, you may notice that strenuous activities are more difficult than when you were younger and it takes longer to catch your breath afterward. This is common. Also, recovery from respiratory illness may take longer.

Influenza

Influenza, also known as *flu* or *grippe*, is a highly contagious respiratory disease caused by viral infection. Symptoms are similar to those of a common cold (fever, chills, cough, stuffy nose, watery eyes, muscular aches, nausea, sore throat), but more severe. The usual treatment for flu is to treat your symptoms while your body fights off the infection.

Flu infection often occurs in epidemics during the "flu season," which generally lasts from late fall to early spring. Flu is spread by inhaling virus-laden droplets when an infected person sneezes, coughs or even talks. You can also get the flu by touching articles contaminated by contact with an infected person. Influenza is most commonly spread in enclosed environments.

Prevention

Getting a "flu shot" reduces the incidence of infection and is particularly important for older adults (see *Immunization Schedule*, p. 327). Drugs called *amantadine* or *rimantadine* can sometimes be effective in preventing or treating influenza type A. Your best natural defense is to maintain overall good health, which gives your body the boost it needs to fight infection.

What you can do

 • Take aspirin, acetaminophen(Tylenol) or ibuprofen to relieve aches and pains. **NEVER give aspirin to children/teenagers. It can cause Reye's syndrome, a rare but often fatal condition.**

 If you have a chronic illness or routinely take prescribed or over-the-counter (OTC) drugs, talk to your doctor or pharmacist before taking any other medications.

- Unless your fluid intake has been limited by your doctor, drink plenty of clear liquids — water, juice, ginger ale — to restore fluids.

- Unless you are on a salt-restricted diet, drink chicken soup, bouillon and other salty liquids to restore fluids and help minimize dizziness when you stand.

- Gargle with warm salt water (one-fourth teaspoon of salt added to eight ounces of water), drink tea with honey or lemon, or use lozenges to soothe sore throat pain.

- Get plenty of rest.

 • Decongestants may help relieve runny nose and watery eyes.

Influenza
DO THESE APPLY:

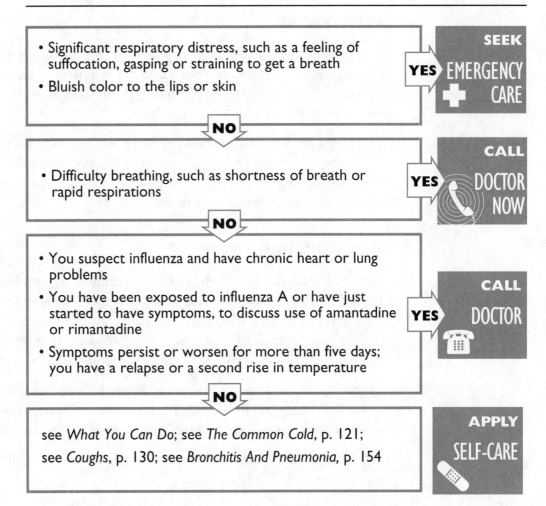

- Significant respiratory distress, such as a feeling of suffocation, gasping or straining to get a breath
- Bluish color to the lips or skin

YES → **SEEK** EMERGENCY CARE

NO

- Difficulty breathing, such as shortness of breath or rapid respirations

YES → **CALL** DOCTOR NOW

NO

- You suspect influenza and have chronic heart or lung problems
- You have been exposed to influenza A or have just started to have symptoms, to discuss use of amantadine or rimantadine
- Symptoms persist or worsen for more than five days; you have a relapse or a second rise in temperature

YES → **CALL** DOCTOR

NO

see *What You Can Do*; see *The Common Cold*, p. 121; see *Coughs*, p. 130; see *Bronchitis And Pneumonia*, p. 154

APPLY SELF-CARE

 If you have a chronic illness or routinely take prescribed or over-the-counter (OTC) drugs, talk to your doctor or pharmacist before taking any other medications.

Wheezing

The respiratory system resembles an upside-down tree with the "trunk" at the throat and the "limbs" (*bronchi*), smaller "branches" (*bronchioles*) and "leaves" (*alveoli* or air sacs) in the lungs. Wheezing is a high-pitched whistle caused by obstruction of air as it moves through the bronchi and bronchioles. The restriction may be due to narrowing of the airway walls or a blockage in the passage. It can be localized in a small area or spread throughout the lungs.

Wheezing can be heard in lung infections such as pneumonia or bronchitis, when a foreign body or mucus blocks an airway, and in people who have asthma. It is also a symptom of allergic reactions or chronic lung disease. Wheezing can be a warning of a very serious problem and needs professional evaluation when it first occurs.

EMPHYSEMA

Emphysema is a *chronic obstructive pulmonary disease* (COPD) in which the alveoli lose their ability to transfer oxygen into the bloodstream and remove carbon dioxide. They become enlarged, trapping air and decreasing the capacity to breathe (see *Bronchitis And Pneumonia*, p. 154).

Most frequently caused by smoking, emphysema results from chronic irritation to the respiratory system. There is no cure for this progressive disease, and treatment is directed toward decreasing the amount of air needed for daily activity and easing the struggle to breathe.

ALLERGIC REACTION

Allergic reactions occur when your body's immune system reacts and goes on the defensive against an element that, under most circumstances, is harmless. Allergens trigger your body's antibodies to counterattack and release chemicals, such as *histamine*, directly into various body tissues. Your symptoms are the result of tissues reacting to these chemicals (see *Allergic Reaction*, p. 107).

Wheezing can be created by spasms in bronchial and bronchiolar walls, swelling in the wall lining and production of excess mucus. **This can be a serious allergic reaction that can quickly become life-threatening and an emergency.**

Wheezing is the prominent symptom in asthma, a serious allergic disorder (see *Asthma*, p. 151).

Prevention

- If you smoke, start taking steps to kick the habit (see *Smoking Cessation*, p. 319).
- Avoid respiratory irritants such as secondhand smoke or chronic exposure to fumes.
- Avoid anything that has triggered an allergic reaction in the past.
- Wear or carry medical-alert identification related to your allergies and any chronic disease.
- Inform all doctors, dentists and pharmacists of your allergies.
- Ask your doctor about pneumonia and flu vaccinations (see *Immunization Schedule*, p. 327).
- Exercise regularly (see *Staying Active*, p. 316). Swimming and water aerobics are especially good for building up your respiratory strength.
- Learn stress management techniques if stress is a factor in your wheezing (see *Stress*, p. 284).
- Maintain normal weight to avoid additional stress on your respiratory system.
- Contact your doctor for information about prevention and treatment of your specific wheezing problem.

What you can do

- Unless your fluid intake has been limited by your doctor, drink at least two quarts of water daily to thin bronchial mucus.
- Maintain a humid environment with a cool-mist vaporizer.
- Learn and use relaxation techniques (see *Stress*, p. 284). Anxiety and panic increase breathing distress and waste energy.
- Use your peak-flow meter, bronchodilators and other medications as directed by your doctor. **DO NOT** wait for early symptoms to go away on their own.

SEE > *Know What To Do*, p. 150

Wheezing
DO THESE APPLY:

- Significant respiratory distress, such as a feeling of suffocation, gasping or straining to get a breath
- Bluish color to the lips or skin
- Signs of a severe allergic reaction; sudden onset of one or more of the following:
  - Loss of consciousness
  - Tightness in chest or wheezing
  - Dizziness, nausea or severe hives
  - Swelling or puffiness around eyes, mouth or throat

YES
SEEK
EMERGENCY
CARE

NO

- Difficulty breathing, such as shortness of breath or rapid respirations
- First episode of acute wheezing
- Wheezing is more severe or not responding to usual treatment
- Fever with wheezing
- Other chronic health problem (such as heart disease) present
- Wheezing soon after dose of new medication
  ▶ Do not take another dose of medicine.

YES
CALL
DOCTOR
NOW

NO

- Chest pain associated with breathing or coughing
- Sputum (phlegm) becomes yellow, gray-green or rust-colored
- Wheezing requires more medication and treatment to control or prevent
- More information and education needed to understand and control wheezing

YES
CALL
DOCTOR

NO

see *What You Can Do*, p. 149
see *Allergic Reaction*, p. 107; see *Hay Fever*, p. 124
see *Asthma*, p. 151; see *Bronchitis And Pneumonia*, p. 154

APPLY
SELF-CARE

Asthma

Asthma is an allergic disease that inflames and constricts the airways to the lungs and causes coughing, wheezing, chest pain and an increased production of mucus. Frequently, an asthma attack gives the feeling of suffocation or even panic. Asthma can lead to bronchitis or pneumonia (see *Bronchitis And Pneumonia*, p. 154).

About half of all asthma cases develop before the age of 10, and about one-third develop before age 40.

If you have allergies, you're particularly susceptible to asthma. Most people with asthma are sensitive to dust, animal dander, pollen, mold and other common allergens. If you're like most people with asthma, appropriate care and drug therapy can help you lead a normal, active life. There is no routine screening to detect the likelihood of developing asthma.

Prevention

If you've experienced asthma attacks, these are some steps you can take to reduce the number and severity of attacks:

- Eliminate or reduce exposure to "triggers" that cause attacks, such as cigarette smoke, pollen, dust and other irritants.

- If pollen triggers attacks, stay inside as much as possible during periods of high pollen count — preferably an inside environment with filtered air.

- Get a flu shot — colds and flu are more serious in those with asthma (see *Immunization Schedule*, p. 327).

- Remove the carpets in your home, and at work if possible, to decrease attacks. Dust mites, which often trigger attacks, thrive in carpeting.

- Enclose your mattress in a plastic zipper bag (make sure there are no openings or tears in it) to reduce your exposure to potential allergens.

- Unless your fluid intake has been limited by your doctor, drink plenty of fluids, which may loosen mucus in your lungs and make breathing easier.

- If your doctor has given you an acute-care regimen and you begin to have an attack, implement the measures immediately. The key to managing an asthma attack is to prevent it from getting out of control.

- Keep a record of daily treatment, acute-care regimen, and pertinent information about symptoms, treatment and your response to treatment.

What you can do

Self-evaluation and self-care are the most important things you can do to control asthma attacks. Discuss a self-care plan with your doctor that includes:

- Daily or routine drug therapy
- Ways to monitor symptoms
- What medications to take when an attack begins
- When to seek medical or emergency care

Final notes

Your doctor will diagnose asthma by taking your medical history and performing a physical examination. In some cases, tests of lung function and chest x-rays also may be used to confirm the diagnosis.

Asthma drugs are often administered using a *metered dose inhaler* (MDI). This tubular device propels small particles of drug through the mouth into the lungs. If you have difficulty using an MDI, your doctor may recommend modifications for proper drug treatment.

know WHAT TO DO

Asthma
DO THESE APPLY:

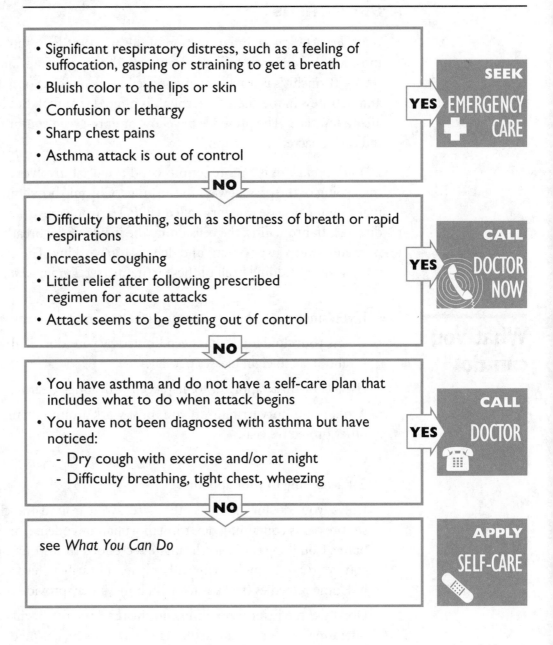

- Significant respiratory distress, such as a feeling of suffocation, gasping or straining to get a breath
- Bluish color to the lips or skin
- Confusion or lethargy
- Sharp chest pains
- Asthma attack is out of control

YES → SEEK EMERGENCY CARE

NO

- Difficulty breathing, such as shortness of breath or rapid respirations
- Increased coughing
- Little relief after following prescribed regimen for acute attacks
- Attack seems to be getting out of control

YES → CALL DOCTOR NOW

NO

- You have asthma and do not have a self-care plan that includes what to do when attack begins
- You have not been diagnosed with asthma but have noticed:
  - Dry cough with exercise and/or at night
  - Difficulty breathing, tight chest, wheezing

YES → CALL DOCTOR

NO

see *What You Can Do*

APPLY SELF-CARE

Bronchitis and pneumonia

BRONCHITIS

Acute bronchitis is an inflammation of the airways that results from irritation or infection. It frequently follows a bout with the flu or a cold, and may last up to two weeks. Bronchitis is usually characterized by a cough accompanied by soreness and tightness in the chest. The cough is often dry at first, but becomes productive after a few days. The presence of yellow or gray-green sputum (phlegm) may indicate a bacterial infection.

Chronic bronchitis is a more serious condition that involves a permanent thickening of the passageways to the lungs. Chronic bronchitis and emphysema make up the disease category called *COPD* (chronic obstructive pulmonary disease). In bronchitis, the cells lining the inside of the breathing passages that normally sweep away mucus and debris stop working. The cough response is the body's way of ridding itself of these irritants (see *Emphysema,* p. 148).

What you can do

- If you smoke, start taking steps to kick the habit (see *Smoking Cessation*, p. 319).
- Unless your fluid intake has been limited by your doctor, drink plenty of liquids — about six to eight glasses per day.
- Use a cool-mist vaporizer to help keep your lungs clear.
- Avoid respiratory irritants. If you must work around them, use a respirator or other protective gear.
- Get plenty of rest to enable your lungs to heal.
- Eat according to your appetite.
- Unless your doctor instructs otherwise, avoid around-the-clock usage of cough suppressants containing dextromethorphan or codeine, or with "DM" in their name. Coughing can help eliminate secretions from your airways. An over-the-counter (OTC) cough syrup will only temporarily relieve a cough; it won't cure it. Home remedies (such as tea with honey) may provide similar relief.
- Don't use medicines containing antihistamines if you will be driving or operating machinery, since these preparations make you drowsy.

 If you have a chronic illness or routinely take prescribed or over-the-counter (OTC) drugs, talk to your doctor or pharmacist before taking any other medications.

PNEUMONIA

Pneumonia is a general term that refers to more than 50 types of lung diseases caused either by viral or bacterial infection. About 2 million people in the U.S. get pneumonia each year, and 40,000 to 70,000 die from it annually. Bacteria-caused pneumonia can be effectively treated with antibiotics, but virus-caused pneumonia isn't helped by such treatment.

Note your symptoms

Most forms of pneumonia are characterized by:

- Chills
- Fever
- Chest pain associated with coughing or breathing
- Coughing
- Bone and joint pain
- Rattling sounds in lungs (*rales*)
- Blue-tinged skin

Other symptoms that may be present are:

- Loss of appetite
- Headache
- Yellow, gray-green or rust-colored sputum (phlegm)

Prevention

A vaccine is available to protect against the leading cause of bacterial pneumonia in adults, and it is recommended for everyone older than 65, those without a spleen or anyone with a chronic disease. Contact your doctor or local public health department (see *Immunization Schedule*, p. 327).

What you can do

- Take aspirin, acetaminophen (Tylenol) or ibuprofen. **NEVER give aspirin to children/teenagers. It can cause Reye's syndrome, a rare but often fatal condition.**

- Unless your fluid intake has been limited by your doctor, drink plenty of clear liquids.

- Unless on a salt-restricted diet, drink chicken soup, bouillon and other salty liquids to restore fluids and minimize dizziness when you stand.

- Use a cool-mist vaporizer.

- Get plenty of rest.

- Eat according to your appetite.

- Check with your doctor to see if there is a risk of infecting others. Stay home if advised to do so.

 If you have a chronic illness or routinely take prescribed or over-the-counter (OTC) drugs, talk to your doctor or pharmacist before taking any other medications.

know
WHAT
TO DO

Bronchitis and pneumonia
DO THESE APPLY:

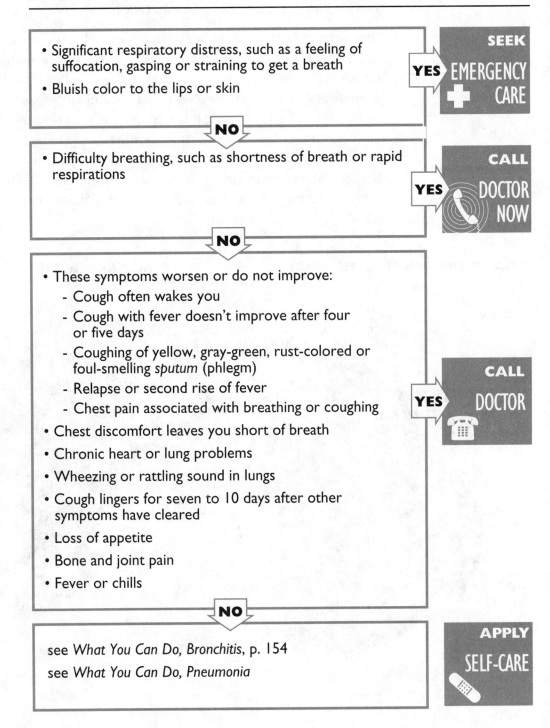

- Significant respiratory distress, such as a feeling of suffocation, gasping or straining to get a breath
- Bluish color to the lips or skin

YES → **SEEK EMERGENCY CARE**

NO ↓

- Difficulty breathing, such as shortness of breath or rapid respirations

YES → **CALL DOCTOR NOW**

NO ↓

- These symptoms worsen or do not improve:
  - Cough often wakes you
  - Cough with fever doesn't improve after four or five days
  - Coughing of yellow, gray-green, rust-colored or foul-smelling *sputum* (phlegm)
  - Relapse or second rise of fever
  - Chest pain associated with breathing or coughing
- Chest discomfort leaves you short of breath
- Chronic heart or lung problems
- Wheezing or rattling sound in lungs
- Cough lingers for seven to 10 days after other symptoms have cleared
- Loss of appetite
- Bone and joint pain
- Fever or chills

YES → **CALL DOCTOR**

NO ↓

see *What You Can Do, Bronchitis,* p. 154

see *What You Can Do, Pneumonia*

APPLY SELF-CARE

HEART CONCERNS

The heart is a tough and remarkable organ. It beats thousands of times each day, carrying blood and oxygen throughout the body.

After years of constant work, it's not surprising that the heart begins to weaken somewhat. The aging heart takes longer to speed up in response to a stimulus or activity. For example, upon standing, more blood needs to be pumped to the brain and throughout the body to maintain blood pressure. In order to do this, the heart beats faster. Because this response becomes slower with age, older adults may occasionally feel lightheaded (indicating a drop in blood pressure) when standing up. This slower response time may also cause you to have the same mildly dizzy sensation when straining to have a bowel movement. Over time, the heart's pumping action becomes less efficient as well. This may cause you to tire more quickly during strenuous activities.

BLOOD FLOW THROUGH THE HEART

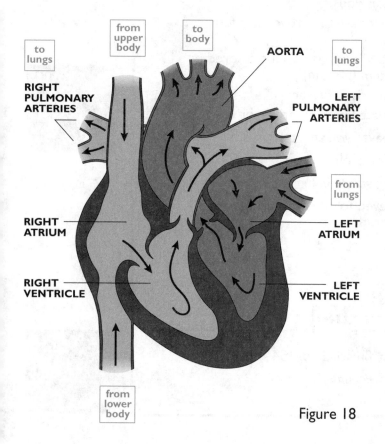

Figure 18

CORONARY ARTERIES

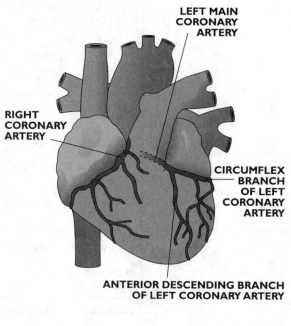

Figure 19

Some factors that affect your risk of developing heart problems are beyond your control — such as family history, gender and age. However, a number of lifestyle changes — including stopping smoking, controlling your weight by eating a low-fat diet and getting regular exercise, keeping diseases like hypertension and diabetes under control, and managing stress — can dramatically improve your chances of avoiding heart disease.

> For more details on preventing heart disease, see
> *Prevention, Chest Pain*, p. 163.

Heart disease

Because more older adults die from heart disease than any other cause, it's important to prevent problems when possible, be familar with symptoms of common heart conditions and be ready to take appropriate action if serious symptoms occur.

CORONARY HEART DISEASE (CHD)

Fatty deposits (*plaque*) can form in the arteries (see Figures 20 and 21), causing a condition known as *atherosclerosis*, or narrowing of the arteries. Blood flow through the heart muscle is restricted. Plaque makes the insides of the arteries less slippery, causing *platelets* (the sticky blood cells that stop bleeding) to stick there, reducing the flow of blood even further. This diminished flow results in *ischemia* (lack of oxygen) to the heart, which causes *angina* (chest pain). If the heart is deprived of enough oxygen for very long, a *myocardial infarction* (heart attack, or death of part of the heart muscle) occurs (see *Heart Attack* and *Heart Pain*, p. 162).

ARTERY WITH NORMAL BLOOD FLOW

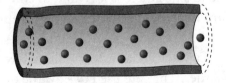

Figure 20

ARTERY WITH REDUCED BLOOD FLOW

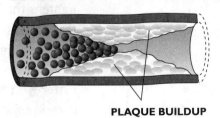

PLAQUE BUILDUP

Figure 21

This group of conditions affecting circulation to the heart is called *coronary heart disease* (CHD).

Nitroglycerin, one of the primary drugs used to treat CHD, helps open up the coronary arteries to increase blood flow to the heart muscle. If your doctor recommends nitroglycerin for occasional chest pain, make sure the two of you discuss the type of symptoms to expect in your particular case, and what you should do if the symptoms or pain change in any way while using this medication.

There are many medications and treatment options commonly used today, including *angioplasty* (a procedure that re-opens clogged arteries by inflating a tiny balloon inside the artery) and bypass surgery.

What you can do

Regardless of age, lifestyle changes that affect how you *nourish and maintain* your body can have a dramatic impact on reducing — and even preventing — CHD. Research shows that controlling your intake of cholesterol is important since high levels in the blood contribute to atherosclerosis.

> To learn more, see the *Prevention* section of this book, p. 309.

CONGESTIVE HEART FAILURE (CHF)

The heart pumps and distributes blood throughout the body, carrying oxygen and nutrients to the tissues (see Figures 18 and 19, p. 158). When the heart is weakened and can no longer pump efficiently, blood begins to back up in the lungs and pools in the extremities and other organs. Breathing becomes difficult when lying down. This condition is known as *congestive heart failure* (CHF), and there are a number of treatments available including medications and diet restrictions.

Treatment options

CHF is treated with medications such as diuretics, cardiac glycosides and ACE inhibitors. *Diuretics* (medications known as water pills that increase fluid loss) remove water from the blood and cause the body to produce more urine. This lightens the heart's workload since there is less fluid to continuously pump throughout the body. *Cardiac glycosides* (Lanoxin) help improve the *contractile force* (pumping action) of the heart muscle. *ACE inhibitors* such as *Enalapril* (Vasotec) and *Captropril* (Capoten) relax artery walls, allowing the heart to work better without working harder. They are used to slow the onset of CHF and decrease the mortality rates with left heart failure.

To minimize the amount of fluid your body retains, your doctor may recommend other options, including limited amounts of fluid and salt in your diet. In some cases, surgery may be needed to repair a faulty heart valve.

PERIPHERAL VASCULAR DISEASE (PVD)

Some degree of *arteriosclerosis* (hardening of the arteries) and atherosclerosis occurs as part of the natural aging process and contributes to poor circulation. Many older adults find that even mildly cold temperatures cause hands and feet to become cold, the result of blood vessels in the fingers and toes narrowing and restricting blood flow. This interference with circulation in the extremities is called *peripheral vascular disease* (PVD).

What you can do

Getting regular exercise, cutting back on caffeine and giving up smoking can help prevent or minimize PVD. To relieve uncomfortable symptoms, try wearing warm socks or gloves, walking, or moving your arms in circles to force more blood into the fingers. Soaking your hands and feet in warm water before bedtime may also bring relief.

Sometimes medications are used to *dilate,* or widen, the arteries to improve circulation.

Chest pain

Chest pain is often associated with the heart and can be a frightening symptom. Although this discomfort may be a warning from your heart and must be handled correctly, there are many other causes of chest pain that are less serious and easier to treat. Knowing the different types of chest pain can help you make safer decisions and get faster relief. **All chest pain should be taken seriously.**

ANGINA

Angina pectoris is a warning that the heart muscle is not getting enough oxygen. Anginal pain is a tightness, squeezing or feeling of pressure over the front of the chest. It may also be felt up in the throat and jaws or down one or both arms. It usually comes on with exertion, stress or overeating and lasts less than 15 minutes. **Any angina means that the heart is in trouble; the pain does not have to be severe to be serious.**

HEART ATTACK

Chest pain that is crushing, squeezing or increasing in pressure may be a warning of heart attack, known as *myocardial infarction.* The pain is like angina, and may not be severe, but it continues for more than 15 minutes and is not eased with rest. It is often accompanied by nausea, sweating, dizziness, shortness of breath and a feeling of doom or danger. The symptoms are caused by a completely blocked coronary artery (see Figure 19, p. 158) that stops blood flow to a part of the heart muscle (see *CHD*, p. 159).

HEART PAIN

Sharp pain from the heart may be caused by an infection in the outer lining (*pericarditis*) or inner lining (*endocarditis*). This often follows an infection in another part of the body. *Palpitations* can cause sudden, brief jabs of pain, usually in the left side of the chest (see *Palpitations,* p. 166).

CHEST-WALL PAIN

The chest wall includes skin, muscles, ligaments, ribs and rib cartilage. Pain can be caused by infection, inflammation, bruises, strains, sprains and broken ribs. Chest-wall pain is usually sharp or knife-like and limited to a small area. It often comes and goes for days; touching, bending, stretching, coughing or taking a deep breath may cause the pain to start or increase.

NON-HEART PAIN

Anxiety is a common cause of chest pain. It may be a sharp jab or dull pressure and it is often located in the left chest area. Pain from *hyperventilation* (excessive rapid breathing) often causes or comes with anxiety (see *Anxiety*, p. 287).

Chest pain can be from the lungs, *pleura* (the thin membranes that cover the lungs), esophagus, diaphragm or several of the organs in the upper abdomen. Pain from the lungs and pleura is similar to chest-wall pain and frequently follows a cold or flu-like illness. Lung diseases like pneumonia, blood clots and asthma may produce chest pain.

If the discomfort is caused by the esophagus or the stomach, there may be an acid taste in the mouth and a burning feeling in the chest that improves with eating.

Prevention

There are many causes of chest pain, and prevention is not possible for all of them. However, good health habits decrease your risk of illness and improve your chances of a quick, full recovery.

- Maintain normal body weight (see *Eating Right*, p. 310).
- Follow a low-fat, well-balanced diet (see *Eating Right*, p. 310).
- Exercise regularly (see *Staying Active*, p. 316).
- If you smoke, begin taking steps to kick the habit (see *Smoking Cessation*, p. 319).
- Have regular checkups to help detect any health problems early (see *Screening Guidelines*, p. 324).
- Learn about any chronic illness you have and follow your doctor's advice (see *A Self-Care Approach*, p. 4; *Steps To Self-Management*, p. 346).
- Learn about stress and stress management (see *Stress*, p. 284).

What you can do

- Learn CPR (see *CPR*, p. 14) and know what to do for emergencies (see *Being Prepared*, p. 12).

- Try to identify what may be causing your pain and avoid that activity or food.

- If chest-wall pain is from an injury, treat with **RICE** process (see *Strains And Sprains*, p. 56) and take aspirin or ibuprofen for pain and inflammation. **NEVER give aspirin to children/teenagers. It can cause Reye's syndrome, a rare but often fatal condition.**

- If pain is from stress or hyperventilation, follow stress management techniques (see *Stress*, p. 284).

- Pain from the stomach or esophagus may be relieved by:

    - Eating smaller meals

    - Stopping smoking

    - Avoiding foods and drugs that seem to trigger pain

    - Raising the head of your bed on four- to six-inch blocks and not eating for at least one hour before bedtime

    - Taking antacids (follow directions on the package)

If you have a chronic illness or routinely take prescribed or over-the-counter (OTC) drugs, talk to your doctor or pharmacist before taking any other medications.

know
WHAT
TO DO

Chest pain
DO THESE APPLY:

- Crushing, squeezing or increasing pressure in chest
- Chest discomfort with:
  - Shortness of breath
  - Dizziness
  - Sweating
  - Nausea or vomiting
  - Pain in jaw, neck, shoulders or arms
  - Rapid or irregular pulse
- Chronic heart disease exists and chest pain is not relieved with nitroglycerin medication
- ▶ Rest quietly with head elevated on pillows; keep warm.
- ▶ Wait for emergency transport or as advised by emergency system.

YES ▶ SEEK **EMERGENCY CARE**

APPLY **EMERGENCY FIRST AID**

NO

- Chest-wall pain with fever
- Chronic heart disease and chest pain is more frequent, more intense or present during times of rest

YES ▶ CALL **DOCTOR NOW**

NO

- Chest pain and cough with yellow, gray-green or rust-colored sputum (phlegm)
- Not diagnosed with angina and having episodes of chest pain with exertion, heavy eating or stress that subside within 15 minutes
- Symptoms worsen or have not improved after 48 hours of self-care

YES ▶ CALL **DOCTOR**

NO

see *What You Can Do*

APPLY **SELF-CARE**

Palpitations

Everyone feels a skip, flutter, flip-flop, thump or pounding in their chest at times. These feelings are palpitations, or *arrhythmias,* and are caused by a change in your normal heart rhythm; they can be very strong, rapid or irregular beats.

Causes of palpitations include hyperventilation, anxiety, fever, excess thyroid hormones, stimulants such as caffeine and nicotine, alcohol and many drugs and medications. Palpitations can occur in some types of heart disease. In most cases, palpitations are brief and harmless, and they go away without treatment.

Prevention

- Exercise regularly (see *Staying Active,* p. 316).
- If you smoke, start taking steps to kick the habit (see *Smoking Cessation,* p. 319).
- Limit the amount of alcohol (see *Use Of Alcohol,* p. 322) and caffeine you drink.
- Read warnings on packages and labels of all drugs you take.
- Do what you can to control your stress (see *Stress,* p. 284).
- Have regular checkups to help detect and treat health problems early (see *Screening Guidelines,* p. 324).

What you can do

- Look for the cause of your palpitations. Do they come after consuming certain foods or beverages? At a specific time of day? During or following a certain activity? Eliminate the possible cause and see if it takes care of the problem.
- Ask your doctor or pharmacist about side effects of your medications.
- Follow the prevention guidelines listed above.
- Relax and remember that most palpitations are harmless.

Palpitations

DO THESE APPLY:

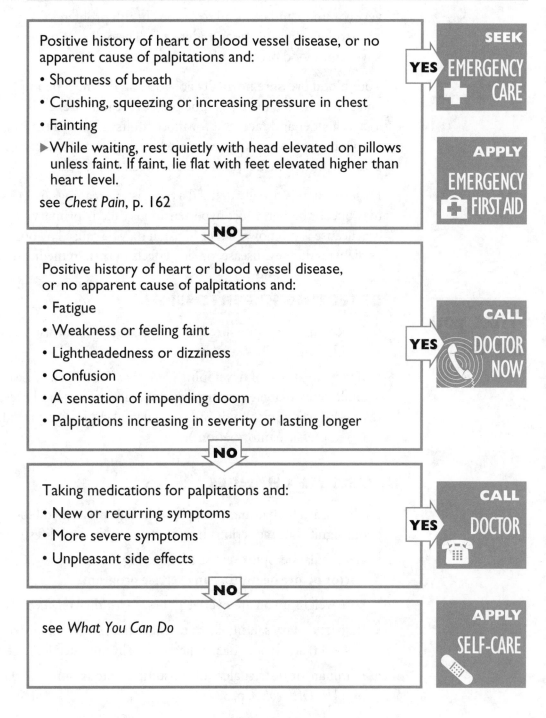

Positive history of heart or blood vessel disease, or no apparent cause of palpitations and:

- Shortness of breath
- Crushing, squeezing or increasing pressure in chest
- Fainting
- ▶While waiting, rest quietly with head elevated on pillows unless faint. If faint, lie flat with feet elevated higher than heart level.

see *Chest Pain*, p. 162

YES → SEEK **EMERGENCY ✚ CARE**

APPLY **EMERGENCY FIRST AID**

NO

Positive history of heart or blood vessel disease, or no apparent cause of palpitations and:

- Fatigue
- Weakness or feeling faint
- Lightheadedness or dizziness
- Confusion
- A sensation of impending doom
- Palpitations increasing in severity or lasting longer

YES → CALL **DOCTOR NOW**

NO

Taking medications for palpitations and:

- New or recurring symptoms
- More severe symptoms
- Unpleasant side effects

YES → CALL **DOCTOR**

NO

see *What You Can Do*

APPLY **SELF-CARE**

Hypertension

Hypertension, or high blood pressure, is known as "the silent killer." Although it is very common and can lead to serious health problems — such as heart attack and stroke — it often goes undetected. The best way to detect hypertension is to have your blood pressure checked regularly.

Your blood pressure normally goes up and down, depending on your activities and emotions. A "normal" blood pressure reading depends on several factors, such as age, gender and race. But for most adults, a normal reading is 120/80. The first number refers to *systolic* pressure, when the heart contracts; the second to *diastolic* pressure, when the heart is at rest between beats.

Hypertension is usually defined as consistent readings of 140 systolic, or 90 diastolic, or higher. Most hypertension is called "primary," which means that the exact cause is unknown. Hypertension may be caused by other conditions — such as diabetes, kidney disease, or side effects of certain medications.

What you can do

DETECTING HYPERTENSION

- Have your blood pressure checked regularly — at least every two years for healthy adults.

- If you are at risk of developing hypertension or heart disease because of high cholesterol, diabetes or family history, have your blood pressure checked once a year. (Screening clinics and some dental clinics can provide easy access to blood pressure information.)

LIFESTYLE CHANGES

Studies indicate that many people with slightly elevated blood pressure can bring about significant reductions in hypertension through lifestyle changes:

- Get regular aerobic exercise (see *Staying Active*, p. 316). **Check with your doctor before beginning an exercise program.**

- Lose weight if you are overweight (see *Healthy Weight*, p. 311).

- Restrict dietary salt intake to no more than 2,400 mg per day (about one teaspoon) and reduce dietary fats, especially saturated fats (see *Eating Right*, p. 310).

- Eliminate or restrict alcohol consumption to less than two ounces per day (see *Use Of Alcohol*, p. 322).

- If you smoke, start taking steps to kick the habit (see *Smoking Cessation*, p. 319).

- The National Heart, Lung and Blood Institute (NHLBI) recommends the Dietary Approaches to Stop Hypertension or "DASH" diet:
  - Eat 8-10 fruits and vegetables per day. One serving is equal to 1 medium apple, 1/2 cup of fruit, 3/4 cup of juice, 1 cup of leafy vegetables or 1/2 cup of other vegetables.
  - Get adequate potassium each day (3.5 mg). Good sources are orange juice, bananas, potatoes and winter squash.
  - Get 2-1/2 to 3 servings of dairy products daily. One serving is 1 cup of milk or yogurt, 1 to 1-1/2 ounces of low-fat cheese, or 2 ounces of processed cheese.

MEDICATIONS

If you are diagnosed with high blood pressure, your doctor may use the "stepped approach" to treatment, beginning with *diuretics* (medications known as "water pills" that increase fluid loss) and progressing to drugs that act directly on the blood vessels, heart and blood chemistry.

The goal of medical treatment is to control hypertension while creating as few side effects as possible.

Final notes

It is crucial that you comply with the treatment program your doctor prescribes if you are diagnosed with hypertension. If you have problems with any part of the program, discuss them with your doctor. Long-term follow-up care is important. Your doctor will decide how often follow-up visits should be scheduled, based on the severity of your hypertension, treatment response and other factors.

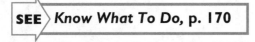

SEE *Know What To Do, p. 170*

know
WHAT
TO DO

Hypertension
DO THESE APPLY:

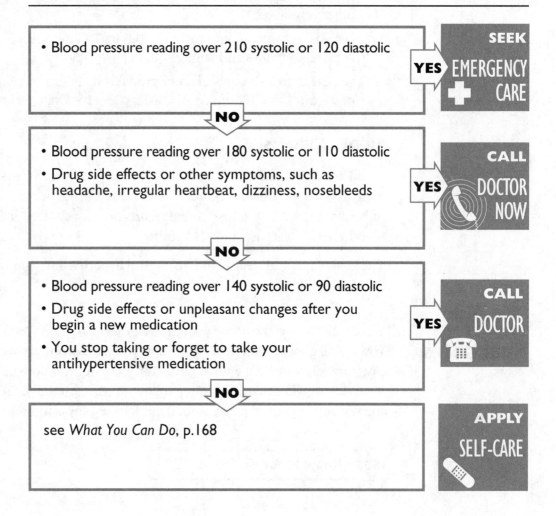

• Blood pressure reading over 210 systolic or 120 diastolic

YES ▸ SEEK EMERGENCY CARE

NO

• Blood pressure reading over 180 systolic or 110 diastolic
• Drug side effects or other symptoms, such as headache, irregular heartbeat, dizziness, nosebleeds

YES ▸ CALL DOCTOR NOW

NO

• Blood pressure reading over 140 systolic or 90 diastolic
• Drug side effects or unpleasant changes after you begin a new medication
• You stop taking or forget to take your antihypertensive medication

YES ▸ CALL DOCTOR

NO

see *What You Can Do*, p.168

APPLY SELF-CARE

ABDOMINAL/GI

Aging brings normal changes in the way your body processes food. Food may take longer to travel down the *esophagus* (the food pipe to your stomach) because of decreased *peristalsis* (muscular contractions) within the esophagus and digestive (gastrointestinal or GI) system. Secretions that aid digestion may also lessen and — along with decreased peristalsis — cause food to move more slowly through the stomach and intestines. The result may be more frequent constipation.

In addition, you may experience *reflux* (or flowing back) of gastric fluids from the stomach into the lower end of the esophagus. This occurs because the *lower esophageal sphincter* (a muscular band at the junction of the esophagus and stomach) weakens as you age, causing the symptoms of gastric reflux that is commonly called *heartburn.*

Your sense of taste and smell may become duller as you get older, causing food to taste flat or unappealing. To compensate for this, many individuals add extra salt to their food. This can lead to problems such as fluid retention, which puts added strain on the heart. (For tips on alternatives to salt, see *Mouth Concerns*, p. 142; *Salt*, p. 314.)

While these physiological changes are a normal part of aging, there are a number of simple ways you can take charge of the situation — including adapting your diet and activity levels — to decrease or even eliminate symptoms. The following chapters will help you understand when these problems can be managed through self-care and when it is appropriate to see your doctor.

GASTROINTESTINAL (DIGESTIVE) SYSTEM

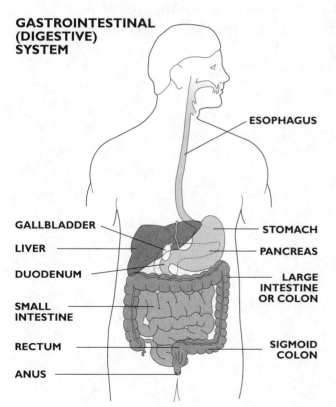

ESOPHAGUS

GALLBLADDER

LIVER

DUODENUM

SMALL INTESTINE

RECTUM

ANUS

STOMACH

PANCREAS

LARGE INTESTINE OR COLON

SIGMOID COLON

Figure 22

Heartburn/gastritis/peptic ulcer

Certain foods, alcohol, beverages that contain caffeine, aspirin, smoking and stress can contribute to several gastrointestinal conditions that range from merely bothersome and uncomfortable — such as heartburn or gastritis — to life-threatening, such as a perforated ulcer.

While occasional minor problems can easily be treated with self-care, chronic and severe symptoms may require immediate medical attention. Chronic gastritis, along with symptoms of fatigue, may indicate bleeding in the gastrointestinal tract, which is a serious condition (see *Peptic Ulcer*, p. 175).

HEARTBURN

Heartburn is caused by the back-flow of gastric acid from the stomach into the esophagus. A burning sensation typically spreads from the upper abdomen into the lower breastbone, and occurs most often after meals or when lying down. Sometimes, sour or bitter material from the stomach is regurgitated, or brought back up, into the mouth. You may experience heartburn with more frequency and severity as you age.

What you can do

Try to rule out other, more serious sources of pain. If you don't suspect a more serious problem, begin self-care:

- Avoid irritants such as coffee, tea, alcohol, aspirin and ibuprofen.

- Avoid foods containing acid, such as citrus fruits and tomatoes.

- If you smoke, start taking steps to kick the habit (see *Smoking Cessation*, p. 319).

- Reduce your stress level, and try to make meals a time of relaxation (see *Stress*, p. 284).

- Sit — don't stand or lie down — while eating.

- Don't lie down right after eating. If nighttime heartburn is a problem, don't eat anything for at least two hours before going to bed. Elevate the head of the bed with four- to six-inch blocks to incline your body and prevent acid from flowing from the stomach and into the esophagus.

- Don't wear tight-fitting clothing, such as tight jeans or girdles.

 • Antacids such as Maalox, Mylanta, Gelusil or Tums can often provide fast, temporary relief. (**If you have high blood pressure or heart disease, don't use antacids with sodium salts without consulting your doctor.**)

- H_2 blockers are medications that decrease the production of stomach acid. These medications include famotidine (Pepcid), ranitidine (Zantac), nizatidine (Axid) and cimetidine (Tagamet). If symptoms persist after two weeks, consult your doctor before taking more of these medications.

Final notes

Some people who are prone to heartburn may suffer repeated attacks. Chronic severe symptoms may lead to complications, including a pre-cancerous condition. However, with self-care you can easily treat the symptoms of simple heartburn with no lasting ill effects.

SEE ▷ *Know What To Do*, p. 176

 If you have a chronic illness or routinely take prescribed or over-the-counter (OTC) drugs, talk to your doctor or pharmacist before taking any other medications.

GASTRITIS

Gastritis is a painful inflammation of the lining of the stomach. This may occur more frequently with advancing age. Causes include acute stress, alcohol abuse, viral or bacterial infections, or nonsteroidal anti-inflammatory drugs (NSAIDs), such as aspirin or ibuprofen.

Symptoms may include upper abdominal pain, diarrhea, nausea and vomiting bright red blood or what looks like coffee grounds. Accompanying fatigue may indicate anemia, which may be caused by blood loss through the gastrointestinal tract (see *Peptic Ulcer*, p. 175).

What you can do

- Try over-the-counter (OTC) antacids to provide possible relief from the pain.
- Moderate your use of tobacco, alcohol and caffeinated drinks (see *Getting And Staying Healthy*, p. 310).
- Avoid foods that may trigger gastritis, such as pickles or spices (the type of food can vary from person to person).
- Avoid NSAIDs (nonsteroidal anti-inflammatory drugs) and other drugs that cause or worsen gastritis (see *Medications That Can Cause Problems . . .*, p. 301; *Home Pharmacy*, p. 303).

Final notes

If over-the-counter (OTC) medications do not relieve the pain, your doctor may recommend a more powerful prescription drug.

Gastritis is generally not serious. In most cases, the pain will stop spontaneously or after minor lifestyle changes.

SEE ▷ *Know What To Do, p. 176*

 If you have a chronic illness or routinely take prescribed or over-the-counter (OTC) drugs, talk to your doctor or pharmacist before taking any other medications.

PEPTIC ULCER

Peptic ulcers are craters or eroded areas in the protective lining of the stomach or intestine that are caused by infection with *Helicobacter pylori* (formerly known as *Campylobacter pylori*), use of NSAIDs and excess stomach acids.

Peptic ulcers cause gastrointestinal bleeding that results in blood loss and *anemia* (a decrease in the number of red blood cells). Often, feeling tired or fatigued is the first symptom noticed and reported (see *Weakness/Fatigue*, p. 78).

The most common type of peptic ulcer is a *duodenal ulcer* in the upper part of the small intestine (see Figure 22, p. 171). Severe ulcers can lead to pain, bleeding and even *perforations* (holes) in the wall of the stomach or intestine. **A perforated ulcer is life-threatening and must be treated immediately with surgery.**

Contributing factors are cigarette smoking, use of alcohol and certain medications. Aspirin, ibuprofen and corticosteroids are known to cause ulcers in some people.

With the significant advances in treatment and with early detection, most people will recover from their ulcer in four to six weeks.

Antibiotics along with antacids in a dosage recommended by your doctor may efficiently treat your ulcer. If these don't work, there are other medications that reduce acid secretions, such as Tagamet, Zantac or Pepcid.

What you can do

To reduce the likelihood of getting an ulcer and to speed the healing process if you already have one:

- Start taking steps to kick the habit if you smoke. Avoid coffee, alcohol, aspirin and ibuprofen (see *Smoking Cessation*, p. 319).

- Avoid hot or spicy foods if they cause discomfort; for the most part you can eat a normal diet.

- Don't drink large amounts of milk. Calcium may stimulate acid production.

- For temporary relief from ulcer pain, try over-the-counter (OTC) antacids such as Maalox or Mylanta.

- Tell your doctor if you have a history of ulcers. Common medications taken for other ailments could increase your risk of ulcer recurrences (see *Medications That Can Cause Problems . . .*, p. 301; *Home Pharmacy*, p. 303).

SEE *Know What To Do, p. 176*

If you have a chronic illness or routinely take prescribed or over-the-counter (OTC) drugs, talk to your doctor or pharmacist before taking any other medications.

know
WHAT
TO DO

Heartburn/gastritis/peptic ulcer
DO THESE APPLY:

- Crushing, squeezing or increasing pressure in chest
  see *Chest Pain*, p. 162
- Back or abdominal pain, especially if associated with shortness of breath, sweating or extreme paleness
- Vomiting bright red blood
- Vomiting what looks like coffee grounds or stool that is deep red (maroon), black or tar-like, with dizziness or feeling weak
- Cold, clammy skin with fainting
  see *Shock*, p. 33

YES →  SEEK EMERGENCY CARE

 NO

- Vomiting what looks like coffee grounds or stool that is deep red (maroon), black or tar-like, without dizziness or feeling weak
- Persistent or moderate to severe symptoms such as heartburn, upper abdominal pain, diarrhea, nausea and vomiting
- Heartburn, and painful or difficult swallowing
- Pain that seems to extend through back

YES →  CALL DOCTOR NOW

NO

see next page

DO THESE APPLY: see previous page

- Burning, aching pain in lower chest or upper abdomen (often relieved by food or antacids)
- Excessive fullness after meals
- Chronic anxiety or stress seems to cause a recurrence of previously treated ulcer
- Heartburn pain — which recurs frequently or lasts more than three days — not relieved by self-care
- A prescribed medication seems to cause heartburn

- Symptoms of gastritis persist or worsen despite use of over-the-counter (OTC) antacids and other self-care

YES
CALL
DOCTOR

NO

see *What You Can Do, Heartburn*, p.173

see *What You Can Do, Gastritis*, p.174

see *What You Can Do, Peptic Ulcer*, p.175

APPLY
SELF-CARE

 If you have a chronic illness or routinely take prescribed or over-the-counter (OTC) drugs, talk to your doctor or pharmacist before taking any other medications.

Nausea and vomiting

Nausea is most often traced to a viral infection or "stomach flu" that produces a queasy stomach, increased salivation and sweating (see *Stomach Flu*, p. 181). When the nausea intensifies, you may begin to vomit. The condition can also be the result of medications, stress, food poisoning or a head injury (see index for specific topic). Because nausea and vomiting can be connected with so many medical problems — some of them serious — it's important to watch your symptoms closely.

Note your symptoms

The most dangerous threat posed by vomiting is dehydration (see *Dehydration*, p. 192), which can occur quickly in older adults. Severe dehydration can be life-threatening, and symptoms should be carefully monitored.

Signs of dehydration include:

- Unusual thirst
- Sunken-looking eyes
- Dry mouth and cracked lips
- Infrequent urination or dark yellow urine
- Skin that is no longer elastic

Also suspect more serious medical conditions if:

- Vomiting bright red blood or what looks like coffee grounds (see *Peptic Ulcer*, p. 175)
- Abdominal pain is severe or pain is localized in one area (see *Abdominal Pain*, p. 194)
- Vomiting is accompanied by headache and stiff neck (see *Meningitis*, p. 213)

Some nausea and vomiting can be traced to food poisoning, which is often confused with viral stomach flu (see *Food Poisoning*, p. 181). Certain foods, when not stored or handled properly, are breeding grounds for bacteria that can inflame the intestines.

Suspect food poisoning if:

- Your symptoms are shared by others who ate the same food.

- Nausea and vomiting begin six to 48 hours after eating food that may not have been stored correctly.

What you can do

GIVE YOUR STOMACH A BREAK

Unless your fluid intake has been limited by your doctor, follow the suggestions below.

- For the first 12 to 24 hours, slowly sip any of the following:

  - Sports drinks, such as Gatorade and Recharge, either full strength or diluted to half drink/half water

  - Non-prescription electrolyte supplements such as Pedialyte (found in the infant formula grocery store aisle)

  - Clear liquids such as water and bouillon (unless your doctor has restricted your sodium)

- Start with a few sips at a time and increase gradually. Do this even if you can't keep anything down for long.

- Suck ice chips if no other liquids stay down.

- Do not eat solid foods while vomiting persists.

- As symptoms improve, offer unbuttered rice, potatoes or noodles; crackers or toast; unsweetened hot or cold cereals; soups with rice and meat; yogurt, bananas and applesauce.

- Resume regular diet several days after symptoms have ceased.

Final notes

While patience and self-care normally do the trick for an upset stomach, it's important to be alert for serious and sudden complications.

SEE *Know What To Do,* p. 180

know
WHAT
TO DO

Nausea and vomiting
DO THESE APPLY:

- Vomiting bright red blood
- Vomiting what looks like coffee grounds, with dizziness or feeling weak

  see *Peptic Ulcer*, p. 175
- Headache and stiff neck

  see *Meningitis*, p. 213
- Signs of dehydration in an adult over 60

  see *Dehydration*, p. 192
- Nausea and vomiting with severe abdominal pain or associated with swollen or tender abdomen

YES → **SEEK EMERGENCY CARE**

NO ↓

- Vomiting what looks like coffee grounds, without dizziness or feeling weak
- Vomiting is severe or in large quantities

  see *Abdominal Pain*, p. 194
- Signs of dehydration in an adult under 60

  see *Dehydration*, p. 192
- Nausea and vomiting occur for more than two hours after head injury

  see *Head/Spinal Injury*, p. 51

YES → **CALL DOCTOR NOW**

NO ↓

- Medication may be cause

YES → **CALL DOCTOR**

NO ↓

see *What You Can Do*, p.179

APPLY SELF-CARE

Stomach flu and food poisoning

Stomach flu and food poisoning have different causes but many of the same symptoms. However, they both fall under the general category of *gastroenteritis*, which is commonly caused by food-borne bacteria, or by viruses spread — hand-to-mouth — by contaminated objects.

Symptoms — vomiting, diarrhea, abdominal cramping and fever — usually take three to 36 hours to develop, with the resulting illness lasting 12 hours to several days.

Prevention

STOMACH FLU

- Maximize your resistance to infection with a healthy diet, plenty of rest and regular exercise.
- Wash your hands frequently.
- Keep your hands away from your nose, eyes and mouth.

FOOD POISONING

- Carefully refrigerate (between 34° F and 40° F) all foods — especially poultry, fish, meats, eggs and salads made with mayonnaise. Don't eat anything that has been kept between 40° F and 140° F for more than two hours.
- Defrost foods in the microwave or refrigerator — not on the kitchen counter.
- Avoid foods made with raw eggs, as well as rare or uncooked meats.
- Be especially careful with large, cooked meats like the holiday turkey. Refrigerate leftovers as soon as dinner is over. Remove thick bones and cut meat into portions less than three inches thick to speed cooling.
- Thoroughly reheat leftover meats before re-serving to destroy any bacteria.
- All utensils that have touched raw meat should be washed in hot, soapy water before reusing. Wash hands, counter tops and cutting boards frequently.
- Follow home-canning and freezing instructions carefully. Throw out any cans or jars that have leaks or bulging lids.

What you can do

Unless your fluid intake has been limited by your doctor, follow the suggestions below.

- For the first 12 to 24 hours, slowly sip any of the following:

  - Sports drinks, such as Gatorade and Recharge, either full strength or diluted to half drink/half water

  - Non-prescription electrolyte supplements such as Pedialyte (found in the infant formula grocery store aisle)

  - Clear liquids such as water and bouillon (unless your doctor has restricted your sodium)

- Start with a few sips at a time and increase gradually. Do this even if you can't keep anything down for long.

- Suck ice chips if no other liquids stay down.

- Do not eat solid foods while vomiting persists.

- As symptoms improve, offer unbuttered rice, potatoes or noodles; crackers or toast; unsweetened hot or cold cereals; soups with rice and meat; yogurt, bananas and applesauce.

- Resume regular diet several days after symptoms have ceased.

- Do not take aspirin or other pain relievers.

- If you suspect food poisoning, check with anyone else who may have eaten the same food. When possible, save a sample of the suspected food in case analysis becomes necessary.

> For additional self-care information, see *Nausea And Vomiting*, p. 178; *Diarrhea*, p. 191; *Dehydration*, p. 192.

> Many forms of bacteria can cause food poisoning, including *salmonella* (typically found in dairy products, eggs, poultry, red meat and seafood) and *E. coli* (most commonly found in improperly cooked ground meats). A rare but fatal form of food poisoning called *botulism* is usually caused by eating foods with a low-acidity content — such as corn and beans — that have been improperly home-canned.

know
WHAT
TO DO

Stomach flu and food poisoning
DO THESE APPLY:

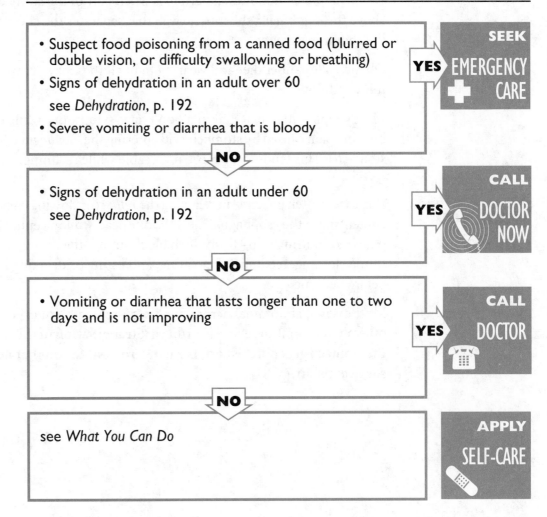

- Suspect food poisoning from a canned food (blurred or double vision, or difficulty swallowing or breathing)
- Signs of dehydration in an adult over 60

  see *Dehydration*, p. 192
- Severe vomiting or diarrhea that is bloody

YES → **SEEK EMERGENCY CARE**

NO

- Signs of dehydration in an adult under 60

  see *Dehydration*, p. 192

YES → **CALL DOCTOR NOW**

NO

- Vomiting or diarrhea that lasts longer than one to two days and is not improving

YES → **CALL DOCTOR**

NO

see *What You Can Do*

APPLY SELF-CARE

Hiatal hernia

Hiatal hernia, or abdominal hernia, is when part of the stomach protrudes above the *diaphragm*, the muscle wall that separates the chest cavity from the abdominal cavity.

Obesity, a low-fiber diet and wearing tight clothes may contribute to this condition.

Most people with a hiatal hernia don't have symptoms, while others experience a burning pain caused by stomach acid entering the *esophagus* (the food pipe to your stomach). This tends to be more noticeable while reclining.

What you can do

Self-care is often effective in relieving the *reflux* (or flowing back) of acidic stomach contents into the esophagus. Elevate your head while sleeping by using extra pillows or putting four- to six-inch blocks under the upper bed legs. Avoid tight-fitting clothing, reclining after eating, and eating or drinking two hours or less before bedtime.

 Most cases of abdominal hernia don't require treatment other than antacids or other medications to relieve heartburn. **Strangulation of the hernia, when part of the stomach gets pinched off, is a dangerous situation that needs immediate surgical repair.**

 If you have a chronic illness or routinely take prescribed or over-the-counter (OTC) drugs, talk to your doctor or pharmacist before taking any other medications.

know **WHAT** **TO DO**

Hiatal hernia
DO THESE APPLY:

- Vomiting bright red blood
- Vomiting what looks like coffee grounds, with dizziness or feeling weak
- Cold, clammy skin with fainting

  see *Shock*, p. 33
- Crushing, squeezing or increasing pressure in chest

  see *Chest Pain*, p. 162
- Diagnosed hernia with weakness, pallor, chest pain, dizziness

YES
SEEK EMERGENCY CARE

NO

- Vomiting what looks like coffee grounds, without dizziness or feeling weak

YES
CALL DOCTOR NOW

NO

- Recurring *reflux* (or flowing back) of stomach contents with discomfort that worsens or persists, even after three days of self-care

YES
CALL DOCTOR

NO

see *What You Can Do*
see *Heartburn*, p. 172
see *Peptic Ulcer*, p. 175

APPLY SELF-CARE

Inguinal hernia

An *inguinal hernia* is when a section of the small intestine protrudes, causing a lump in the groin. In men, the hernia often protrudes into the *scrotum*, the "sac" of skin that holds the testes. An inguinal hernia usually results from weak abdominal muscles and increased pressure in the abdomen. The combination forces a loop of intestine out through the weak area in the muscle wall. Obesity, heavy lifting and prolonged coughing can bring on a hernia or make it worse.

Symptoms can include swelling in the groin that goes away when lying down or when gentle pressure is applied, and groin pain when bending or lifting.

Strangulation of the hernia, which is when part of the intestine gets pinched off, is an emergency and needs immediate surgical repair.

What you can do

Surgery is the only cure for this type of hernia. Until the hernia is repaired, avoid heavy lifting.

know
WHAT
TO DO

Inguinal hernia
DO THESE APPLY:

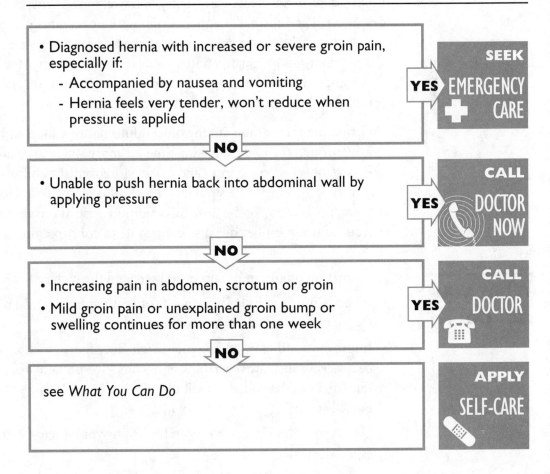

• Diagnosed hernia with increased or severe groin pain, especially if:
  - Accompanied by nausea and vomiting
  - Hernia feels very tender, won't reduce when pressure is applied

YES → SEEK **EMERGENCY CARE**

NO

• Unable to push hernia back into abdominal wall by applying pressure

YES → CALL **DOCTOR NOW**

NO

• Increasing pain in abdomen, scrotum or groin
• Mild groin pain or unexplained groin bump or swelling continues for more than one week

YES → CALL **DOCTOR**

NO

see *What You Can Do*

APPLY SELF-CARE

Constipation

Constipation is a decreased frequency of bowel movements characterized by hard, dry stools. The "normal" frequency of bowel movements varies from person to person. It may be once a day for one person and once every three days for another. Other symptoms of constipation include difficulty passing stools, abdominal pain and fullness, bloating and gas. Occasional changes in stools (color, consistency, texture and bulk) are generally not serious.

Constipation is common among older adults because food and water move more slowly through the body, allowing time for more water to be absorbed into the body so stools become harder and drier. Moreover, the ability of the *rectum* (see Figure 22, p. 171) to store stool increases with age, so you may not have bowel movements as often. Some medical conditions, use of certain medications, lack of exercise and a low-fiber diet also contribute to constipation.

What you can do

Constipation often can be successfully treated through self-care:

- If your eating habits have changed (other than for medical reasons), go back to the diet you had before the problems began.

- Improve your diet by adding more high-fiber foods, such as whole grains, bran, beans, leafy and raw vegetables, and fruits — especially dried fruits. A high-fiber diet has the added benefit of reducing your blood-cholesterol level and possibly reducing your risk of colon cancer.

- Unless your fluid intake has been limited by your doctor, drink plenty of fluids, especially water.

- Increase your daily exercise, especially if you sit all day.

- Investigate ANY medications you are taking to see if they cause constipation. **DO NOT stop taking a prescribed medication without consulting your doctor.**

If these steps don't work, consider over-the-counter (OTC) remedies such as bulk laxatives that draw water into the stool, milk of magnesia (**not for individuals with kidney problems**), or stool softeners.

A reduction in the frequency of bowel movements with no other symptoms does not necessarily require treatment.

HEMORRHOIDS

Hemorrhoids are swollen, inflamed veins that can be around the outside or the inside of the *anus.* They are extremely common and can be caused or aggravated by constipation, straining to move bowels, obesity or a sedentary lifestyle.

Symptoms may include pain, itching, burning, swelling, bleeding and a sense of incomplete emptying in the rectum. Frequently, hemorrhoidal bleeding is seen as bright red blood on the toilet paper or in the toilet bowl after moving the bowels.

What you can do

Simple self-care is usually the key to initial treatment:

- Keep the anal area clean with pre-moistened towels or "baby wipes."
- *Sitz baths* (soaking in hip-high water) can be soothing.
- Avoid sitting for long periods of time, if possible, or sit on a rubber donut. Stretch frequently.
- Over-the-counter (OTC) hydrocortisone creams can reduce swelling and inflammation. Avoid creams with topical anesthetics, since they may slow healing.

 - Take steps to avoid constipation and straining to move bowels. Eat high-fiber foods or take over-the-counter (OTC) fiber supplements. Unless your fluid intake has been limited by your doctor, drink plenty of fluids and exercise regularly (see *Eating Right,* p. 310; *Staying Active,* p. 316). The occasional use of a mild laxative might be of value, but a better choice is a simple stool softener. Ask your doctor if any medications you are taking could be causing constipation (iron is notorious for this), and if you can take a stool softener to decrease this side effect.

SEE Know What To Do, p. 190

 If you have a chronic illness or routinely take prescribed or over-the-counter (OTC) drugs, talk to your doctor or pharmacist before taking any other medications.

Constipation
DO THESE APPLY:

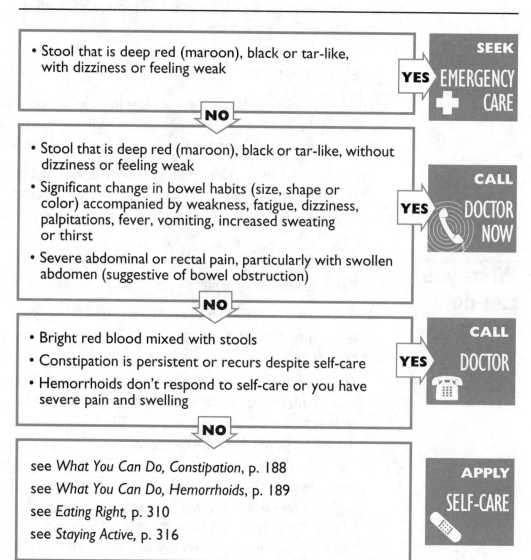

• Stool that is deep red (maroon), black or tar-like, with dizziness or feeling weak

YES → **SEEK EMERGENCY CARE**

NO

• Stool that is deep red (maroon), black or tar-like, without dizziness or feeling weak

• Significant change in bowel habits (size, shape or color) accompanied by weakness, fatigue, dizziness, palpitations, fever, vomiting, increased sweating or thirst

• Severe abdominal or rectal pain, particularly with swollen abdomen (suggestive of bowel obstruction)

YES → **CALL DOCTOR NOW**

NO

• Bright red blood mixed with stools

• Constipation is persistent or recurs despite self-care

• Hemorrhoids don't respond to self-care or you have severe pain and swelling

YES → **CALL DOCTOR**

NO

see *What You Can Do, Constipation*, p. 188

see *What You Can Do, Hemorrhoids*, p. 189

see *Eating Right*, p. 310

see *Staying Active*, p. 316

APPLY SELF-CARE

Diarrhea

Diarrhea (frequent, watery stools) takes place when solid waste is pushed through the intestines before the water in the waste has time to be reabsorbed by the body. Excessive loss of water, called *dehydration* (see *Dehydration*, p. 192), is the biggest health risk to having diarrhea.

Diarrhea is most commonly caused by viral infections. Other causes include bacterial infections and irritations of the digestive tract. It is frequently accompanied by nausea and vomiting (see *Nausea And Vomiting*, p. 178).

Many medications may cause diarrhea, including antibiotics, blood pressure drugs, digitalis, anti-cancer drugs, gold compounds and nonsteroidal anti-inflammatory drugs (NSAIDs) (see *Home Pharmacy*, p. 303).

What you can do

- Slowly sip any of the following:
  - Sports drinks, such as Gatorade and Recharge, either full strength or diluted to half drink/half water
  - Non-prescription electrolyte supplements such as Pedialyte (found in the infant formula grocery store aisle)
  - Clear liquids such as water and bouillon (unless your doctor has restricted your sodium)
- Avoid juices and sodas since these can actually worsen diarrhea, cause an imbalance of salt in the blood, and increase the risk of dehydration.
- As symptoms improve, offer unbuttered rice, potatoes or noodles; crackers or toast; unsweetened hot or cold cereals; soups with rice and meat; and yogurt, bananas and applesauce.
- For several days, avoid spicy foods, alcohol and foods high in fat.

- You may take over-the-counter (OTC) preparations like Pepto-Bismol and Kaopectate that will make the stools more solid. However, these medications should be avoided for about the first six hours (since diarrhea sometimes helps speed recovery from certain ailments).

 If you have a chronic illness or routinely take prescribed or over-the-counter (OTC) drugs, talk to your doctor or pharmacist before taking any other medications.

DEHYDRATION

Dehydration is excessive loss of water in the body and is a dangerous risk of both vomiting (see *Nausea And Vomiting*, p. 178) and diarrhea. It can occur quickly, particularly in older adults. Dehydration also depletes the body of two essential minerals, sodium and potassium, which are *electrolytes*. Severe dehydration can be life-threatening, and symptoms should be carefully monitored.

Signs of dehydration include:

- Unusual thirst
- Sunken-looking eyes
- Dry mouth and cracked lips
- Infrequent urination or dark yellow urine
- Skin that is no longer elastic

What you can do

To prevent dehydration from occurring or getting worse:

- Drink clear liquids like water and bouillon after vomiting is under control (see *Nausea And Vomiting*, p. 178).

- At the first sign of dehydration, increase your fluid intake to eight to 10 large glasses of water a day. You may also drink a rehydration fluid like Rehydralyte to replace lost electrolytes (because of the sodium content, consult your doctor first if you have high blood pressure, heart disease, diabetes, glaucoma or a history of stroke).

- If you regularly take a *diuretic* (medication known as "water pills" that increases fluid loss) and you think you may be dehydrated due to recent illness, ask your doctor if you should continue taking your medicine. **Never abruptly stop taking medication without first consulting your doctor.**

know
WHAT
TO DO

Diarrhea
DO THESE APPLY:

- Stool that is deep red (maroon), black or tar-like, with dizziness or feeling weak
- Severe abdominal pain
- Signs of dehydration in an adult over 60

  see *Dehydration*, p. 192

YES → **SEEK EMERGENCY CARE**

NO

- Stool that is deep red (maroon), black or tar-like, without dizziness or feeling weak
- Signs of dehydration in an adult under 60

  see *Dehydration*, p. 192

YES → **CALL DOCTOR NOW**

NO

- Suspect medications are causing diarrhea
- Diarrhea persists for three days or more
- Recent travel to a foreign country

YES → **CALL DOCTOR**

NO

see *What You Can Do, Diarrhea*, p. 191

see *What You Can Do, Dehydration*

APPLY SELF-CARE

Abdominal pain

One interesting aspect of aging is that conditions that may have caused a great deal of pain when you were younger may result in only minor pain, discomfort or pressure as you get older. This is because the number of nerve endings decrease and the response time of the remaining nerve endings is slowed. What this means to you is that the *degree of your pain* may not be a good indicator of the *severity of your condition*. As a result, it's important to pay attention to even minor symptoms and seek medical attention when appropriate.

APPENDICITIS

Appendicitis, the most common abdominal emergency, most frequently strikes males between the ages of 15 and 25 but can occur in older adults as well. Accurate diagnosis and rapid treatment can greatly reduce the likelihood of complications and death, usually caused by a burst appendix.

Symptoms ordinarily occur in this order:

- Vague discomfort around and just above the navel; later, a sharper pain in the lower right quadrant of the abdomen
- Possible nausea, vomiting, loss of appetite
- Tenderness in the lower right abdomen
- Fever
- Constipation and, less commonly, diarrhea

Once appendicitis is confirmed, the appendix will probably be removed. This surgery, called an *appendectomy*, is relatively low in risk.

What you can do

If you suspect appendicitis, seek immediate medical attention. DO NOT use laxatives or apply heat to the area. Both can cause the appendix to rupture more quickly.

SEE > *Know What To Do, p. 197*

GALLBLADDER DISEASE

The gallbladder stores bile that is made in the liver, then passes the bile on to the intestines to help digest fats. With a high amount of fat and cholesterol in the system, some of the bile may turn into stones. As the bile flows from the gallbladder to the intestines through the bile ducts, these *gallstones* can block the ducts, causing severe pain, local inflammation or *jaundice* (yellow skin). If the stones stay in the gallbladder, they cause no discomfort.

The pain usually occurs in the pit of the stomach or the upper right side of the abdomen and radiates to the upper right side of the back. It usually begins one to three hours after a meal and persists for several hours. It may be accompanied by nausea and vomiting.

What you can do

The greatest risk factors for gallbladder disease are eating a high-calorie, high-fat diet (which increases bile production), obesity and extreme dieting. Avoid fatty foods and overeating to help prevent a gallbladder attack.

SEE ⟩ *Know What To Do*, p. 197

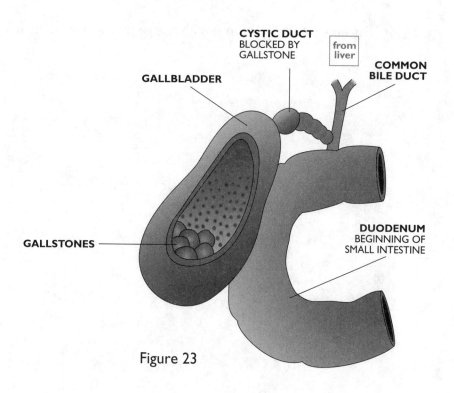

Figure 23

GAS

Everyone produces intestinal gas (*flatus*) that is expelled during a bowel movement. It is perfectly normal to pass gas throughout the day. In most cases, excess gas is not the result of disease and is not a serious condition — but it can be bothersome and embarrassing.

What you can do

- Limit foods that may cause excess gas, such as beans and other legumes, wheat and wheat bran, oats, Brussels sprouts, sauerkraut, cabbage, corn, rutabagas, apricots, bananas and prunes. (To minimize gas in beans, soak dry beans overnight, then use fresh water to cook them.) If dairy products give you gas, try cultured milk products such as yogurt and buttermilk, or add a *lactase* supplement (lactase breaks down lactose so it can be more easily digested) to your milk to aid digestion.

- Consume a high-fiber diet and, unless your fluid intake has been limited by your doctor, drink plenty of water to avoid constipation.

- Add an anti-gas product such as Beano to high-fiber foods.

- Cut back on fried foods, fatty meats, cream sauces and gravies, which can increase gas and bloating.

- Limit use of *fructose* and *sorbitol*, two sugar substitutes that can contribute to gas.

- Eat slowly and chew thoroughly. Large pieces of food are harder to digest.

Abdominal pain
DO THESE APPLY:

- Chest, back or abdominal pain, especially if associated with shortness of breath, sweating or extreme paleness
- Abdominal pain with a swollen, tender abdomen
- Abdominal pain and persistent or unusually forceful vomiting, or vomiting bright red blood or greenish bile
- Abdominal pain is severe or associated with chills, fever, rapid pulse, constipation, weakness or fatigue, or a sickly appearance
- Vomiting what looks like coffee grounds or stool that is deep red (maroon), black or tar-like, with dizziness or feeling weak

YES  SEEK EMERGENCY CARE

NO

- Vomiting what looks like coffee grounds or stool that is deep red (maroon), black or tar-like, without dizziness or feeling weak
- Moderate to severe abdominal pain and you sustained a recent injury or blow to the abdomen
- Abdominal pain persists for more than 24 hours
- Symptoms are suggestive of appendicitis

YES  CALL DOCTOR NOW

NO

- Abdominal pain leads to a sustained loss of appetite or weight loss
- You have been diagnosed with gallstones and an "episode" persists for longer than three hours
- Gas pains are not relieved with self-care
- Abdominal pain and jaundice

YES CALL DOCTOR

NO

see *What You Can Do, Appendicitis*, p. 194

see *What You Can Do, Gallbladder Disease*, p. 195

see *What You Can Do, Gas*

 APPLY SELF-CARE

Diverticulosis and colon cancer

Digestion is completed in the *colon*, or large intestine, where water is removed from the digested food and the remaining waste is formed into *feces* (stool). The final two sections of the colon are called the *sigmoid colon* and the *rectum* (see Figure 22, p. 171). During a bowel movement the muscles in the abdominal wall tighten, causing pressure inside the colon to move the stool into the rectum toward the *anus* (rectal opening). The stool is expelled when the *anal sphincter*, a ring of muscle at the end of the rectum, relaxes.

DIVERTICULOSIS

Small sac-like pouches called *diverticula* often develop in the wall of the colon. The condition of having these diverticula is called *diverticulosis*, and its cause is unknown. This condition is usually not serious, and often there are no symptoms. Constipation or heavy straining with a bowel movement can increase the pressure in your colon, causing the pouches to become stretched or filled with stool. This may result in mild cramping and pain, especially in the lower left side of your *abdomen*, or belly.

If the diverticula become infected or inflamed, the condition is called *diverticulitis*. This can become a very serious illness. Symptoms of diverticulitis may be only mild cramping at first. The cramping may slowly increase over a few days to become severe abdominal pains with fever and nausea. The colon can become completely blocked, and the infection may spread throughout the abdominal cavity.

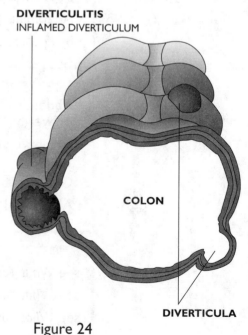

DIVERTICULITIS
INFLAMED DIVERTICULUM

COLON

DIVERTICULA

Figure 24

Note your symptoms

- Diverticulosis often has no symptoms; symptoms may indicate diverticulitis
- Abdominal cramping; pain may be mild at first and slowly become severe

- Pain may be more severe on lower left side of abdomen
- Fever or chills
- Nausea or vomiting
- Intermittent pain or pain relieved by a bowel movement
- Tender, full, tight abdomen
- Constipation

What you can do

- Treatment of diverticulosis is primarily directed at preventing constipation:
  - Eat a diet high in fiber (see *Eating Right*, p. 310).
  - Unless your fluid intake has been limited by your doctor, drink eight glasses of water daily.
  - Use fiber or bulk laxatives regularly to prevent chronic constipation.
  - Avoid straining with bowel movements.
- Avoid small indigestible seeds such as poppy, raspberry, strawberry, etc.
- **If you suspect diverticulitis: DO NOT eat solid foods, and call your doctor.**

COLON CANCER

Colorectal (colon-rectum) cancer, also called colon cancer, is a common form of cancer in older adults. The cause of colorectal cancer is not known, but there is a large incidence in countries where diets are high in animal fat and low in fiber. Your risk is increased if you have a family history of colorectal cancer, previous history of colon *polyps* (protruding growths or tumors) or have *ulcerative colitis* (inflammatory disease of the bowel). Colorectal cancers are curable when detected and treated early (see *Screening Guidelines*, p. 324).

What you can do

- Eat a high-fiber, low-fat diet.
- Exercise regularly and drink plenty of water (unless your fluid intake has been limited by your doctor) to keep the bowels functioning appropriately.
- Partake in regular screening tests for colorectal cancer (testing for blood in the stool every year, with a *sigmoidoscopy* and/or a *colonoscopy* every five years or on doctor's advice).
- Report any change in bowel patterns or any rectal bleeding to your doctor.

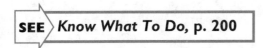

SEE *Know What To Do, p. 200*

If you have a chronic illness or routinely take prescribed or over-the-counter (OTC) drugs, talk to your doctor or pharmacist before taking any other medications.

Diverticulosis and colon cancer
DO THESE APPLY:

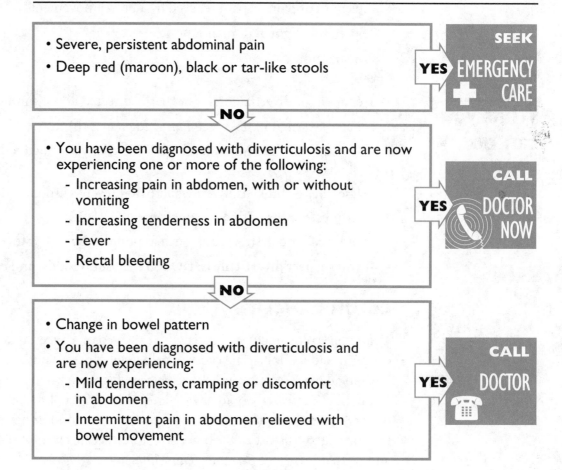

- Severe, persistent abdominal pain
- Deep red (maroon), black or tar-like stools

YES → **SEEK EMERGENCY CARE**

NO

- You have been diagnosed with diverticulosis and are now experiencing one or more of the following:
    - Increasing pain in abdomen, with or without vomiting
    - Increasing tenderness in abdomen
    - Fever
    - Rectal bleeding

YES → **CALL DOCTOR NOW**

NO

- Change in bowel pattern
- You have been diagnosed with diverticulosis and are now experiencing:
    - Mild tenderness, cramping or discomfort in abdomen
    - Intermittent pain in abdomen relieved with bowel movement

YES → **CALL DOCTOR**

DIABETES AND THYROID CONCERNS

The *endocrine system* consists of ductless glands that produce and secrete hormones. The normal aging process causes some changes within this complex system. For example, the thyroid gland can decrease its production of thyroid hormones by as much as 50%. *Glucose metabolism* (the body's ability to convert glucose into energy) also slows with age. Because of these normal changes, disorders are often difficult to diagnose. This is why it is so important to promptly and accurately report symptoms listed in the following pages to your doctor.

Diabetes

Modern medical treatment and proactive self-care emphasizing healthy living habits have changed the way we look at diabetes, a disease that was once fatal.

Diabetes is an imbalance in body chemistry. Normally, the sugars and starches you eat (*carbohydrates*) are converted by the body into *glucose*, a sugar, which the body then uses for energy. With diabetes, the body's ability to store and use glucose is impaired.

Insulin is an important key to the chemical imbalance. Insulin is a hormone produced in a gland called the *pancreas*, which controls the conversion of blood glucose into fuel for the body. With diabetes, either the body does not produce enough insulin, or the insulin is blocked from working correctly (*insulin resistance*). The result in both cases is too much glucose in the blood. This can cause damage to the heart, blood vessels, eyes, kidneys, nerves and other body organs. The exact cause of diabetes is still unknown. Genetics and autoimmune diseases may play a part in juvenile onset diabetes. Weight gain, lack of exercise and a family history of diabetes are all contributing factors to adult onset diabetes.

3

DIABETES TYPE I AND TYPE 2

There are two types of diabetes (although they have similar symptoms and treatments). With *diabetes type 1*, the pancreas does not produce enough insulin. Without insulin, blood sugar rises rapidly, yet the cells are not able to use the sugar. Looking for a new energy source, the cells draw on fat for their needs. When fat is broken down under these conditions, serious medical problems arise. It is most common in young men and boys.

Diabetes type 2 is most common among overweight adults, especially women over 40 years of age. About one-third of diabetics of this type have a family member with the disease. Approximately 18% of people over age 65 and 25% over age 85 have diabetes. In diabetes type 2, insulin production is reduced, and the insulin that is produced by the pancreas is not properly used or absorbed. Blood sugar levels rise. This increase occurs gradually, and the symptoms come on more slowly. The consistently elevated levels of blood sugar are damaging, however, and can lead to a number of severe problems.

Note your symptoms

Both types of diabetes have similar symptoms. However, the symptoms develop at different speeds, with diabetes type 1 coming on rapidly (usually in childhood) and diabetes type 2 typically developing over a period of years.

Almost half of older adults with diabetes don't know they have it. The following are some common symptoms:

- Frequent urination
- Bladder and/or urinary tract infections
- Increased thirst, overeating
- Fatigue, low energy
- Nausea, vomiting
- High blood pressure
- Weight loss (most typical in children and young adults)
- Tingling in the hands and feet
- Blurred vision
- Lowered resistance to infection
- Impotence in men (occasionally)
- No menstrual periods in premenopausal women (occasionally)

What you can do

Once diagnosed, individuals with diabetes play a very important role in managing their disease and maintaining good health. It's crucial to follow the doctor's treatment plan. While some individuals can control diabetes with diet and exercise alone, others require a combination of insulin or oral hypoglycemic medications along with a controlled diet and exercise plan. The treatment goal is to maintain acceptable levels of blood glucose in the body throughout the day.

Diet and aerobic exercise are the foundation of treatment for adults. As weight is lost, the blood has a remarkable tendency to normalize glucose levels. The goal of any weight loss plan is to limit calories with a nutritionally balanced food selection. A reasonable guideline is to lose one pound a week, which typically means reducing calorie intake by 500 calories per day. Frequent monitoring of progress with a doctor is important. Once acceptable levels of weight and blood sugar are achieved, the risk of heart disease can be further lowered by reducing fat intake to less than 30% of caloric intake and saturated fat to less than 10% of total calories (see *Eating Right*, p. 310; *Staying Active*, p. 316). **Consult your doctor prior to modifying your diet and exercise.**

Exercise, a valuable tool in managing diabetes, helps burn off calories and reduce the appetite. It helps to normalize blood sugar levels and assists the body in combating insulin resistance. Diabetics are at risk of coronary heart disease, and exercise reduces this risk (see *Heart Disease*, p. 159). If you have diabetes, you'll want to develop a diet and exercise program that suits your specific health status. People with diabetes may have associated problems that make some forms of exercise more appropriate than others. Heart attack, detached retina and foot damage are all associated with diabetes and may affect the type of exercise plan that is developed.

Cuts, blisters or sores on the feet may be slow to heal if you have diabetes. Check your feet every day, keep them clean and warm, trim toenails and wear shoes to help prevent injuries.

SEE ⟩ *Know What To Do, p. 208*

DIABETIC RETINOPATHY

Vision loss is one of the serious complications of diabetes. Seven percent of blindness in the U.S. is caused by diabetes, but vision loss is not inevitable. With diabetes, high levels of blood glucose may cause blood vessels in the eyes to break, blurring vision. Untreated diabetes can also lead to growth of abnormal blood vessels in the eye — further impairing vision. Consistent management of blood sugar and regular visits (at least yearly) to an eye specialist, or *ophthalmologist*, can help minimize and avoid damage to the eye.

HYPOGLYCEMIA

Monitoring and controlling blood glucose is crucial to the successful management of diabetes. When glucose drops too low, *hypoglycemia* occurs. Symptoms include hunger, weakness, dizziness, headache, shakiness and confusion. Hypoglycemia can be triggered by taking too much insulin, exercising too strenuously or getting off schedule on a meal plan.

What you can do

If you have symptoms of hypoglycemia, take a quick-acting sugar right away. Hard candy, orange juice or sugar cubes are good sources. **If symptoms don't go away, seek immediate care.**

SEE > *Know What To Do, p. 208*

Thyroid problems

The *thyroid* is a small, butterfly-shaped gland located in the neck. For a little gland, it has a big job. You could call it a "chemical commander" that sends activity messages to the brain, heart, liver, kidney and bones. The thyroid controls how the body burns fuel to produce energy. Increased amounts of thyroid hormones can speed up the body's chemical reactions. Lowered amounts can slow down activity. Either way, thinking and physical activity can be affected. Thyroid problems are common among older adults, yet these problems sometimes go undetected. Symptoms such as hair loss, dry skin, fatigue and weakness can develop slowly and be dismissed as part of the aging process. Thyroid problems are not a stage of life. They can and should be treated.

HYPOTHYROIDISM

With *hypothyroidism*, there's a decrease in the amount of thyroid hormone produced. The complex communication system between the hypothalamus and pituitary gland in the brain somehow breaks down, and as a result, the thyroid cuts back on hormone production. Hypothyroidism occurs four times more often in women than men, most frequently between the ages of 35 and 60. The most common cause of hypothyroidism is a disease called *Hashimoto's*, where the immune system turns against the thyroid gland. Viruses and bacteria can also hinder production of the thyroid hormone. For some people on medication for an overactive thyroid (*hyperthyroidism*), the drug can make the gland produce too little hormone, resulting in hypothyroidism.

Note your symptoms

The symptoms of hypothyroidism can develop slowly over months, which is why some of the following symptoms may go unnoticed:

- Fatigue and lack of energy
- Difficulty in performing mental tasks
- Slowed heart rate
- Constipation
- Weight gain in spite of less food
- Dry, lifeless hair
- Increased susceptibility to cold temperatures

- Numbness or tingling in the hands
- Poor memory, reduction in mental prowess
- Muscle cramps
- Poor hearing, hoarse voice, speech problems
- In women, heavy and/or prolonged menstrual periods
- In men, impotence

What you can do

It is common to feel "slowed down" at times. However, if you experience one or more of the above symptoms consistently, check with your doctor. Hypothyroidism can be treated with medication. Long-term follow-up is important, and annual checkups are a must. If you change doctors, be sure to notify your new doctor of this condition.

HYPERTHYROIDISM

Hyperthyroidism, or too much thyroid hormone, is most commonly caused by an autoimmune condition called *Graves' disease.* No one knows what triggers this disease, which is seven times more common in women than in men. Hyperthyroidism can also follow a viral infection. Thyroid problems are common in the later years of life. The danger is to ignore the symptoms because you think they are a common occurrence of growing older.

Note your symptoms

Too much thyroid hormone, or a hyperthyroid gland, can result in one or more of the following symptoms:

- Feelings of anxiety, inability to sit still
- Difficulty in relaxing or getting to sleep
- Shaky hands
- Reduced sensitivity to cold temperatures
- Increased sweating

- Irregular, faster heartbeats
- Shortness of breath after mild exertion
- Diarrhea
- Itchy eyes
- Unexpected weight loss
- Extreme weakness
- Swelling of the thyroid gland itself (*goiter*)
- In premenopausal women, few or no menstrual periods

Less common symptoms include a gritty feeling in the eyes, or eyes that appear to bulge out, as well as blurred vision.

What you can do

It is possible to recover completely from hyperthyroidism with treatment. The most common treatment for this disorder is radioactive iodine. It is consumed in the form of a clear, salty drink, and acts upon the thyroid gland to slow it down. Surgery may also be required to remove either part or all of the overactive thyroid and is highly successful in 90% of the cases. Whichever treatment is recommended, the chances of reversing the problem are excellent.

Final notes

Both hypo- and hyperthyroidism are treatable. Diagnosis in the early stages is important. Warning signals of these problems can be missed, ignored or misdiagnosed. Staying tuned into your own body and its signals will help you and your doctor maintain the best health regimen.

SEE *Know What To Do, p. 208*

Diabetes/thyroid problems
DO THESE APPLY:

- A person with diabetes loses consciousness

- A person with diabetes develops symptoms of hyperglycemia (high blood sugar):
    - Sudden and severe increase in thirst or urination
    - Sweet or fruity-smelling breath
    - Weakness or drowsiness
    - Nausea, vomiting or diarrhea

- A person with diabetes shows signs of hypoglycemia (low blood sugar) even after eating something containing sugar. Symptoms of hypoglycemia:
    - Weakness, drowsiness or hunger
    - Trembling or nervousness
    - Dizziness
    - Cold sweat or pallor
    - Blurred vision
    - A tingling sensation in the hands or feet

YES → **SEEK EMERGENCY CARE**

NO

- A person with diabetes type 1 is having symptoms of an illness that are affecting the blood sugar levels

YES → **CALL DOCTOR NOW**

NO

- You think you have symptoms that are suggestive of diabetes

- You have diabetes and your glucose levels are consistently elevated

- You have diabetes and are having difficulty complying with your treatment plan or you need additional information about medication or diet

- You think you have symptoms of hypo- or hyperthyroidism

YES → **CALL DOCTOR**

MUSCLES/BONES/JOINTS

It is normal to experience some loss of strength, endurance and flexibility as you age. Muscle mass decreases, bones weaken and joints stiffen. However, it's possible to significantly *slow* these effects of aging — and the development of chronic conditions such as arthritis and osteoporosis (see *Osteoporosis*, p. 216) — by maintaining a healthy diet (see *Eating Right*, p. 310) and a physically active lifestyle that keeps your body strong and vital (see *Staying Active*, p. 316).

Getting regular exercise such as walking, swimming, golfing, aerobic dancing or riding a bicycle can help you minimize pain and maximize movement. For details on preventing and self-managing chronic illness, see *Managing Illness*, p. 335.

Arthritis

Arthritis (joint inflammation) refers to several diseases that cause joint pain, swelling and stiffness. There are more than 100 different types of arthritis, but the majority of them fall into one of four categories (see *Major Types Of Arthritis*, p. 211).

Osteoarthritis (also called degenerative joint disease) is common among older adults. The *cartilage* (a material that cushions bones at the joints) begins to wear out, and bone rubs against bone. Pain is the first symptom and is often worsened by exercise. Osteoarthritis starts slowly and usually begins on one side of the body only. Morning stiffness may follow periods of inactivity, and joint discomfort often occurs before a change in the weather. As the disease progresses, the joints become swollen and inflexible, and a grating sensation may accompany movement. Over time the inflammation may deform joints; this is especially noticeable in the hands where knuckles become enlarged.

Rheumatoid arthritis usually starts between the ages of 30 and 40. It can affect as many as 15 or 20 joints at a time, as well as the lungs, spleen, skin and brain. Tenderness in all active joints is one of the earliest recognizable signs. Unlike osteoarthritis, rheumatoid arthritis frequently affects both sides of the body, such as both feet or both hands. The affected joints are painful and warm to the touch during initial attacks and subsequent flare-ups. Small lumps called *nodules* — ranging in size from a pea to a walnut — may occur under the skin near the elbows, nose, scalp or knees, or under the toes, although they are not usually painful. Other symptoms may include fatigue and weight loss.

Most arthritic conditions cannot be cured, but their detrimental effects can be limited with consistent self-care and medical support.

Prevention

While you can't prevent arthritis, it is possible to delay the onset and slow the degenerative process.

- Avoid trauma, overuse and repetitive or jarring activities. Vary your exercise and activity schedule to allow changes in the pressure and stress on joints.

- Exercise regularly. Aerobic exercise increases blood flow to nourish joint tissues. Exercising with weights strengthens muscles that support and protect joints. Stretching and range-of-motion exercise help maintain joint flexibility (see *Staying Active*, p. 316).

- Control your weight. Excess pounds place stress on weight-bearing joints such as knees (see *Eating Right*, p. 310).

What you can do

After arthritis has developed in a joint, self-care can help you maintain joint function and decrease pain, swelling and inflammation.

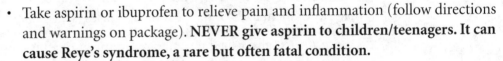

- Take aspirin or ibuprofen to relieve pain and inflammation (follow directions and warnings on package). **NEVER give aspirin to children/teenagers. It can cause Reye's syndrome, a rare but often fatal condition.**

- Rest sore joints. If you must continue to put weight or stress on the joint, take breaks and rest.

- For inflamed, swollen joints, apply an ice pack for 10 to 15 minutes every hour for two hours, then leave ice off for two hours. Repeat this cycle for 48 hours or until swelling is gone. For protection, place a washcloth between bare skin and ice. Do not use heat as long as there is swelling.

- If joint is not swollen, apply warm, moist heat for 20 to 30 minutes, three or four times a day. Follow heat with gentle full-range-of-motion exercises and gentle massage.

 If you have a chronic illness or routinely take prescribed or over-the-counter (OTC) drugs, talk to your doctor or pharmacist before taking any other medications.

- When joint pain and inflammation subside, continue the prevention measures listed on the previous page.
- Become informed about your type of arthritis. Ask your doctor for self-care treatments specifically for you. Learn about resources in your community such as support groups, physical therapy, occupational therapy and stores that carry medical supplies (see *Resources*, p. 360).

MAJOR TYPES OF ARTHRITIS

Osteoarthritis	Rheumatoid Arthritis	Gout	Ankylosing Spondylitis
Cause			
Cartilage in joints wears out (degenerates)	Membrane lining of joint is inflamed, but cause still unclear	Buildup of uric acid crystals in joint fluid	Inflammation in spine, other joints; thought to be genetically linked
Symptoms			
Pain, stiffness, swelling in joints, especially fingers, may improve with rest; bony growth spurs can occur	Pain, stiffness, swelling in joints, with low-grade fever; doesn't subside with rest	Pain, stiffness, swelling, especially in big toe, ankle or knee	Pain, stiffness in back, neck and other torso joints such as hips
Commonly Affects			
Men and women, worsens with age	Middle-aged women most often	Men more often; aggravated by foods high in purines (such as organ meats) or alcoholic beverages	Men in their 30s, but stiff back can last a lifetime

For information about Lyme disease as a cause of arthritis, see *Tick Bites*, p. 49.

When to seek help

Although arthritis is a slowly progressive disease that can be managed well with self-care, there are three problems that require medical help quickly:

- Infection in a joint
- Broken bone near arthritic joint
- Nerve damage

Call your doctor if you have:

- Sudden swelling, heat or redness in joint(s)
- Joint pain that is severe or interfering with usual activities

- Joint pain that requires you to take aspirin, ibuprofen or any other pain reliever daily or frequently to ease the pain. **NEVER give aspirin to children/teenagers. It can cause Reye's syndrome, a rare but often fatal condition.**
- Pain upon motion of the joint, or limited movement
- Frequent joint pain and a history of ulcer or a bleeding disorder
- Joint symptoms and a rash or fever
- Inability to move or use joint
- Sudden pain in joint with numbness or tingling in limb below, back pain with numbness in legs, or loss of control in bowels or bladder
- Possible fracture (see *Broken Bones*, p. 59)
- Arthritis that worsens or does not improve after six weeks of self-care (see *What You Can Do*, p. 210)

 If you have a chronic illness or routinely take prescribed or over-the-counter (OTC) drugs, talk to your doctor or pharmacist before taking any other medications.

Neck pain

Most neck pain is caused by straining the muscles or tendons in the neck and generally can be treated at home. But there are many reasons for neck pain. Neck pain caused by an accident or injury, such as whiplash from a car accident, can indicate a serious or even life-threatening injury to the spinal cord (see *Head/Spinal Injury*, p. 51). Chronic neck pain can be the indirect result of the aging process, resulting in degenerative disc disease.

Other frequent causes of neck pain are arthritis (see *Arthritis*, p. 209), meningitis or a pinched nerve.

MENINGITIS

Meningitis is an infectious disease that can be life-threatening. The classic symptoms are fever, headache and an extremely stiff neck — so stiff that you can't touch your chin to your chest. It can also cause intense muscle spasms in the neck. **If you have these symptoms, seek immediate emergency care.**

PINCHED NERVE

A pinched nerve can be caused by arthritis or a neck injury. The pain may extend down the arm or cause numbness or tingling in the arm or hand. **If you suspect a pinched nerve, call your doctor.**

What you can do

Environmental factors — your surroundings — can contribute to or cause neck pain. An uncomfortable mattress, a pillow that's too high or an ill-fitting desk chair or work area can take a toll on the neck muscles.

If your neck hurts more in the morning:

- Try a firmer mattress on your bed, or use a bed board under your mattress to make a soft mattress firmer.
- Use a pillow designed to protect your neck, or no pillow at all.
- Fold a bath towel lengthwise into a four-inch strip and wrap it around your neck. Secure it with a safety pin while you sleep.

If your neck hurts more at night:

- Consider whether poor posture can be contributing to your pain. Walk, stand and sit with your ears, shoulders and hips in a straight line.

- Make any necessary adjustments to your office chair or work area.

- Keep elbows at a 90° angle for typing.

- Consider doing simple neck exercises every two hours, such as:

  - Sit or stand with an extremely erect posture to stretch the muscles in the back of your neck. Do it gently, repeating six times.

  - Squeeze your shoulder blades together gently six times.

  - Starting from an extremely erect posture, gently and slowly drop your head backward and repeat six times.

  - Gently drop your head backward, forward and side to side with gentle pressure from your hands, repeating six times.

If your neck hurts anytime:

 - Aspirin or ibuprofen can help relieve pain and inflammation. **NEVER give aspirin to children/teenagers. It can cause Reye's syndrome, a rare but often fatal condition.**

- Apply an ice pack for 10 to 15 minutes every hour for two hours, then leave ice off for two hours. Repeat this cycle for 48 hours or until swelling is gone. For protection, place a washcloth between bare skin and ice. Do not use heat as long as there is swelling.

- Heat from a heating pad (on the low setting) or shower may be helpful if muscle swelling is not a problem (see *Heating Pad, First-Aid Supplies*, p. 307).

Also see *Headaches*, p. 75.

 If you have a chronic illness or routinely take prescribed or over-the-counter (OTC) drugs, talk to your doctor or pharmacist before taking any other medications.

Neck pain

DO THESE APPLY:

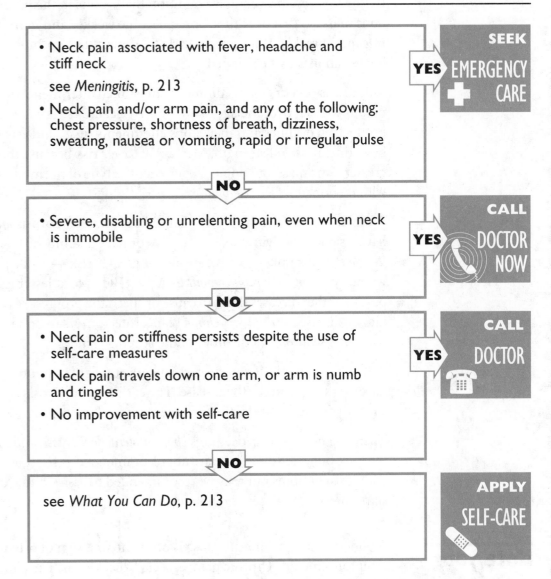

• Neck pain associated with fever, headache and stiff neck

see *Meningitis*, p. 213

• Neck pain and/or arm pain, and any of the following: chest pressure, shortness of breath, dizziness, sweating, nausea or vomiting, rapid or irregular pulse

YES → **SEEK EMERGENCY CARE**

NO

• Severe, disabling or unrelenting pain, even when neck is immobile

YES → **CALL DOCTOR NOW**

NO

• Neck pain or stiffness persists despite the use of self-care measures

• Neck pain travels down one arm, or arm is numb and tingles

• No improvement with self-care

YES → **CALL DOCTOR**

NO

see *What You Can Do*, p. 213

APPLY SELF-CARE

Osteoporosis

Osteoporosis is a preventable condition that results in the progressive loss of bone mass, so that over time bones become weaker and more susceptible to *fractures* (breaks). With proper early treatment the continuous "thinning" of the bones can usually be stopped.

This disease occurs most commonly in women after menopause and affects one in four women over the age of 60. This is because *estrogen* (a female hormone) production declines and then stops after menopause, and estrogen contributes to bone thickness and strength. Men are at lower risk because they generally have greater bone mass and do not experience the type of hormonal changes associated with menopause (see *Menopause*, p. 255).

Women who are the most likely candidates for osteoporosis are Asian or white, have a slender body frame, are inactive or have a family history of the disease. Women who smoke or drink are also at greater risk — while postmenopausal women on *hormone replacement therapy* (HRT) are at lesser risk (see *Menopause*, p. 255). Other diseases that can cause or speed the progress of osteoporosis include kidney disease, *multiple myeloma* (cancerous tumors in bone), liver disease and *Cushing's syndrome* (a disorder of the adrenal gland).

Talk to your doctor if you suspect you are at risk of developing osteoporosis or have any symptoms of the disease. The earlier osteoporosis is diagnosed, the sooner you and your doctor can take steps to slow its progress.

There are now x-ray procedures (*bone mineral density tests* and *CT scans*) that can measure bone density. These are not recommended as routine screening for people without symptoms but may be recommended to assist with a decision whether to start hormone replacement therapy.

Note your symptoms

A bone breaking with little cause is often the first sign of osteoporosis. Other symptoms include chronic pain, especially back pain. The pain may result from *compression fractures* in which *vertebrae* (bones of the spine) weakened by osteoporosis partially collapse, leading to stooping, a loss of height and an increased curve in the spine (a condition called *scoliosis*). The curve may become so pronounced that it becomes a hump *(gibbus)*.

What you can do

Taking preventive measures prior to menopause is the most effective way of preventing or reducing the effects of osteoporosis — especially if you are at high risk. However, you can realize benefits whenever you begin.

- Get plenty of aerobic, weight-bearing exercise — walking, running, jumping, aerobic dancing, climbing stairs — to keep your bones strong. (Swimming is an excellent aerobic exercise, but it's not particularly helpful in strengthening weight-bearing bones.)

- Make sure your diet includes plenty of calcium to help reduce bone loss. Women who are premenopausal or who are on estrogen need 1,000 mg daily, while postmenopausal women who are not on estrogen, and all women over age 65, need 1,500 mg. Low-fat dairy products or calcium supplements are good sources. The antacid Tums is an inexpensive and easy way to get calcium.

- Vitamin D helps your bones absorb calcium. Get out in the sun regularly; it's a good source of vitamin D. (Wearing sunscreen with an SPF of at least 15 will help protect your skin from the sun's damaging rays.) Vitamin D fortified milk and cereals are other good sources. Postmenopausal women need 400-600 IU per day of vitamin D.

- If you smoke, start taking steps to kick the habit.

- Keep alcohol consumption to a minimum.

- If you are a woman, consider hormone replacement therapy (HRT) to replace estrogen loss resulting from menopause (see *Menopause*, p. 255).

- Take special care to avoid sudden movements or falls that can cause bones to fracture (see *Safety*, p. 328; *Hip Pain*, p. 234).

Final note

The drug Fosamax (*alendronate*) has been recently approved to treat osteoporosis in postmenopausal women. Daily treatment with Fosamax has been shown to increase bone mass throughout the body, including the spine and hips. This drug is also effective in reducing vertebral fractures and slowing the development of vertebral deformities and progressive height loss in postmenopausal women with osteoporosis. However, Fosamax may cause minor side effects and should only be taken in combination with a proper diet and a regular exercise program. Ask your doctor if Fosamax is a treatment option for you.

 If you have a chronic illness or routinely take prescribed or over-the-counter (OTC) drugs, talk to your doctor or pharmacist before taking any other medications.

Back pain

Four out of five adults have back pain severe enough to interrupt their daily routine at least once in their life. A common and frustrating problem to treat, there is no quick, easy cure; recovery is slow; the pain often recurs; and prevention and treatment require life-long commitment.

Self-care is the major factor in preventing and treating back pain. Understanding the anatomy of the back and the most common injuries may help you decrease your risk of back pain and, if it occurs, promptly begin treatment.

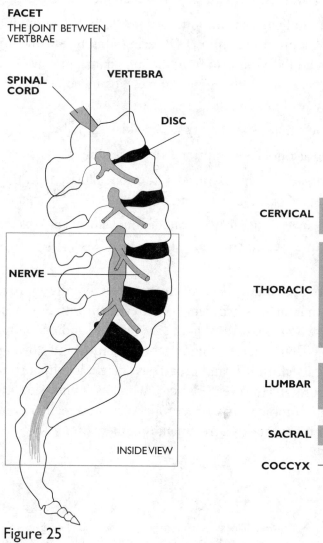

Figure 25

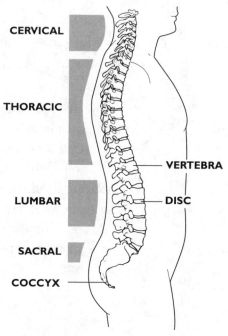

Figure 26

Your backbone consists of 30 small, round, donut-shaped bones called *vertebrae*. Stacked up in an "S" arrangement (see Figures 25 and 26, p. 218), the vertebrae form a protective tunnel for your *spinal cord*. The spaces between vertebrae are filled by *discs*, packets of tough cartilage with a jelly-like filling, that cushion and absorb impact. Your spinal cord, a bundle of major nerves, leaves your brain through the *vertebral tunnel* and sends branches around the discs out to the rest of your body. Large muscles and ligaments support the spine as it twists, bends, stretches, turns and maintains an upright posture.

CAUSES

There are many causes of back pain: muscles can be strained, torn or go into spasm; ligaments and tendons may be overstretched and sprained; discs become worn down, move out of alignment (*slipped disc*) or rupture (*herniated disc*); bones wear down or change, such as in arthritis or a fracture (see *Osteoporosis*, p. 216); and, occasionally, infection and tumors can be the sources of pain. In addition, back pain may not originate from the back itself but may be *referred pain* from problems in the prostate in men or reproductive organs in women, or from kidney infections or disorders in the stomach and intestines (see *Kidney Stones*, p. 226).

Pain from strains, sprains and minor disc damage is usually sudden and sharp, and it eases over two to three days with self-care. The sharp pain from a herniated disc or fractured vertebra usually lasts several weeks and requires medical care. A steady ache is often a sign of disease, such as arthritis or referred pain.

Any back problem that causes swelling or a shifting in the alignment of the spine can put pressure on a nerve. Numbness, weakness or tingling are signs of nerve irritation. Nerves in the neck will produce symptoms in the arms and upper body, while spinal nerves in the middle and lower back affect the back, buttocks, legs and feet. Pressure on the *sciatic nerve* causes sharp, shooting pains down the back of the leg into the foot. Back pain can be constant or come only with movement.

Prevention

- Maintain good posture and keep the right amount of curve in your lower back:
  - Stand tall with your ear, shoulder, hip and ankle in a line. Do not lock your knees. Balance weight evenly on your feet.
  - Avoid wearing high heels.
  - Sit tall with your shoulders back and your lower back supported. Keep knees even with or higher than hips. Avoid sitting in one position for longer than one hour.

- Use correct posture when lifting:
  - Bend your knees and lift with your leg muscles. Keep your back straight.
  - Never bend forward to lift. Keep the load close to your body.
  - Avoid turning or twisting while holding a heavy object.
  - Avoid lifting heavy loads above your waist.
- Sleep on a firm surface. Provide support for your lower back and under your knees if it feels more comfortable.
- Rise up from a prone position correctly. Rising is actually lifting your body's weight. Roll to your side and use your arms and legs to lift up.
- Maintain correct body weight. Obesity or a large abdomen can pull your lower back out of alignment.
- Exercise to maintain good muscle tone in your back and abdomen. Walking, swimming and biking are all good activities.
- Learn stress management (see *Stress*, p. 284) and muscle-relaxation techniques such as yoga.

CHOOSING AN EXERCISE PROGRAM FOR YOUR BACK

By maintaining good muscle tone in your back and abdomen, you significantly reduce your chances of suffering a new back injury, or aggravating an old one. A daily routine focused on strengthening and stretching will go far in helping you stay active and pain-free.

Performing back-saving exercises (described on the following pages) for about 30 minutes a day will produce the greatest benefits. Sporadic, intense bouts of exercise may do more harm than good. Set aside 15 minutes in the morning and 15 minutes at night for best results.

If you find that an exercise causes more back pain or aggravates an injury, stop and reevaluate your back pain and exercise technique with your doctor or physical therapist. Of course, you should always check with your doctor before starting any exercise program, especially if you are recovering from a back problem. Most therapeutic exercise programs are graduated, and your doctor will likely want to alter the exercises as you progress.

SEE > *Know What To Do, p. 227*

A. Knee-to-chest raise, to help loosen a tense back or hips: Lie on your back on the floor and bring your right knee to your chest. Clasp your hands over your shin, hold the position and count to five. Repeat with left leg, then with both legs.

Figure A

B. Pelvic tilt, to reduce a swayed back by strengthening the abdominal and back muscles: Lie on your back on the floor. Press your lower back to the floor and simultaneously tighten your abdominal muscles and buttocks. This movement should be very small. Hold the position and count to five, then release. Repeat five times.

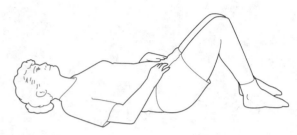

Figure B

C. Hamstring stretch, to help stretch and loosen the muscles on the back of the thigh: Lie on your back on the floor. Slowly raise your right leg in a straight position, supporting it with your hands until you feel a stretch. Stop before you feel any pain or discomfort. Hold the position and count to five. Slowly lower the leg to the floor and repeat the exercise five times. Then repeat five times with left leg. **Caution: Be sure to use your hands to guide your outstretched leg toward you.**

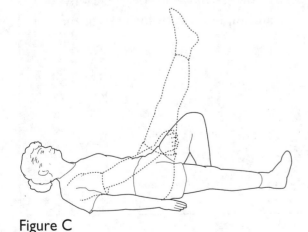

Figure C

D. Half sit-ups, to help strengthen abdominal muscles: Lie on your back, knees bent, feet flat on the floor. Reach forward toward your knees slowly raising your head and neck until your shoulders barely lift off the floor. Hold and count to five. Slowly lower yourself to starting position and repeat five times. **Caution: Keep head in line with shoulders.**

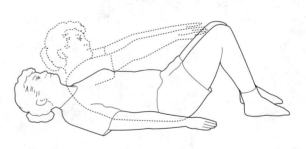

Figure D

E. Lower back rotation, to limber and strengthen back muscles: Lie on your back with both feet on the floor. Rotate your head to one side while dropping your knees to the opposite side. Hold and count to five. Slowly return to starting position. Then, alternating sides, repeat 10 times.

F. Elbow props, to strengthen low back muscles and help maintain the normal lumbar curve: Lie on your stomach, turn your head to one side and relax your arms at your sides. Stay in this relaxed position for three to five minutes. Then, prop yourself up on your elbows and hold for two to three minutes. Lie back down in starting position for one minute. Repeat five times. **Caution: Keep your lower back completely relaxed.**

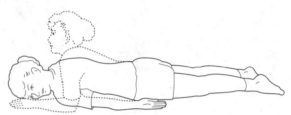

Figure E

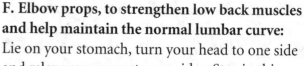

Figure F

ADVANCED EXERCISES

If you have a back injury, check with your doctor or physical therapist before doing these exercises.

G. Hip hyperextension, to strengthen and limber hip, buttock and back muscles: Lie on your stomach, arms folded under your chin in front of you. Straighten and tighten left leg, then slowly raise it from your hip. Return leg to the floor and repeat five times with the same leg. Switch legs and repeat exercise five times with right leg. **Caution: Don't lift pelvis to raise leg. Keep each leg straight and stiff.**

H. Press-ups, to strengthen lower back muscles and help maintain the normal lumbar curve: Lie on your stomach with hands placed on the floor, as pictured. Do a partial push-up while keeping your pelvis on the floor. Hold this raised position and count to five. Slowly lower yourself to the starting position. Repeat five times. **Caution: Relax your lower back and legs.**

Figure G

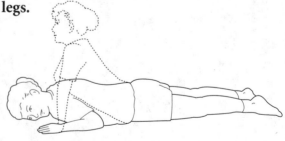

Figure H

EXERCISES TO AVOID

Some common, but potentially harmful exercises are:

- Leg lifts (extending both legs and lifting them simultaneously while lying on your back)

- Heavy weightlifting with the upper body

- Sit-ups done with straight legs

- Knee-to-chest exercises and/or bent-knee sit-ups done during severe back pain

- Any stretching done sitting with legs in a V position (frequently part of aerobic class routines)

Note your symptoms

If you have injured your back and are unsure whether to see your doctor or treat the pain at home, take a moment to answer the following questions:

- Does the back pain follow an *impact* (forceful contact or collision) injury or accident?

- Have you had pain for more than a few days?

- Is your pain worse after a few days of rest?

- Does your back pain interfere with sleep, work or any other daily activity?

- Do you have shooting pains, tingling, numbness or weakness in your legs?

- Do you have trouble raising your feet while going up the stairs?

If you answered *no* to each of these questions, then you are an ideal candidate for resolving your back problem on your own. If you answered *yes* to one or more questions, your chances of self-care are still very good, but you should see a doctor to determine the most appropriate treatment plan for your injury. Even with a doctor's help, a self-care program is an important part of your recovery.

SEE > *Know What To Do, p. 227*

What you can do

If you have back pain, try doing the exercises shown below. If you can successfully complete all four, then you can probably cautiously resume your normal activities. Be sure to maintain good posture and to avoid any exaggerated movements. As long as it does not increase your pain, repeat all four exercises two to three times throughout the day. If one exercise in particular aggravates your injury, skip it and focus on the other three.

FIRST AID FOR BACK PAIN

I. Stand with hands on hips and lean backward, gently stretching your back.

Figure I

J. Sit in a flat-footed squat and relax as much as possible. Don't bounce. Hold this position for 20 to 40 seconds. This exercise is particularly helpful for muscle strains.

From this position, go directly to Figure K. Standing up from the squat can aggravate disc-pain problems.

Figure J

K. Lie flat on your stomach with your arms placed at your sides. Turn your head to one side and relax as much as possible.

Figure K

L. After one or two minutes flat on your stomach, prop yourself up on your elbows, arching your back. Hold for two to five minutes. Stop if you feel severe or increasing pain.

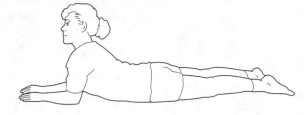

Figure L

What you can do

If you're still worried or in pain:

- Restrict activity. One or two days in bed may be needed in severe cases. Resume normal activity very slowly. Avoid any activity that puts stress on your back. Immediately stop any activity that causes or increases pain. Complete recovery may take up to six weeks.

- Apply ice or cold packs for 20 minutes every two hours for acute pain; decrease to 20 minutes twice daily once pain has lessened. For protection, place a washcloth between bare skin and ice.

- Once pain has lessened, take warm showers with water directed at the painful area.

- Take aspirin or ibuprofen to ease pain and inflammation (follow directions on the package). **NEVER give aspirin to children/teenagers. It can cause Reye's syndrome, a rare but often fatal condition.**

- Sleep on a firm surface. If possible, place a piece of plywood between the mattress and box springs.

- Support your back while sleeping. Place a pillow under your knees or lie on your side, knees bent and with a pillow between them.

- If back pain starts with no known cause, look for signs of a problem in another area of your body that may be causing referred pain.

- For minor muscle soreness in your back, apply heat (such as from a heating pad on low setting) for 20 to 30 minutes, three or four times a day (see *Heating Pad, First-Aid Supplies*, p. 307).

SEE *Know What To Do, p. 227*

 If you have a chronic illness or routinely take prescribed or over-the-counter (OTC) drugs, talk to your doctor or pharmacist before taking any other medications.

KIDNEY STONES

Kidney stones are usually chronic, most often affecting adults between the ages of 30 and 40. They vary in size from microscopic to several centimeters in diameter. Most are made of calcium.

Note your symptoms

- Severe pain in the *flank* (the small of the back just above the hip) and/or pubic region
- Nausea, vomiting (usually with severe pain) or abdominal bloating
- Pain traveling along the urinary tract and into the genitalia, as the stone passes out of the body
- Chills, fever, frequent or difficult urination (less common)

What you can do

Kidney stones cannot be "cured" by self-care, but increasing fluids by three to five quarts per day and making some dietary modifications (ask your doctor for recommendations, especially if you are on a fluid-restricted diet) reduce recurrences in many people.

Final notes

Most kidney stones will pass spontaneously, requiring only fluids and a pain reliever, with no further treatment. Medication may be prescribed to help dissolve existing stones and prevent new ones. For a small percentage of kidney stones, additional medical treatment may be required.

know
WHAT
TO DO

Back pain
DO THESE APPLY:

- Loss of bladder or bowel control
- Leg weakness or limited movement following a back injury
- Sudden tearing pain in upper back without muscle soreness
- Severe pain in back and abdomen
- Unable to urinate and disabling pain
  see *Kidney Stones*

YES →

SEEK
EMERGENCY
✚ CARE

APPLY
EMERGENCY
⊞ FIRST AID

 NO

- Severe pain that goes down into the leg, groin or testes
- ▶Keep the person still. Avoid movement. Slide firm support under total body if possible without moving.
- Recent abdominal surgery
- Taking an *anticoagulant* (medicine that prevents or delays the blood from clotting)
- Severe pain following a fall or accident
- Fever, back pain or you see bloody urine and/or symptoms suggestive of kidney stones

YES →

CALL
DOCTOR
NOW

 NO

- Numbness or tingling in leg or foot
- Burning or painful urination; brown, red or cloudy urine
- Disabling pain or unable to move back for more than 24 hours
- Unexplained fever, chills, nausea, vomiting or weight loss
- Chronic pain that does not improve after two weeks of self-care

YES →

CALL
DOCTOR
☎

NO

see *What You Can Do* (including exercises), *Back Pain*, pp. 220-225

see *What You Can Do, Kidney Stones*

APPLY
SELF-CARE

Arm pain

Arm pain usually centers around the soft tissues near the shoulder, elbow or wrist — the muscles, ligaments, tendons and *bursae* (little fluid-filled sacs at the joints that help muscles slide over other muscles or bones).

BURSITIS

Through injury or overuse, the bursae can become inflamed and cause considerable pain. This condition, which is called *bursitis,* usually develops over several days from the time of injury or overuse.

Bursitis in the shoulder usually begins with a nagging ache that develops into more severe pain. Sometimes there is swelling at the tip of the shoulder. Bursitis in the elbow may result in an egg-sized swelling at the end of the elbow.

TENDINITIS

Tendons are thick cords that attach muscles to bones. Tendons transmit power generated by the muscles to move the bones. Inflammation or irritation of a tendon is called *tendinitis.*

Rotator cuff tendinitis is an irritation of the tendons and muscles around the shoulder. Inflammation and pain can result from activities such as pitching a baseball, playing golf, working in the yard, reaching overhead or carrying a heavy suitcase, or from injuries such as falling on your shoulder.

The shoulder is the largest joint not supporting the body's weight, and has a complicated set of motions. Any inflammation or injury to the joint limits movement — a problem known as *frozen shoulder.* A combination of resting the shoulder and passive, *range-of-motion exercises* (moving the joint gently through its full range of normal motions) will contribute to healing and minimize the development of scar tissue.

Tennis elbow is a common condition resulting from overuse of the muscles of the forearm, causing pain and inflammation where the tendons attach at the outside of the elbow. Overuse of these muscles occurs in tennis and other sports that require a forced forward motion of the wrist or hand. Gardening, using tools or clenching your hand excessively also may cause inflammation and pain. For tennis players, using a two-handed backhand is one of the best ways to prevent the condition.

Golfer's elbow occurs from overuse of the muscles and tendons affecting the inner side of the elbow. Pain is usually felt in the inner part of the elbow and while bending fingers or wrists.

What you can do

If you experience bursitis or tendinitis in the arm, you may get relief from:

- Resting the part of the arm that hurts, and avoiding the motion or activity that causes the condition

- Putting ice or cold packs on the area. At the first sign of trouble, apply an ice pack for 10 to 15 minutes every hour for two hours, then leave ice off for two hours. Repeat this cycle for 48 hours or until swelling is gone. For protection, place a washcloth between bare skin and ice. Do not use heat as long as there is swelling.

- Taking ibuprofen or aspirin. **NEVER give aspirin to children/teenagers. It can cause Reye's syndrome, a rare but often fatal condition.**

- Maintaining strength and motion by gently moving the affected part through its full range of motion. The goal is to keep your arm from stiffening.

CARPAL TUNNEL SYNDROME

Carpal tunnel syndrome results from compression of the *median nerve* (the central or middle nerve) of the wrist. It is usually caused by repetitive motions such as using a computer keyboard, exposure to vibration (using a jackhammer, for example) or an injury to the wrist.

Hobbies that often cause symptoms include knitting, gardening, weightlifting, painting and playing certain musical instruments. Medical conditions that result in swelling of the wrist — diabetes, certain thyroid conditions, pregnancy, arthritis — and excessive use of alcohol also may cause carpal tunnel syndrome.

Neglecting this condition can lead to permanent nerve damage and loss of hand function.

If you have a chronic illness or routinely take prescribed or over-the-counter (OTC) drugs, talk to your doctor or pharmacist before taking any other medications.

Note your symptoms

The pain associated with carpal tunnel syndrome is often described as burning, and can be accompanied by tingling, numbness or weakness of the hand, as well as shooting pain (particularly in the thumb and first two fingers). The pain is frequently worse at night and in the early morning. Unless an injury has occurred, the pain usually comes on gradually.

What you can do

If you suspect you have carpal tunnel syndrome, the first step is to identify the activity causing the symptoms.

If you discover that the cause is related to certain tasks:

- Try modifying your project or workspace. Adjust your worktable, desk, chair or keyboard height, or use a wrist rest.
- Avoid repetitive hand motions with your wrist bent (the way you hold scissors, for example).
- Take periodic breaks and stretch your hands and fingers.

For relief:

- Apply an ice pack for 10 to 15 minutes every hour for two hours, then leave ice off for two hours. Repeat this cycle for 48 hours or until swelling is gone. For protection, place a washcloth between bare skin and ice. Do not use heat as long as there is swelling.
- Rest and elevate the hand and forearm above the level of the heart.
- Splint the wrist in a neutral position to immobilize it. The splint can be worn 24 hours a day if necessary, or only in bed.
- Hang arm over the bed if problem occurs while you sleep.
- Limit salt intake.

- Try using over-the-counter (OTC) nonsteroidal anti-inflammatory drugs (NSAIDs), such as ibuprofen or aspirin. **NEVER give aspirin to children/ teenagers. It can cause Reye's syndrome, a rare but often fatal condition.**

 If you have a chronic illness or routinely take prescribed or over-the-counter (OTC) drugs, talk to your doctor or pharmacist before taking any other medications.

Arm pain

DO THESE APPLY:

• Sudden arm pain accompanied by one or more of the following:
- Chest pain
- Shortness of breath
- Sweating
- Dizziness
- Restlessness
- Anxiety or panic
- Nausea or vomiting

• Sudden arm pain in person with history of high blood pressure, coronary heart disease or heart attack

see *Chest Pain*, p. 162

YES → SEEK **EMERGENCY CARE**

NO

• You experience signs of infection
- Redness around the area or red streaks leading away
- Swelling
- Warmth or tenderness
- Pus
- Fever
- Tender or swollen lymph nodes

YES → CALL **DOCTOR NOW**

NO

• Numbness or tingling in fingers
• Suspect carpal tunnel syndrome, and symptoms do not improve after one month of self-care

YES → CALL **DOCTOR**

NO

---

see *What You Can Do, Bursitis* and *Tendinitis*, p. 229
see *What You Can Do, Carpal Tunnel Syndrome*

APPLY **SELF-CARE**

Leg pain

Most leg pain is caused by injury or straining the muscles and ligaments in the leg. Other conditions that cause leg pain are thrombophlebitis, intermittent claudication, shin splints and varicose veins.

THROMBOPHLEBITIS

Thrombophlebitis is inflammation and blood clots in the veins, which usually cause the leg to ache. This aching generally occurs after a period of inactivity, such as prolonged bed rest, taking a long plane ride or sitting through a long meeting. Sometimes a vein in the calf feels firm and tender, but not always. Swelling can also be difficult to detect.

The danger is a blood clot that can break off and go to the lungs. This is called a *pulmonary embolism* and is life-threatening.

If thrombophlebitis is suspected, call your doctor now.

INTERMITTENT CLAUDICATION

When arteries in the legs narrow, the resulting pain is called *intermittent claudication.* The pain is "intermittent" because it's brought on by exercise and stops after a few minutes of rest.

When arteries narrow, blood cannot reach the muscles efficiently. During increased activity, such as walking, pain occurs. Older adults and heavy smokers are susceptible to this condition and are sometimes bothered even during such mild exercise as walking (see *PVD*, p. 161).

If you suspect intermittent claudication, consult your doctor.

VARICOSE VEINS

Varicose veins are a common and treatable condition in which bluish, swollen and twisted veins develop on the legs. They usually begin to appear on the back of the calves or on the insides of the legs when a person is between the ages of 20 and 40. They are almost always more unsightly than they are disabling. While they can't be cured, they can be treated.

Varicose veins are caused by long-term swelling of the leg veins near the skin's surface. This happens when leg muscles and the valves responsible for pumping blood back to the heart fail and allow blood to pool or collect in the veins. The veins then become distorted and swollen, particularly during prolonged standing. Feet and ankles may swell, and the calves and other affected areas may ache or feel heavy. These symptoms may worsen in women before or during menstruation.

In severe cases, the skin around the veins may itch and develop eczema (see *Eczema*, p. 98) or *ulcers* (open sores).

Varicose veins tend to run in families. They can be aggravated by prolonged standing or sitting, by being overweight and by numerous pregnancies.

What you can do

Varicose veins are common and usually mild enough for people to treat on their own. To lessen swelling and discomfort and to prevent the condition from worsening:

- Walk regularly.
- Wear elastic support hose that reach all the way to the knee. Put them on after elevating legs for 10 to 15 minutes or as soon as you get out of bed in the morning.
- Wear shoes that support your feet well.
- Lose weight if you are overweight.
- Avoid standing or sitting for prolonged periods. If this can't be avoided, develop a habit of contracting and relaxing calf and leg muscles, and bending knees and ankles several times a day.
- Avoid crossing your legs, wearing tight clothing or doing anything that inhibits the flow of blood from the legs to the heart.
- Never scratch an itchy varicose vein, since an ulcer can develop.
- If symptoms are bothersome, elevate legs above chest level twice a day or more for 30 minutes each time. Put pillows under your calves (not knees) so your ankles are higher than your heart.

See your doctor if, despite self-care measures, varicose veins develop ulcers, worsen or interfere with normal activities. Severe pain, tenderness and warmth in the area may indicate a blood clot. Call your doctor immediately and elevate the leg until it can be examined. If you suspect a blood clot, avoid massaging or rubbing the leg and avoid unnecessary walking.

HIP PAIN

Common causes of hip pain include overuse of the joint (starting a new exercise program or walking a long distance, for example), arthritis in the hip (see *Arthritis*, p. 209), infections in the joint and fractures.

Hip fractures are common among older adults whose bones are weakened and brittle, and even more common among people who have osteoporosis, which weakens the bones further (see *Osteoporosis*, p. 216). Fractures can result from a fall, or even from a sudden contraction of the muscles of the leg. In some cases it's hard to tell which came first — the fall or the fracture.

A hip fracture used to mean months of bed rest — which could lead to weakness and complications such as pneumonia, bed sores and blood clots. A surgical procedure called *ORIF* (open reduction and internal fixation) has dramatically improved the chances of a relatively speedy and effective recovery — but it's still a good idea to avoid a fracture in the first place.

> For tips on ways to prevent falls and other accidents that can result in a hip fracture, see *Safety*, p. 328.

What you can do

If pain is due to overuse:

- Take it easy and rest.

- Apply an ice pack for 10 to 15 minutes every hour for two hours, then leave ice off for two hours. Repeat this cycle for 48 hours or until swelling is gone. For protection, place a washcloth between bare skin and ice. Do not use heat as long as there is swelling.

- Take aspirin or ibuprofen. **NEVER give aspirin to children/teenagers. It can cause Reye's syndrome, a rare but often fatal condition.**

- **If symptoms persist, call your doctor**.

If you have a chronic illness or routinely take prescribed or over-the-counter (OTC) drugs, talk to your doctor or pharmacist before taking any other medications.

know
WHAT
TO DO

Leg pain
DO THESE APPLY:

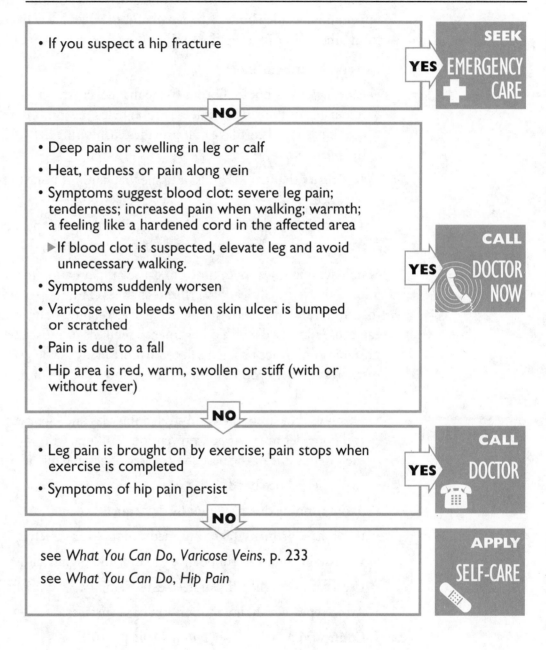

• If you suspect a hip fracture

YES → **SEEK EMERGENCY CARE**

NO

• Deep pain or swelling in leg or calf

• Heat, redness or pain along vein

• Symptoms suggest blood clot: severe leg pain; tenderness; increased pain when walking; warmth; a feeling like a hardened cord in the affected area

  ▶ If blood clot is suspected, elevate leg and avoid unnecessary walking.

• Symptoms suddenly worsen

• Varicose vein bleeds when skin ulcer is bumped or scratched

• Pain is due to a fall

• Hip area is red, warm, swollen or stiff (with or without fever)

YES → **CALL DOCTOR NOW**

NO

• Leg pain is brought on by exercise; pain stops when exercise is completed

• Symptoms of hip pain persist

YES → **CALL DOCTOR**

NO

see *What You Can Do, Varicose Veins,* p. 233

see *What You Can Do, Hip Pain*

APPLY SELF-CARE

Knee pain

The knee — the body's largest and one of its most complex joints — connects the upper and lower leg bones (the *femur* and *tibia*) and acts like a hinge. It is unique from other joints in its ability to slide and glide, swivel and bend.

Parts of the knee include:

- *Cartilage*, the smooth, fibrous tissue that covers the ends of the bones and the underside of the *patella* (kneecap) and helps the joint move smoothly. The crescent-shaped cartilage that provides cushioning between the bones is called the *meniscus.*

- *Ligaments*, the strong bands of tissue that connect bone to bone and support the knee.

- The muscles of the knee (*quadriceps* in the front and the *hamstring* in the back), which move the knee and provide stability and strength.

Simple wear and tear over time can cause inflammation to any part of the knee joint. This eventually leads to *arthritic* changes (a buildup of tissue within the joint) that stiffen and limit movement. Being overweight, or any injury — new or old — can cause increased strain on ligaments, tendons or muscles and lead to an unstable joint. Knee problems become more likely as you get older, but preventive measures can help you minimize your chances of pain or injury.

Prevention

- Exercises that strengthen and stretch muscles and ligaments around the knee and upper leg are your best prevention. Walking, with warm-up and cool-down exercises, is one of the best choices (see *Staying Active,* p. 316).

- Avoid deep-knee bends.

- Avoid running downhill rapidly or frequently.

- If you have arthritis, take your medication — as directed.

- Wear stabilizing and supportive shoes. Avoid high heels.

- Use a cane or walker if you need extra stability.

- Avoid repeated, jarring motions on hard surfaces.

- Control your weight (see *Eating Right,* p. 310).

What you can do

- If knee pain occurs after an injury, rest and immobilize your knee. Start **RICE** treatment immediately (see *Strains And Sprains*, p. 56).

- Pay attention to the pain and avoid any activity that may cause or increase it.

- Use a cane to take weight off the sore knee.

- **DO NOT** put a pillow only under your knee at night; this may cause the joint to stiffen. Elevate the entire leg.

- If pain is caused by arthritis, see *Arthritis*, p. 209.

 - Take aspirin or ibuprofen to ease pain and inflammation. **NEVER give aspirin to children/teenagers. It can cause Reye's syndrome, a rare but often fatal condition.**

Also see *Strains And Sprains*, p. 56.

SEE *Know What To Do, p. 238*

 If you have a chronic illness or routinely take prescribed or over-the-counter (OTC) drugs, talk to your doctor or pharmacist before taking any other medications.

know
WHAT
TO DO

Knee pain
DO THESE APPLY:

- Severe pain following an injury
- Knee deformed or bent in an abnormal way
- Knee rigidly locked in one position
- Unable to bear any weight on knee
- Bone protruding or can be seen through the skin
- ▶Immobilize knee. Elevate leg if possible. Apply sterile dressing if there is an open wound. Apply ice. For protection, place a washcloth between bare skin and ice.

see *Broken Bones*, p. 59

YES →
SEEK
EMERGENCY
CARE

APPLY
EMERGENCY
FIRST AID

NO

- Unstable, wobbly or very weak knee
- Popping sound, snapping or locking sensation during or after injury
- Pain in knee with swelling or pain in calf
- Knee is red, painful and feels hot when touched
- Knee pain with fever from no other apparent cause
- Severe knee pain even when not standing or putting weight on it
- Knee pain combined with another medical problem such as gout, or kidney, heart or liver disease

YES →
CALL
DOCTOR
NOW

NO

see next page

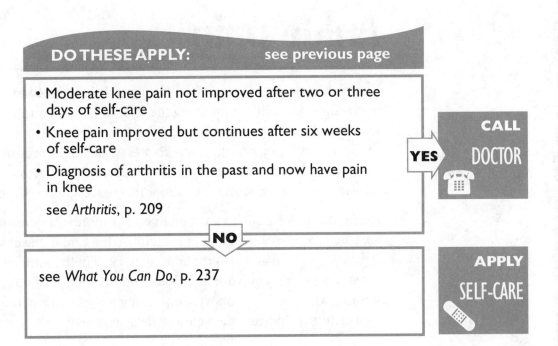

DO THESE APPLY: see previous page

- Moderate knee pain not improved after two or three days of self-care
- Knee pain improved but continues after six weeks of self-care
- Diagnosis of arthritis in the past and now have pain in knee

  see *Arthritis*, p. 209

YES → **CALL DOCTOR**

NO

see *What You Can Do*, p. 237

APPLY SELF-CARE

Ankle pain

Your ankle is a very complex, versatile joint. It is designed to keep your foot aimed in one direction while supporting the total weight of your body when you take a step. When it is not under pressure, the ankle allows the foot to flex and rotate. Problems develop when the ankle rotates while under pressure, such as twisting when you step; or the joint is injured by repeated high pressure, such as when you are running on hard surfaces or supporting excess body weight.

Ankle pain may be due to a sprain in one or more ligaments (see *Strains And Sprains*, p. 56), inflammation in a tendon, a fracture in the ankle bone (see *Broken Bones*, p. 59), or damage to the sliding surfaces in the joint (see *Arthritis*, p. 209). Whatever the cause of your ankle pain, it is a message to relieve the pressure, rest the joint and provide support. Continuing to walk on a painful ankle without treatment may increase damage and delay recovery.

ANKLE SWELLING

There is frequently swelling with pain in an ankle injury due to damage to muscles and ligaments. Ankle swelling without pain or injury is often from the accumulation of fluid that has leaked out of the *circulatory* (blood and lymph) *system*. Fluid retention (*edema*) is caused by the buildup of excess pressure in the veins that forces the fluid out into the surrounding tissue.

Anything that interferes with the flow of blood from the legs back to the heart can result in ankle swelling. Some causes — including prolonged standing or sitting with pressure on the back of your legs, tight clothing such as garters or knee-high stockings, varicose veins (see *Varicose Veins*, p. 232), or a diet high in salt or sodium — can be helped with self-care. When ankle swelling is a sign of a more serious health problem — such as a blood clot (see *Thrombophlebitis*, p. 232), heart failure (see *Congestive Heart Failure*, p. 160), liver or kidney disease — treatment requires medical attention with individualized self-care.

Prevention

- Wear shoes, clothing and sporting gear that fit well, have adequate support and are appropriate for each activity.
- Wear stabilizing shoes. Avoid or limit wearing high heels.
- Avoid trauma, overuse or jarring activities such as running on hard surfaces.
- Exercise regularly. Always do warm-up (including range-of-motion) and cool-down exercises.

- Walk or do leg exercises a few minutes every hour when standing or sitting for long periods.

- Avoid wearing clothing that restricts blood flow. Wear support stockings.

- Control your weight and limit sodium in your diet if it seems to be a factor (see *Eating Right*, p. 310).

- Take all medications as directed. **Check with your doctor before decreasing or stopping any prescription drugs** (see *Using Medications*, p. 298).

What you can do

- If ankle pain follows an injury, start **RICE** immediately (see *Strains And Sprains*, p. 56).

- Avoid or limit exerting weight on ankle (use a cane or crutches if necessary). Pay attention to the pain. If it hurts, decrease activity.

- Support an unstable or weak ankle with high-topped shoes or elastic wrap. Wrap ankle firmly, but not tightly, with elastic bandage. Start at the lower part of your foot, just above the toes, wrapping around the foot and then around the ankle in a figure-eight turn. Repeat figure-eight turns until the foot, ankle and lower leg (not the toes) are bandaged. Do not wrap too tightly or obstruct the blood flow. Loosen and rewrap periodically or if there is any tingling, numbness, change in color of toes or increased swelling.

 - Take aspirin or ibuprofen to ease pain and inflammation (follow instructions on the package). **NEVER give aspirin to children/teenagers. It can cause Reye's syndrome, a rare but often fatal condition.**

- Elevate swollen ankles as often as possible with feet at least above hip level or preferably above heart level.

- When pain decreases, gently exercise ankle a few times a day:
  - Sit with leg hanging freely and gently; move foot up and down, in and out.
  - As ankle becomes stronger, support it with elastic wrap and walk on tiptoes, then on heels, to stretch and strengthen the joint.
  - Gradually increase the duration and frequency of exercise periods.

SEE *Know What To Do, p. 242*

 If you have a chronic illness or routinely take prescribed or over-the-counter (OTC) drugs, talk to your doctor or pharmacist before taking any other medications.

Ankle pain
DO THESE APPLY:

- Bone protruding or can be seen through torn skin
- Ankle appears to be twisted, out of joint or bent in an abnormal position
- Severe pain following a serious injury to ankle
- ▶Immobilize ankle. Elevate leg if possible. Apply sterile dressing if there is an open wound. Apply ice. For protection, place a washcloth between bare skin and ice.

see *Broken Bones*, p. 59

YES

SEEK
EMERGENCY
CARE

APPLY
EMERGENCY
FIRST AID

 NO

- Injury to ankle and severe pain even when not bearing weight
- Ankle unstable following injury with immediate pain and sound of snapping or sensation of tearing
- Ankle unable to bear weight for 24 hours or longer
- Swollen ankle with chronic kidney, heart or liver disease
- Ankle painful, red and warm to touch or fever

YES

CALL
DOCTOR
NOW

NO

- Ankle pain and difficulty bearing weight for 72 hours or longer
- Ankle pain and swelling or discomfort in other joints

YES

CALL
DOCTOR

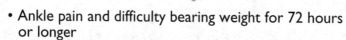 **NO**

see *What You Can Do*, p. 241

APPLY
SELF-CARE

Foot pain

Most foot pain is caused by shoes that do not fit well. Problems can be easily prevented and usually respond to self-care.

MORTON'S NEUROMA

Morton's neuroma is swelling in one of the nerves that supplies sensation to the front half of your foot and toes. These nerves run parallel along the five long bones in your foot and end in the toes. Tight-fitting shoes squeeze the bones together and pinch a nerve. This pressure causes swelling with intense pain in the ball of the foot and numbness between the toes.

PLANTAR WARTS

Warts are caused by a virus and usually appear on the surface of the skin. A *plantar wart* appears on the ball of the foot and grows inward so it feels like you are stepping on a pebble. This wart looks like an area of thick skin with small black dots scattered throughout and a center core beneath the surface. Unfortunately, they tend to recur.

CALLUSES

Calluses are hard, thickened layers of dead skin caused by friction. They often follow blisters and are a result of the skin thickening to protect an area against ongoing pressure. The ball of the foot is a very common site for calluses, especially if you wear high heels. Calluses can also occur on hands, fingers, toes or anywhere friction occurs.

SEE *Know What To Do, p. 246*

Prevention

- Wear shoes that fit correctly. Avoid shoes that are too tight or loose, or that rub or slip.

- Wear high heels as little as possible. If unavoidable, alternate with pairs of shoes that have lower heels.

- Ease pressure areas with moleskin patches (available at drugstores).

- Limit your risk of contracting or spreading a foot virus by wearing slippers or bath shoes and avoiding going barefoot.

What you can do

- For calluses, soak your feet in warm water for 15 minutes, then rub the area with a pumice stone to remove thickened skin. Follow treatment by applying a moisturizing lotion. Repeat process daily until calluses disappear.

- Warts and calluses can be removed with an adhesive patch containing 40% salicylic acid, which is available at most drugstores. Put the patch on the affected area at night after soaking your foot. Remove it in the morning and rub off the whitened skin. Protect with a moleskin patch.

 - Take aspirin or ibuprofen to ease pain and inflammation (follow directions on the package). **NEVER give aspirin to children/teenagers. It can cause Reye's syndrome, a rare but often fatal condition.**

SEE ⟩ *Know What To Do,* p. 246

 If you have a chronic illness or routinely take prescribed or over-the-counter (OTC) drugs, talk to your doctor or pharmacist before taking any other medications.

Heel pain

Most heel pain is due to injury from repeated stress and trauma to the tissues that connect the bones of the feet and lower leg. These tissues bear your total body weight; are pulled in steps, twists and turns; are pounded in activities such as running and jogging; and often are stuffed into poorly fitting shoes with inadequate support. Is it any wonder that they sometimes hurt?

There are two primary causes of heel pain: plantar fasciitis and bursitis.

PLANTAR FASCIITIS

The *plantar fascia* is a tough band of tissue that stretches from your heel bone to the ball of your foot. It can become inflamed (resulting in *plantar fasciitis*) when it is over-stretched or torn by feet that flatten or roll inward while walking, feet with high arches, excessive running or sudden turning.

Shoes that fit improperly, offer inadequate support, or have soles that are too stiff or thin increase your risk of plantar fasciitis. This pain is usually felt in small spots just behind the ball of your foot, right in front of your heel or along either side of the sole. There may be some swelling in the painful areas. Repeated plantar fasciitis or extreme overstretching can lead to the development of calcified fascia splinters, or *bone spurs*, in the area.

BURSITIS

Bursae (*bursa* for one) are little fluid-filled sacs at the joints that help muscles slide over other muscles or bones. The *calcaneal bursae* surround the back and underside of the heel. Inflammation of the bursae (*bursitis*) is most often due to pressure from shoes or landing hard on the heel. Pain and swelling are felt directly underneath or on the back of the heel.

Prevention

- Wear shoes that fit properly and have adequate arch support; flexible, well-padded soles; and sufficient padding in the heel cup.
- Remember to stretch and warm up before exercising, including prolonged walking on hard surfaces (see *Staying Active*, p. 316).
- Ease pressure areas with moleskin patches.
- Wear footwear appropriate to the sport or exercise.
- Maintain normal weight (see *Healthy Weight*, p. 311).

What you can do

- Rest the area. Stop or decrease any activity that causes heel pain.

- Apply an ice pack for 10 to 15 minutes every hour for two hours, then leave ice off for two hours. Repeat this cycle for 48 hours or until swelling is gone. For protection, place a washcloth between bare skin and ice. Do not use heat if there is swelling.

 - Take aspirin or ibuprofen to ease pain and inflammation (follow directions on the package). **NEVER give aspirin to children/teenagers. It can cause Reye's syndrome, a rare but often fatal condition.**

- Wear extra padding in shoes to protect and support tender areas.

Foot and heel pain
DO THESE APPLY:

- Signs of infection: redness around the area or red streaks leading away; swelling; warmth or tenderness; pus; fever; tender or swollen lymph nodes
- Severe heel pain with redness and swelling
- Severe heel pain and fever with no apparent cause

YES → CALL **DOCTOR NOW**

↓ **NO**

- Severe pain in ball of foot and numbness in toes not relieved after three weeks of self-care
- Heel pain is worsening or has not improved after four weeks of self-care

YES → CALL **DOCTOR**

↓ **NO**

see *What You Can Do, Foot Pain*, p. 244
see *What You Can Do, Heel Pain*

APPLY SELF-CARE

 If you have a chronic illness or routinely take prescribed or over-the-counter (OTC) drugs, talk to your doctor or pharmacist before taking any other medications.

Toe pain

Although toes are small, they contain many bones, ligaments, tendons and joints. In addition to being susceptible to all the diseases and injuries that occur in larger joints and bones, toes are often pinched, stubbed, jammed and have things dropped on them. What's more, they usually receive very little attention and care *until* they hurt.

BUNIONS

A *bunion* is a swelling of the joint at the base of the big toe. The toe turns inward toward the other toes and may even overlap. This forces the joint outward, causing it to rub against shoes. Thick skin forms in the pressure area and, if the pressure is not relieved, a bony spur develops. The deformed joint often becomes inflamed and very painful.

CORNS

Corns are hard, thickened areas of skin caused by pressure from under the skin surface. The most common site for a corn is the top of toes where the tissue is squeezed between the bones in the toe and tight-fitting shoes. Corns are usually yellow with a clear core and may become soft, moist or red.

HAMMER TOES

A toe that bends up permanently at the middle joint is called a *hammer toe*. The tendency to develop hammer toes is inherited.

INGROWN TOENAILS

When the edge of a toenail grows out into the soft flesh surrounding the nail bed, there is usually inflammation, swelling, pain and a high risk of infection. *Ingrown toenails* are caused by trimming the sides of the toenail too short, wearing shoes that are too tight, or injury to the toe or toenail.

Prevention

- Wear shoes that fit properly and have good arch support. Low-heeled shoes with a roomy toe box are best.

- If there is a high risk of trauma or injury to your toes, wear shoes with a reinforced toe box.

- Cut toenails *straight across*. Do not cut or file down the sides.

What you can do

- Relieve pressure over the painful area by wearing shoes that are roomy or open.

- Cushion area with moleskin or pads (available at drugstores) to ease friction.

- For corns, soak your feet in warm water for 15 minutes, then rub the area with a pumice stone to remove thickened skin. Follow treatment by applying a moisturizing lotion. Repeat process daily until corn disappears.

- Corns may also be removed with "corn plasters," an adhesive patch containing 40% salicylic acid, which is available at most drugstores. Put the patch on the area at night after soaking your foot. Remove it in the morning and rub off the whitened skin. Protect with a moleskin patch.

- For an ingrown toenail:
  - Soak foot in warm water for 10 to 15 minutes.
  - Wedge a small piece of cotton under the corner of the nail to train it to grow outward.
  - Repeat process daily until nail has grown out and can be trimmed straight across.

 - Take aspirin or ibuprofen to relieve pain and inflammation (follow directions and warnings on package). **NEVER give aspirin to children/teenagers. It can cause Reye's syndrome, a rare but often fatal condition.**

 If you have a chronic illness or routinely take prescribed or over-the-counter (OTC) drugs, talk to your doctor or pharmacist before taking any other medications.

know
WHAT
TO DO

Toe pain
DO THESE APPLY:

- Signs of infection in ingrown toenail
  - Redness around the area or red streaks leading away from toenail
  - Swelling
  - Warmth or tenderness
  - Pus
  - Fever
  - Tender or swollen lymph nodes

YES → CALL DOCTOR NOW

 NO

- Chronic illness such as diabetes or circulatory problems
- Sudden severe pain in big toe and no previous diagnosis of gout

  see *Gout, Major Types Of Arthritis*, p. 211
- Severe pain interferes with walking or daily activities
- Big toe begins to overlap second toe
- Symptoms worsen or do not respond after three weeks of self-care

YES → CALL DOCTOR

NO

see *What You Can Do*

 APPLY SELF-CARE

WOMEN'S HEALTH

As a woman ages, her body undergoes a natural transformation from the childbearing years. *Menopause*, or the gradual loss of fertility, results in lower hormone levels, which in turn effect changes in body tissues and cause a decrease in bone strength (see *Menopause*, p. 255; *Osteoporosis*, p. 216). However, advancing age or decreased levels of hormones have little effect on sexual desire. Most older women continue to enjoy the patterns of sexual expression they had when they were younger.

Today, good preventive care such as regular breast exams and Pap smears — combined with possible hormone replacement therapy (HRT) — promotes well-being in older women.

Breast lumps

About 50% of all women will develop a breast lump before they reach menopause. The vast majority of these lumps are harmless. In fact, 80% of all lumps that are *biopsied* (tested) are *benign* (noncancerous). But some lumps are *malignant* (cancerous). With early detection, there may be more options for treatment and a better chance to catch any cancer that may spread to other parts of the body.

Men can develop breast cancer, but it's extremely rare.

Although some risk factors for breast cancer have been identified, 70% of all women who develop the disease have no known risk factors. Having one or more of the following risk factors *does not* mean that breast cancer is inevitable:

- Over 50 years old
- Having a mother or sister who has had breast cancer, especially if the cancer was in both breasts or developed at an early age
- Early menstruation and/or late menopause
- Having a first child after the age of 30, or having no children
- A previous diagnosis of breast cancer

FIBROCYSTIC BREAST LUMPS

Some women have naturally lumpy breasts (called *benign fibrocystic breasts*). Fibrocystic breasts will feel lumpy and tender, and several lumps will be detected. Fibrocystic breast lumps do not require treatment. Most associated pain or discomfort can be relieved by:

- Using mild analgesics such as aspirin, ibuprofen and acetaminophen (Tylenol). **NEVER give aspirin to children/teenagers. It can cause Reye's syndrome, a rare but often fatal condition.**

- Wearing a larger or more supportive bra during the premenstrual phase

- Eliminating caffeine

Because the presence of cysts may make it more difficult to find a potentially dangerous lump, it is very important to examine your breasts on a monthly basis. However, women who have benign breast lumps are not at higher risk for breast cancer.

Note your symptoms

A mass in the breast tissue may be hard or soft and can have a smooth or irregular contour. The size can range from microscopic to quite large. While some lumps are tender or painful, most are painless.

Fibroadenomas are another common type of breast lesion, characterized by a rubbery, firm, smooth mass. They are most often found in women under 30 and are almost always benign. Surgical removal of the lump cures the problem.

If you have a chronic illness or routinely take prescribed or over-the-counter (OTC) drugs, talk to your doctor or pharmacist before taking any other medications.

Prevention

THREE-PART SCREENING PROGRAM

Monthly breast self-examination: By taking a few minutes to check your breasts each month, you will become familiar with how they normally feel and will be able to identify changes. If you still menstruate, the best time to examine yourself is two to three days after your menstrual period has ended. If you no longer menstruate, choose the same day each month to do the exam (the first day of the month, for example). Follow the six steps on the following page. Call your doctor if you discover any lumps, have discharge from nipples or have any concerns.

Professional breast examination: Recommended for all women during routine checkup, beginning annually at age 40, or at age 35 if there is a family history of premenopausal breast cancer in mother or sister.

Regular mammography: A *mammogram* — an x-ray of the breast — is generally recommended for all women beginning at age 40. It is not recommended that women under 40 have routine screening by mammogram unless there is a history of premenopausal breast cancer in mother or sister.

Final notes

Call your doctor as soon as possible if you think you have a breast lump, have unusual nipple discharge or have unusual pain or tenderness in your breast. The call could save your life.

Breast Self-Exam
Make these six steps a monthly habit

IN FRONT OF THE MIRROR

1. Stand up straight, arms at your sides, and visually inspect your breasts. *Check for discharge from the nipples or puckering, dimpling or scaling of skin.*

2. Clasp your hands behind your head and press your hands forward. You will feel your chest muscles tighten. *Check for any change in the normal shape and contour of your breasts.*

3. Press your hands firmly on your hips and lean forward. At the same time, move your shoulders and elbows forward. *As in step 2, check for any change in shape or contour that seems different from the way your breasts normally look.*

Figure 27

IN THE SHOWER OR BATH

4. Raise one arm and with your opposite hand, press breast firmly with your fingers flat. Make small circles, moving from the outer edge toward the nipple each time until you have worked your way around the entire breast. *Check for any unusual lump or mass, especially between the breast and underarm, including the underarm.*

5. Gently squeeze the nipple. *Check for a discharge.* **If you have a discharge at any time, call your doctor.**

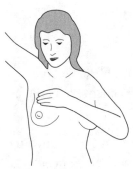

Figure 28

LYING DOWN

6. Repeat steps 4 and 5 lying on your back. Slip a pillow or folded towel under the shoulder of the raised arm. This flattens the breast and makes examination easier.

Repeat steps 4, 5 and 6 for the other breast.

For information from the National Cancer Institute call 1-800-4-CANCER.

Adapted from the National Institutes of Health

Pap smear

Examination of the female reproductive organs (a *pelvic examination*) gives your doctor essential information about your gynecological health. One of the most important elements of this exam is the *Pap smear*, which tests for the presence of cancer in the cervix and may identify endometrial or ovarian cancer.

A *speculum*, a plastic or metal duck-billed instrument, spreads the walls of the vagina so that a scraping of the cervix and a sample of vaginal secretions can be taken.

These cells are then sent to a laboratory where a trained technician studies them under a microscope and assigns them one of five classes:

Class I: No abnormal cells (negative Pap smear)

Class II: Atypical cells caused by inflammation, infection or benign growths

Class III: Abnormal or premalignant (precancerous) cells

Class IV: Severely altered cells (likely to be cancer)

Class V: Indication of cancerous cells

A Pap smear is a reliable screening procedure that detects about 90% of cervical cancers. Since cervical cancers are slow-growing, there is an excellent chance regular Pap smears will detect the cancer before it spreads.

How frequently you should be examined should be determined by you and your doctor. Age, lifestyle and health history all play a role. The American Cancer Society recommends a Pap smear every three years after two consecutive normal screenings, until the age of 65. Annual Pap smears are recommended if there is a history of STDs or multiple sex partners. After the age of 65, the screening interval should be determined by you and your doctor (see *Screening Guidelines*, p. 324).

Menopause

Menopause, also called the "change of life," is a natural event — not an illness — that marks the end of a woman's menstrual cycles and her ability to bear children. It occurs for most women between the ages of 47 and 55, when production of the female hormone *estrogen* begins to decline. Low hormone levels in older women affect bone strength (see *Osteoporosis*, p. 216) as well as breast size and shape, skin tone and the linings of the vagina and *urethra* (the tube that allows urine to pass from the bladder out of the body). If the lining of the urethra becomes too thin, urinary incontinence may result (see *Urinary Incontinence, Women's Health*, p. 266). The lining of the vagina may become thin and dry enough to cause bleeding or make sexual intercourse painful (see *Vaginal Dryness*, p. 256).

Menopause can last a few months or several years, and it is considered complete when a woman has not menstruated for a full year. Menopause eliminates the need for any form of contraception, although doctors usually recommend continuing birth control until one year after a woman's last period.

What you can do

IRREGULAR PERIODS

Menstrual periods usually become lighter — but can become heavier — and irregular before they stop completely. Keep a written record of your periods, including dates, in case you need to discuss them with your doctor.

HOT FLASHES

These sudden feelings of intense heat, accompanied by sweating and flushing, normally last a few minutes. They are most common at night — although they can occur any time. Hormone imbalance caused by menopause can result in insomnia and subsequent fatigue (see *Insomnia*, p. 293). For most women, hot flashes gradually decrease over a period of a few years and eventually disappear.

To manage symptoms of hot flashes:

- Wear loose, lightweight clothing — preferably in layers — that can be easily removed.

- Drink plenty of fluids unless your fluid intake has been limited by your doctor. Avoid caffeine and alcohol if they seem to bring on hot flashes.

- Exercise regularly to help stabilize your hormones and prevent insomnia (see *Staying Active*, p. 316).

VAGINAL DRYNESS

Estrogen helps stimulate the production of natural lubricants in the vagina, so the loss of estrogen can result in vaginal dryness — which can make intercourse painful and lead to *vaginitis* and an increased urge to urinate (see *Vaginitis*, p. 263).

Water-based lubricants (K-Y Jelly, Lubifax, Surgilube) provide relief for many women. Do not use Vaseline or other petroleum-based products. In addition, many women find that regular sexual activity decreases problems with soreness during intercourse.

MOOD SWINGS

Hormonal and physical changes related to menopause may result in moodiness, depression, lethargy and nervousness. The best approach is to try to understand that this is a normal part of menopause and to be as accepting of yourself — and your moods — as possible.

OSTEOPOROSIS

The thinning of bones (*osteoporosis*) that is caused by reduced estrogen levels results in weakened bones that are easily broken. This silent disease usually has no symptoms and goes undiagnosed until a bone suddenly breaks. You are more likely to be a candidate for osteoporosis if you are Asian or white, have a slender body frame, are inactive and have a family history of the disease. Women who smoke or drink are also at greater risk (see *Osteoporosis*, p. 216).

HORMONE REPLACEMENT THERAPY (HRT)

Treatment option

This treatment is currently the mainstay for treating symptoms of menopause. For some women, the use of HRT offers protection against osteoporosis and cardiovascular disease by reducing and even reversing bone loss, and improving cholesterol levels (see *Heart Disease*, p. 159; *Osteoporosis*, p. 216). New studies show hormones may also reduce the risk of colon cancer.

In 1975, a link between developing *endometrial* (uterine) cancer and estrogen replacement was discovered. In order to reduce this risk and gain the positive effects of estrogen, the hormone is given in smaller doses along with another female hormone, *progesterone*.

Risks and benefits

HRT may be the answer if you are:

- Having difficulty with symptoms of menopause
- A prime candidate for osteoporosis
- At risk for heart disease

HRT may not be best for you if you:

- Have a personal or family (your mother or sister) history of breast cancer
- Have had recent uterine or ovarian cancer
- Have an active blood-clotting disorder
- Are experiencing undiagnosed vaginal bleeding
- Have liver disease (such as hepatitis), gallbladder disease or migraine headaches

Here are some points to consider as you work with your doctor in determining the combination of hormones and dosage that's right for you:

- A combination of estrogen and progesterone is needed to minimize estrogen's potentially cancer-causing effect on the uterus.
- Women who have had a hysterectomy need only take estrogen, either daily or for the first 25 days of the month.
- Most women on combination therapy take daily estrogen and add progesterone for nine to 14 consecutive days each month. This restores monthly cyclic bleeding, and may cause such symptoms as bloating, cramps, breast tenderness or even migraines.
- Another option is to take smaller doses of progesterone along with estrogen every day. This method may prevent monthly bleeding and other symptoms, but can take up to six months to work, causing irregular and unexpected bleeding in the meantime (see *Postmenopausal Uterine Bleeding*, p. 259).
- Natural progesterone derived from soybeans tends to preserve estrogen's positive effect on cholesterol levels. At this time, the amount of progesterone within these capsules may vary since they are not being regulated by the Food and Drug Administration (FDA). Women who decide to take this type of progesterone should be monitored carefully.
- An estrogen skin patch is available for women with a low risk of heart disease, who can't take oral estrogen due to liver disease or who have an increased risk for gallstones. Those who need combined therapy must also take progesterone pills.

It might take time to find the right combination and dosage of hormones that are best suited to your body. Continue to work with your doctor until you find a satisfactory treatment.

Also see *Uterine Bleeding While On HRT,* p. 260.

SURGICAL MENOPAUSE

Surgical menopause is caused by the removal of the uterus (*hysterectomy*) with ovaries (*oophorectomy*). In oophorectomy there is a dramatic fall in estrogen levels, often resulting in severe and abrupt symptoms. To help offset these symptoms, estrogen replacement therapy (ERT) is generally begun immediately after surgery.

Menopause
DO THESE APPLY:

• You experience even minor vaginal bleeding, and:
  - You haven't menstruated in more than a year and aren't taking hormone replacement therapy
  - You are taking hormone replacement therapy and experience any unexplained vaginal bleeding
• Menopausal symptoms become intolerable or interfere with daily life
• You are avoiding social contacts or otherwise are unable to enjoy yourself

YES → CALL DOCTOR

NO

see *What You Can Do,* p. 255

see *Breast Lumps,* p. 250

see *Postmenopausal Uterine Bleeding,* p. 259

see *Depression,* p. 289

APPLY SELF-CARE

Postmenopausal uterine bleeding

Postmenopausal uterine bleeding is unexpected, menstrual-like bleeding that occurs approximately one year or more after menstruation ends. You are at increased risk of experiencing this condition if you are a woman over age 60. This is because blood vessels become more fragile as you age, and the vaginal lining becomes thinner. A recent vaginal infection is also a risk factor (see *Vaginal Discharge*, p. 262).

Postmenopausal uterine bleeding may be an indication of a minor problem or a serious one, so it's important to get prompt medical diagnosis and treatment. Possible causes of the bleeding include:

- Irritation, infection or thinning of the membranes that line the *vulva* (the female external genitalia). *Atrophic vaginitis*, an inflammation of vaginal tissue due to aging of the tissue and loss of estrogen, may result in bleeding with intercourse.

- *Hormone replacement therapy* (HRT) that stimulates the *endometrium* (uterine lining), causing sloughing away of blood and tissue similar to normal menstruation (see *Uterine Bleeding While On HRT*, p. 260)

- *Fibroid tumors*, which are growths in the uterus that are almost always noncancerous (see *Fibroid Tumors*, p. 260)

- *Polyps* (grape-shaped growths that are usually noncancerous), *myomas* (polyps on the inner lining of the uterus) or tumors of the *cervix* (the narrow outer end of the uterus)

- Cancer of the reproductive system

Diagnostic tests your doctor may recommend include blood studies, a Pap smear, *endometrial aspiration* (inserting a thin tube into the uterus and taking a sample of the uterine lining) or *dilatation and curettage* (known as a D & C), which involves dilating the cervix and scraping the surface lining of the uterus.

Treatment of postmenopausal uterine bleeding may include medications or surgery, depending on the cause.

UTERINE BLEEDING WHILE ON HRT

With some hormone replacement therapy (HRT), it is common to have monthly periods; ask your doctor what to expect. If you are on HRT (estrogen and progestin) and have monthly cycles, you should call your doctor if:

- You are on *cyclic estrogen plus progestin therapy* and bleeding occurs other than at the time of expected withdrawal bleeding (days 10 to 15 of the month if progestin is given on days 1 to 10 of the month).

- You are on *continuous estrogen plus progestin therapy* and bleeding is heavy (heavier than a normal menstrual period), prolonged (longer than 10 days at a time), or frequent (more often than monthly), or bleeding persists longer than 10 months after beginning therapy.

If you have decided on HRT, you'll want to work closely with your doctor to find the right combination of treatment for you. It may take patience, but persistence usually pays off.

> For more information on the risks and benefits of HRT, see *HRT*, p. 256.

What you can do

- If you are on HRT and cycle monthly, track your monthly cycles.
- Try lubricants if you have atrophic vaginitis (see *Vaginal Dryness*, p. 256).

FIBROID TUMORS

Fibroid tumors — or fibroids — consist of bundles of smooth muscle and connective tissue that develop slowly within the wall of the uterus. These growths are almost always noncancerous and can vary from the size of a pea to that of a grapefruit (the size of the entire uterine cavity).

More than 75% of women with fibroids experience no symptoms. When symptoms do occur, they may include heavy bleeding, frequent urination or incontinence, abdominal pain or pressure in the lower back, constipation or pain during sexual intercourse.

These tumors can remain unchanged for long periods of time and often stop growing without intervention. After menopause, fibroids tend to decrease in size due to the decrease in estrogen. On the other hand, fibroids have the potential to develop into multiple, fast-growing tumors and — in rare cases — can be *malignant* (cancerous). Fibroid tumors can recur when you are on HRT.

Postmenopausal uterine bleeding
DO THESE APPLY:

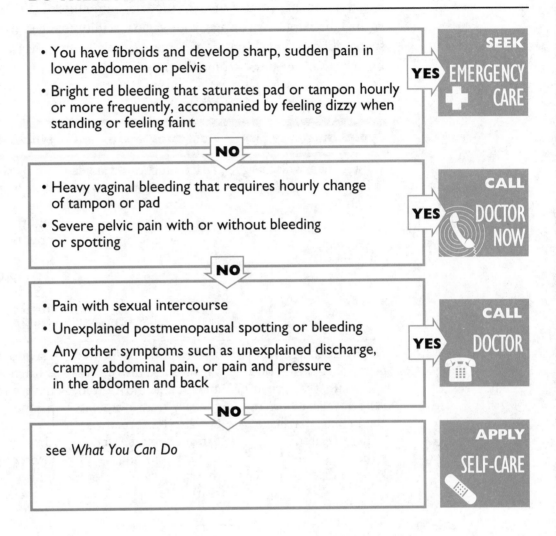

- You have fibroids and develop sharp, sudden pain in lower abdomen or pelvis
- Bright red bleeding that saturates pad or tampon hourly or more frequently, accompanied by feeling dizzy when standing or feeling faint

YES → **SEEK EMERGENCY CARE**

NO ↓

- Heavy vaginal bleeding that requires hourly change of tampon or pad
- Severe pelvic pain with or without bleeding or spotting

YES → **CALL DOCTOR NOW**

NO ↓

- Pain with sexual intercourse
- Unexplained postmenopausal spotting or bleeding
- Any other symptoms such as unexplained discharge, crampy abdominal pain, or pain and pressure in the abdomen and back

YES → **CALL DOCTOR**

NO ↓

see *What You Can Do*

APPLY SELF-CARE

Vaginal discharge

Healthy women produce small or moderate amounts of odorless, non-irritating vaginal discharge. As you age, your vaginal acidity changes, making you more susceptible to vaginal infections. Abnormal discharge is very common and has many possible causes — some that require a doctor's care.

Symptoms	Possible Cause	Know What To Do
White, cheesy discharge; itching; burning with urination	Yeast infection (candida, monilia) or other forms of nonspecific vaginitis	Apply self-care if you have been diagnosed with a yeast infection before and think you have one now (see *What You Can Do, Vaginitis*, p. 264); if symptoms do not respond to self-care in three or four days, call doctor
Frothy discharge that is profuse, strong in odor, and white, gray-green or yellow; vaginal burning and itching; may have urinary-related symptoms (see *UTIs, Women's Health,* p. 265)	Trichomonas, a form of vaginitis and urinary tract infection, is most often sexually transmitted; it can also be spread via damp towels, shared bathing suits and — theoretically — toilet seats	Call doctor now; if diagnosed with trichomonas, alert sex partner(s) and encourage them to see a doctor; abstain from all sexual intercourse until you no longer have symptoms (see *UTIs, Women's Health,* p. 265)
Murky white, gray or yellow discharge; distinct "fishy" odor; itching	Bacterial vaginosis or nonspecific vaginitis	May go away on its own; apply self-care for vaginitis (see *What You Can Do, Vaginitis*, p. 264); call doctor if symptoms do not improve in three or four days

Symptoms	Possible Cause	Know What To Do
Vaginal discharge accompanied by severe lower abdominal pain, fever, or recurrent or significant amounts of bloody discharge	May indicate a serious condition	Call doctor now (see *Sexually Transmitted Diseases*, p. 279)
Discharge in postmenopausal woman who is not on hormone replacement therapy (HRT)	May indicate other problems	Call doctor

VAGINITIS

Abnormal vaginal discharge is the hallmark symptom of *vaginitis*, which can be the result of stress, antibiotics (that kill protective bacteria) or excessive douching. It can also be transmitted through sexual intercourse. If you have diabetes, you are especially susceptible.

In addition to vaginal discharge, symptoms of vaginitis may include burning and itching, general pelvic discomfort, pain during intercourse, and painful or more frequent urination.

Prevention

- Wear cotton underpants that allow for air exchange in crotch and thighs. Avoid tight-fitting pants.
- Avoid douching and use of feminine deodorant sprays and other perfumed products.
- Wipe from front to back after using the toilet.
- If you are on hormone replacement therapy (HRT) and having periods, change tampons at least three times a day during your period. Alternate with pads and be sure to remove the last tampon when your period is over.
- If you are prone to vaginitis, consume more acidophilus milk, buttermilk, cranberry juice and yogurt with live cultures to help the vagina maintain its natural chemical balance.

What you can do

Some types of vaginitis can be treated with self-care. If you have been diagnosed with a yeast infection in the past and you suspect one now, and/or you have minimal symptoms and suspect nonspecific vaginitis, here are some self-care measures:

- For a suspected yeast infection, try over-the-counter (OTC) antifungal creams such as Gyne-Lotrimin or Monistat. (If you have never seen a doctor for a vaginal infection, consult your doctor before using these products.)

- Avoid intercourse — along with douches and tampons — while you have vaginitis to allow time for vaginal tissue to heal.

- Try not to scratch the area. Apply cold-water compresses or ice packs to reduce inflammation and soothe irritation. For protection, place a washcloth between bare skin and ice. Warm *sitz baths* (sitting in hip-high water) may also offer you some relief.

- Call your doctor if symptoms persist or worsen after three or four days of self-care, or if you are unsure what is causing your problem or what you should do.

Final notes

In most cases, symptoms of vaginitis disappear quickly with treatment. However, vaginitis does tend to recur, and some women simply seem to be more susceptible than others. Complications can be avoided by paying attention to abnormal vaginal discharge and sensations, and getting prompt treatment.

> If you experience burning and pain with urination and feel like you need to urinate more than usual, see *UTIs, Women's Health*, p. 265.

Urinary problems

Burning or stinging pain with urination, frequent or urgent urination, or blood in the urine may all be signs of an infection in the lower urinary tract or inflammation around the *urethral* opening (the urethra is the tube that carries urine from the bladder out of the body).

URINARY TRACT INFECTIONS (UTIs)

Urinary tract infections are also known as *UTIs*, *cystitis* and *bladder infections*. They are most common among women, but can also affect children, infants and men (see *UTIs, Men's Health*, p. 272).

Symptoms may include a frequent and urgent need to urinate, pain or a burning sensation during urination, cloudy or foul-smelling urine, pain or itching in the urethra, pressure in the lower abdomen, and lower back pain.

Between 80% and 90% of UTIs are caused by *E. coli* bacteria, which are generally found in the digestive system. Because the female anus and urethra are very close together, bacteria can find their way from the anus into the urethra and bladder. Any irritation to the genital area (such as sexual intercourse or wearing tight pants) can increase the likelihood of developing an infection.

What you can do

To prevent UTIs and minimize infection once you feel symptoms coming on:

- Drink plenty of fluids (eight or more glasses of water a day), unless your fluid intake has been limited by your doctor. Cranberry juice also may be helpful.
- Avoid alcohol, coffee, tea, carbonated beverages and spicy foods.
- Wear cotton underwear, cotton-lined pantyhose and loose clothing.
- Wipe from front to back after using the toilet (to reduce the spread of bacteria from the anus to the urethra).
- Avoid sexual intercourse when symptoms are present.
- Try to urinate before and after intercourse.

- Empty bladder frequently.
- Avoid bubble bath or bath oil, especially when symptoms are present.
- Avoid frequent douching and do not use vaginal deodorants or perfumed feminine hygiene products.
- If your doctor prescribes antibiotics, be sure to take the entire prescription as directed to help prevent a relapse or recurrence (see *Using Medications*, p. 298).

TRICHOMONAS

Trichomonas is a form of vaginitis that is usually sexually transmitted, and it can also affect the bladder and urethra. Symptoms include painful or more-frequent-than-usual urination, and a large amount of frothy vaginal discharge that is offensive in odor and white, gray-green or yellow in color. The *vulva* (the female external genitalia) may itch and there may be a burning sensation in the vagina with spotting of blood. The pelvic area may feel uncomfortable and swollen, and sexual intercourse may be painful.

URINARY INCONTINENCE

Between 5% and 10% of people over age 65 — approximately 2 million people in the U.S. — are affected by *urinary incontinence*, or the inability to control bladder function. In women, decreased hormone levels may result in a thinning of the tissue lining the urethra. This causes the urethra to weaken and leak urine. The effects of childbirth and aging also can cause the uterus and pelvic floor to sag, putting pressure on the bladder. However, there are many preventive measures and treatments for this condition.

What you can do

- If you are overweight, losing weight may help reduce pressure on your bladder (see *Healthy Weight*, p. 311).

- Check with your doctor to see if your bladder has shifted. A mechanical lift inserted into the vagina may help correct your bladder's position.

- Ask your doctor to check for thinning in the lining of your urethra and vagina. A topical estrogen cream or estrogen supplements in pill form can treat this situation (see *HRT*, p. 256).

- *Kegel exercises* strengthen the muscles that surround the openings of the urethra, vagina and anus. Follow these instructions:

  - While urinating, try to stop the flow of urine. Start and stop it as often as you can.

  - Contract your muscles as if you were stopping your urine stream, but do it when you're not urinating — while sitting, standing, walking or driving.

  - Tighten your rectal muscles as if trying not to pass gas. Contract your anus, but don't move your buttocks.

  - Do these exercises every morning, afternoon and evening. Start with five repetitions and gradually work up to 20 or 30 repetitions each time. Hold each position while slowly counting to five. Try not to move your buttocks, stomach muscles or legs.

- Some medications such as *diuretics*, or "water pills" (often prescribed for congestive heart failure and high blood pressure to increase fluid loss), can cause *urge incontinence*, when you feel the need to urinate but can't hold back long enough. Ask your doctor about changing your medication or the time of day you take it.

- Check with your doctor if you experience pain, frequency of urination, or blood in the urine. You may have an infection (see *UTIs, Women's Health*, p. 265).

Also see *Vaginal Discharge*, p. 262.

SEE *Know What To Do*, p. 268

know
WHAT
TO DO

Urinary problems
DO THESE APPLY:

- Chills, fever, *flank* (the small of the back just above the hip) pain or nausea/vomiting — especially if symptoms develop rapidly
- Urinary incontinence comes on suddenly

YES

NO

- Symptoms of urinary tract infection or trichomonas
- Visible blood in the urine
- Symptoms not relieved 48 hours after beginning antibiotics

see *What You Can Do, UTIs*

- Leakage of urine to any degree

YES

NO

see *What You Can Do, UTIs*, p. 265
see *What You Can Do, Urinary Incontinence*, p. 267
see *Kidney Stones*, p. 226

MEN'S HEALTH

Although men do not experience menopause, physiological changes take place as men age that affect their health and sexuality in subtle, but important ways. As the male sexual hormone, *testosterone*, begins to decline, sexual function may change. It may take more time to achieve an erection, and the penis may stay erect for a shorter period (see *Sexual Health*, p. 278). Illness and certain medications, as well as alcoholism, can affect this process. The prostate tends to enlarge with age and may or may not cause any symptoms (see *Prostate Problems*, p. 273). Preventive care in the form of regular genital care and prostate examinations, as well as a healthy lifestyle, is a man's prescription for sexual health and well-being.

Genital health

Three minutes of your time each month can go a long way toward early detection of infections and cancers of the penis or testes. Early detection is the key to early treatment and cure. (Cancer of the testicle is one of the most easily treated cancers if caught right away.)

Washing the penis daily, particularly under the *foreskin* that covers the tip of an uncircumcised penis, can prevent bacterial infection and reduce the risk of developing penile cancer.

Men should also examine their penis and testes each month for any changes that could indicate infection or cancer.

Prevention

After a warm bath or shower:

- Stand with your right leg on the side of the tub or on the toilet seat.
- Gently roll the right testicle between the thumbs and fingers of both hands. Check for:
  - Hard lumps or nodules
  - An enlargement or change in the consistency of the testicle
  - A pain or dull ache in the groin or lower abdomen

3

- Repeat this procedure on your left side.

- Feel the *epididymis*, the spongy tube on the top and the back side of the testicle. Pain could mean an infection.

- Examine the foreskin of the penis and the head of the penis for anything unusual, including sores, warts, redness or discharge.

WHEN TO CALL YOUR DOCTOR

Testicular cancer spreads quickly — within a few months — so it is important to see your doctor to rule it out as soon as possible after you find any testicular lumps or nodules.

Also discuss an enlarged testicle, groin pain or any penile discharge with your doctor.

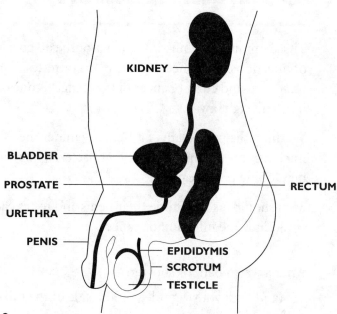

Figure 29

PAINFUL OR SWOLLEN TESTES OR PENIS

Pain, lumps, swelling or changes of any kind — even if they do not cause pain — in the testes or penis may be a sign of a problem that needs prompt attention.

Possible causes include:

- Torsion — or twisting — of the testicle
- Internal damage to the testicle, due to an injury of some kind
- Infection of the lymph glands
- A recent case of mumps
- Accumulation of fluid
- A cyst or tumor

Genital health
DO THESE APPLY:

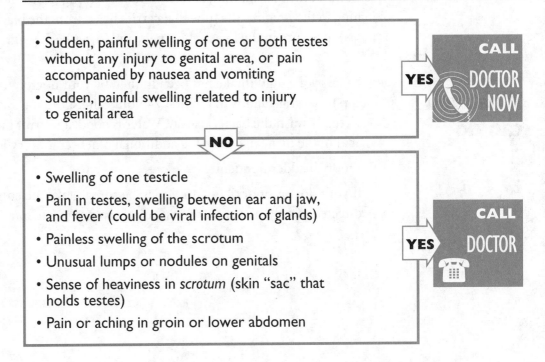

- Sudden, painful swelling of one or both testes without any injury to genital area, or pain accompanied by nausea and vomiting
- Sudden, painful swelling related to injury to genital area

YES → CALL DOCTOR NOW

NO

- Swelling of one testicle
- Pain in testes, swelling between ear and jaw, and fever (could be viral infection of glands)
- Painless swelling of the scrotum
- Unusual lumps or nodules on genitals
- Sense of heaviness in *scrotum* (skin "sac" that holds testes)
- Pain or aching in groin or lower abdomen

YES → CALL DOCTOR

Urinary problems

Problems with urination — difficulty getting urine started or completely stopped (dribbling), frequent or painful urination, decreased force of the urine stream, incomplete bladder emptying, blood in the urine — can have a variety of causes, ranging from a urinary tract infection to prostate cancer.

URINARY TRACT INFECTIONS (UTIs)

Urinary tract infections (also known as *UTIs*, *cystitis* and *bladder infections*) are most common among women (see *UTIs, Women's Health*, p. 265), but can also affect men, children and infants. In men, most UTIs are caused by obstructions or structural problems in the urinary tract. In men over 50 years old, the problem is often caused by an enlarged prostate gland that hinders the flow of urine out of the bladder and becomes the perfect breeding ground for bacteria.

Symptoms may include a frequent and urgent need to urinate, pain or a burning sensation during urination, cloudy or foul-smelling urine, blood in urine, pain or itching in the *urethra* (the tube that carries urine from the bladder out through the penis), pressure in the lower abdomen, and lower back pain.

What you can do

- Unless your fluid intake has been limited by your doctor, drink plenty of fluids (up to several gallons in the first 24 hours after noticing symptoms). This can virtually wash the bacteria away. Water is good, and fruit juices that put more acid in the urine may provide additional relief (cranberry juice is best).

- Empty bladder frequently.

- If your doctor prescribes antibiotics, be sure to take the entire prescription as directed to help prevent a relapse or recurrence (see *Using Medications*, p. 298).

Trichomonas is more common in women but does occur in men. It is an infection caused by a single-celled microorganism called *trichomonas vaginalis*. The infection is most frequently spread through sexual intercourse.

Symptoms are uncommon in men but can include mild pain while urinating and discomfort in the urethra. In addition, there may be an unusual discharge from the penis.

Call your doctor now if you think you have trichomonas. If you are diagnosed with the infection, alert your sex partner(s) and encourage them to seek medical care (see *Vaginal Discharge*, p. 262).

PROSTATE PROBLEMS

The *prostate* (see Figure 29, p. 270), which produces some of the fluid in semen, is a donut-shaped gland that sits below the bladder and surrounds the urethra. The three most common prostate problems are prostate infection (*prostatitis*), prostate enlargement (*benign prostatic hypertrophy*) and prostate cancer.

Prostate infection (*prostatitis*) is an infection of the prostate that may occur with a urinary tract infection as a result of bacteria traveling up the urethra. The prostate becomes swollen, constricting the urethra and causing urinary problems.

Symptoms include difficulty starting or stopping urination (dribbling), a strong and frequent urge to urinate while passing only small amounts of urine, pain or discomfort in the area behind the *scrotum* (the "sac" of skin that holds the testes), low back or abdominal pain, and pain and burning during urination or ejaculation. Fever and chills, a general ill feeling, and blood in the urine or pus-filled discharge are also possible.

The prostate can also become inflamed without bacterial infection (*prostate syndrome* or *prostatodynia*). The hallmark symptom is pain behind the scrotum or in the lower back. The condition is often related to stress or anxiety.

What you can do

Prostate infection requires a doctor's diagnosis and antibiotics, although self-care may be helpful as well; prostatodynia may respond to self-care alone.

- Unless your fluid intake has been limited by your doctor, drink lots of water and fruit juices.

- Avoid alcohol, caffeine, carbonated beverages and spicy foods.

- Ejaculate three or four times a week.

 - Try warm baths or over-the-counter (OTC) pain relievers, such as aspirin, acetaminophen (Tylenol) or ibuprofen, to soothe the pain. **NEVER give aspirin to children/teenagers. It can cause Reye's syndrome, a rare but often fatal condition.**

- Practice stress management techniques (see *Stress*, p. 284).

Prostate enlargement (*benign prostatic hypertrophy* or *BPH*) is a noncancerous increase in the size of the prostate gland that appears to be part of the normal aging process; four out of five men between 50 and 60 years of age have this condition. It is not usually a serious problem, but it can become severe enough to compress the urethra and hinder the flow of urine as you urinate.

The hallmark symptom of BPH is *nocturia,* which is the need to get up at night to urinate. Other common symptoms include difficulty starting, stopping (dribbling) or maintaining the flow of urine; a decrease in the force or volume of the flow; or increased frequency of urination. Symptoms that develop as a result of the condition include increased fatigue, due to difficulty getting back to sleep at night because of nocturia, and mild dehydration (if fluid intake is decreased to avoid having to get up at night).

What you can do

- Avoid the use of caffeine, alcohol and any over-the-counter (OTC) medications such as decongestants that have warnings related to causing urine retention.

- If you regularly take a *diuretic* (medication known as "water pills" that increase fluid loss), ask your doctor if you should continue taking your medication. **Never abruptly stop taking a medication without first consulting your doctor.**

- Take plenty of time to urinate. Sit on the toilet instead of standing.

- Unless your fluid intake has been limited by your doctor, try to drink two quarts of water and other fluids throughout the day to help prevent urinary tract infections.

- Don't drink fluids after the evening meal. Empty your bladder before bedtime.

 If you have a chronic illness or routinely take prescribed or over-the-counter (OTC) drugs, talk to your doctor or pharmacist before taking any other medications.

- If you have nocturia, leave a night-light on and make sure the path to the bathroom is clear to decrease the risk of falls. You might prefer to keep a urinal at the bedside to avoid getting up at all — especially if you tend to feel dizzy or light-headed when you first get out of bed.

Prostate cancer grows slowly in many cases, remaining within the prostate and causing no health problems. In other cases, however, it can spread aggressively and become life-threatening (prostate cancer is the second leading cause of cancer death in men in the U.S.).

Symptoms include decreased strength of the urine stream, difficulty getting urine started or completely stopped (dribbling), frequent and painful urination, hip or lower back pain, and blood or pus in the urine.

What you can do

While prostate surgery is successful in many cases for localized prostate cancer, it can also result in impotence and *urinary incontinence* (see *Urinary Incontinence, Men's Health*, p. 276). As a result, men who are diagnosed with the disease may face a difficult dilemma: whether to undergo treatment and take the risk of side effects, or opt for "watchful waiting" and risk the possibility that the cancer will spread.

Watching and waiting — a process in which your doctor closely monitors your condition without treating it — may be appropriate if your tumor is small and appears to be growing slowly. (It is also common to do nothing in the way of follow-up for men who are older or in less than optimal health.)

If you and your doctor decide to watch and wait, you'll want to discuss how often you need to go in for checkups. Over time, if your doctor notices a steady increase in your *prostate-specific antigen* (PSA) level (a sign that the cancer could be spreading), it may be time to discuss a different treatment path.

Important questions to ask your doctor include the following:

- What are my treatment options?
- What are the risks, benefits and possible side effects of each option?
- How will treatment affect my sex life?
- Will the treatment be painful, and if so, how will you treat the pain?
- Will I need to change my normal activities? If so, how and for how long?
- How often will I need to have checkups?

> If there is pain associated with urination or ejaculation and an unusual discharge from the penis, see *Sexually Transmitted Diseases*, p. 279.

URINARY INCONTINENCE

Urinary incontinence (the inability to control urine) is not a normal aspect of aging, but it does affect millions of people (between 5% and 10% of people over age 65). With the treatments available today, most can be spared the embarrassment commonly associated with this condition. Urinary incontinence is treatable in about 95% of cases and often can be completely cured. When it can't be cured, it can usually be controlled.

Types of urinary incontinence include *urge incontinence* (leaking urine as soon as you feel the urge to go to the bathroom), *stress incontinence* (leaking urine when the bladder is stressed, such as when you laugh, cough or make a sudden move — usually a temporary situation for men following prostate surgery) and *overflow incontinence* (feeling like the bladder never empties completely).

Common causes of urinary incontinence include:

- Enlargement of the prostate gland (see *Prostate Problems*, p. 273)
- Damage to the urethra while treating prostate problems, such as during surgery or radiation treatment for cancer (see *Prostate Problems*, p. 273)
- Central nervous system disorders such as Parkinson's disease (see *Parkinson's Disease*, p. 88) or stroke (see *Stroke*, p. 82)
- Diabetes (see *Diabetes*, p. 201), urinary tract infections and certain medications

What you can do

Urinary incontinence requires a visit to your doctor, who will take your medical history and possibly conduct some tests. Medications you are taking may be aggravating the condition, so talk to your doctor about that possibility.

Once a diagnosis is made, your doctor may prescribe medication to help stimulate bladder muscle contractions, or recommend surgery to tighten certain muscles or remove blockages.

In addition to a doctor's evaluation and treatment, self-care techniques you may find helpful include:

- Training your bladder to urinate on a schedule. To do this, start urinating at regular times. Gradually work your way up to longer and longer periods between urination.
- Emptying your bladder as much as you can, waiting a few minutes, then emptying it again. This is called *double-voiding*.
- Practicing *Kegel exercises* to strengthen the muscles that control urination (see *Urinary Incontinence, Women's Health*, p. 266).

If you've seen the doctor but still experience some urinary leakage on occasion, try keeping a urine receptacle close by or using incontinence pads to absorb urine, protect clothing and prevent odor. Comfortable, inconspicuous and disposable pads are readily available at grocery stores or drugstores.

know
WHAT
TO DO

Urinary problems
DO THESE APPLY:

- Inability to urinate at all
- Chills, fever, *flank* (the small of the back just above the hip) pain or nausea/vomiting — especially if symptoms develop rapidly
- Urinary incontinence comes on suddenly

YES → **CALL DOCTOR NOW**

NO

- Leakage of urine to any degree
- Visible blood in the urine
- Symptoms of urinary tract infection, trichomonas or prostate problem
- Symptoms not relieved 48 hours after beginning antibiotics

YES → **CALL DOCTOR**

NO

see *Kidney Stones*, p. 226

see *Painful Or Swollen Testes Or Penis*, p. 271

see *What You Can Do, UTIs*, p. 272

see *What You Can Do, Prostate Infection*, p. 273

see *What You Can Do, Prostate Enlargement*, p. 274

see *What You Can Do, Prostate Cancer*, p. 275

see *What You Can Do, Urinary Incontinence*

APPLY SELF-CARE

SEXUAL HEALTH

Just as diet and exercise are important for a healthy heart, maintaining sexual health is important for overall well-being. Sexuality is part of an individual's identity. While many physiological changes may occur with aging, the desire for sexual intimacy (*libido*) does not diminish. Research shows that most men and women remain as sexually active in their later years as they were as young adults.

Many postmenopausal women fear that they will no longer have the desire for sex. Yet many report a renewed interest — partly attributed to the freedom from becoming pregnant and parenting kids that are now grown and out of the home. Lubricants and hormone replacement therapy (HRT) can help eliminate discomfort caused by menopausal symptoms.

Men often worry that they will no longer be able to achieve and maintain an erection. While it is true that this process may take a little longer, this is not a sign of impotence. Although the fear people feel of having a heart attack from sex shouldn't be discounted, studies show that the risk is no greater than that caused by getting out of bed in the morning. However, anxiety about sex can lead to lower performance and decreased enjoyment.

The key, for any age, is communication. Taking time for communication and foreplay allows a woman's natural lubrication process to work, and assists a man in achieving an erection. Taking time also creates a greater sense of intimacy and joy.

Sexual health in older adults is a function of a greater understanding of the physiological and emotional changes of aging as well as genital health and an awareness of safe-sex practices (see *Prevention, STDs*, p. 281). While sperm counts generally decline in older men, the ability to father a child continues. Birth-control practices may still be necessary if the female partner is of child-bearing years. Likewise, age does not protect against sexually transmitted diseases (STDs). Older adults having sexual relations outside of a long-term relationship will want to take the same precautions as younger adults (see *Prevention, STDs*, p. 281; *HIV*, p. 282).

Illness and certain medications can cause sexual impotency and other problems; these issues should be discussed with your doctor.

Sexually transmitted diseases (STDs)

Most sexually transmitted diseases (STDs) can be prevented by following basic safe-sex practices (see *Prevention*, p. 281). The *human immunodeficiency virus* (HIV) that causes *acquired immunodeficiency syndrome* (AIDS), can also be transmitted by needles and from mother to fetus (see *HIV*, p. 282). Although genital herpes is an incurable STD, it can be managed with self-care and medical treatment. **Always consult your doctor for diagnosis and treatment.**

SEXUALLY TRANSMITTED DISEASES

Disease	Cause	Signs	Diagnosis	Final Notes
Chlamydia	Bacteria	General pelvic pain, vaginal discharge, discomfort during sexual intercourse, and/or burning urination (which can occur in both men and women); scrotal swelling or pain in men	Pelvic exam and/or test or culture from the cervix or penis, examination of tissue or biopsy	Treated with antibiotics; if untreated chlamydia can cause pelvic inflammatory disease (PID), infertility and complications in pregnancy; and prostatitis, epididymitis or urethritis in men
Genital Herpes	Virus	Clusters of blisters in genital, anal or mouth areas; turn into ulcers or sores and heal in one to three weeks; accompanied by mild flu-like symptoms	Physical exam	Treated with *Acyclovir* (Zovirax) for first-time outbreaks; self-care includes warm sitz baths, cool compresses soaked in Burrow's solution, witch hazel compresses, a hair dryer set on low to dry blisters, non-prescription pain relievers

Continued on next page

 If you have a chronic illness or routinely take prescribed or over-the-counter (OTC) drugs, talk to your doctor or pharmacist before taking any other medications.

SEXUALLY TRANSMITTED DISEASES

Disease	Cause	Signs	Diagnosis	Final Notes
Genital Warts (HPV)	Virus	Small, fleshy growths in genital, anal or mouth areas; singular or in clusters	Physical exam	Cryotherapy, topical medications, surgical removal; genital warts often reappear after treatment
Gonorrhea	Bacteria	Men: mucous- and/or pus-filled discharge from penis; slow, painful or difficult urination; Women: mucous- and/or pus-filled vaginal discharge; vaginal itching; painful or burning urination	Physical exam and lab tests of vaginal culture	Untreated gonorrhea can lead to pelvic inflammatory disease (PID) or cause arthritis, infertility and other serious problems
Human Immuno-deficiency Virus (HIV) (see *HIV*, p. 282)				
Syphilis	Bacteria	Painless sore on genitals, anus or in mouth two to four weeks after infection, hardening into a painless ulcer then disappearing; swollen lymph nodes, fever, and/or rashes four to six weeks after infection	Blood test, examination of fluid from sores	Untreated syphilis can lead to blindness, brain damage and heart disease

Prevention

You can greatly reduce the likelihood of STDs by practicing safe sex:

- Always use a latex condom — if having sex outside of a long-term relationship
- Limit the number of sex partners
- Ask your partner to be tested for STDs
- Avoid sex with infected individuals

Final notes

These resources can provide you with more information:

- Centers for Disease Control and Prevention National AIDS Hotline: 1-800-342-2437
- Centers for Disease Control and Prevention National STD Hotline: 1-800-227-8922
- National Herpes Hotline: 1-919-361-8488

Human immunodeficiency virus (HIV)

The *human immunodeficiency virus* (HIV) causes *acquired immunodeficiency syndrome* (AIDS). If you test positive for HIV, you carry the virus and can infect others but may not have symptoms of the illness for some time. For adults, the average period from infection with the virus to development of AIDS is six to 10 years. After AIDS develops, death usually occurs within two or three years.

Currently there are 34 million people estimated to have HIV/AIDS worldwide.

Note your symptoms

Some people experience symptoms of an acute viral infection within a few months after exposure. The symptoms typically last one to two weeks and resemble *infectious mononucleosis*: swollen glands, sore throat, fever, malaise and/or skin rash (see *Swollen Glands,* p. 135). Years may pass before early symptoms of AIDS appear, which include:

- Prolonged, unexplained fatigue
- Fever lasting more than 10 days
- Night sweats
- Swollen glands or rapid weight loss
- Persistent diarrhea, colds, unexplained dry cough or sore throat
- Easy bruising or unexplained bleeding

TRANSMISSION

HIV is spread by unprotected sexual intercourse, by sharing needles or syringes with someone who has HIV, receiving contaminated blood, blood products, organs for transplantation or semen for artificial insemination; from mother to fetus during pregnancy; and from mother to infant through breast-feeding.

Prevention

You can prevent infection with HIV by eliminating risky behaviors:

- Limit your number of sex partners or abstain from sexual intercourse.
- Avoid unprotected sexual intercourse (oral, vaginal, anal). Always use latex condoms unless you are in a monogamous relationship, and you and your partner have tested negative for HIV for six months or longer.
- Don't use intravenous (IV) drugs, or share needles or syringes.

NOTE: HIV does not appear to be transmitted through saliva, tears, sweat or stool. Nor can it be transmitted through mosquito bites, donating blood or contact with inanimate objects such as toilet seats. An infected person who is coughing, talking or eating poses no risk of spreading HIV to others.

TESTING FOR HIV

- Do you suspect you have been exposed to HIV? If so, get tested immediately and repeat the test in six months. Continue testing every three to six months for as long as your high-risk behavior continues.
- Is your HIV test positive but you have no symptoms of AIDS? Schedule follow-up visits and tests with your doctor.
- Cooperate with your doctor and public health officials in identifying your sex partner(s) so they may be alerted to the possibility of exposure to HIV.

What you can do

There is no vaccine for HIV infection and no drug that is effective against the virus. Your best strategy for dealing with HIV is to prevent exposure by abstaining or by practicing safe sex.

Final notes

Drug treatments for HIV and AIDS are aimed at prolonging life by preventing replication of the virus. In general, combinations of drugs appear to be most effective. People who test positive for HIV often experience depression and job-security issues, as well as major social and financial challenges. For more information on counseling resources, contact the Centers for Disease Control and Prevention National AIDS Hotline, 1-800-342-2437. **Always consult your doctor for diagnosis and treatment.**

For more information, see *Sexually Transmitted Diseases*, p. 279.

MENTAL HEALTH

Aging has its rewards — time to travel, pursue hobbies and enjoy friends and family. But the challenges of growing older — retirement, possible physical problems, the use of certain medications and the loss of friends and loved ones — can contribute to stress, anxiety, depression and grief.

By staying physically and mentally fit through exercise, a nutritious diet, work or other intellectually stimulating activities, you will be better prepared for what could be some of the best years of your life.

Stress

Anyone who has been late for an important appointment or struggled with the family finances knows that stress is a normal and even useful reaction.

In stressful situations or emergencies, our bodies automatically increase production of certain hormones. This results in a rise in heart rate and blood pressure, a tensing of muscles to prepare the body for action, an increase in perspiration to cool the body, faster respiration to raise the oxygen supply and a dilation of the pupils to improve vision. These responses, known as "fight or flight," were once vital to the survival of the human race.

Studies show that some older adults tend not to have a "fight or flight" reaction, but rather a passive "freeze" reaction to stress. Inactivity, acceptance, contemplation, apathy and neutrality are quieter responses to common crises such as illness, loss of loved ones, moving or retirement. Others react to stress differently through increased muscle tension or anxiety.

Stress in itself is neither good nor bad, but how a person reacts to stress can have a huge impact on their well-being. *Anxiety*, fear or dread without obvious cause or threat, is one way to react to stress (see *Anxiety*, p. 287). *Grief* is a response to the loss of a loved one, or something dear to us (see *Grief*, p. 291).

In extreme cases of stress, such as during war or a natural disaster, *post-traumatic stress disorder* (PTSD) can develop. It's characterized by the persistent "re-experiencing" of the stressful event with flashbacks and sometimes hallucinations. Other symptoms include avoiding thoughts and feelings about the event, emotional withdrawal, insomnia, irritability and an exaggerated startle response.

What you can do

The physical symptoms of stress can be alleviated after you recognize the sources of stress. For example, if isolation and inactivity are contributing to persistent joint tension or pain, you cannot solve the problem by simply treating the pain. The key is to find ways to minimize or manage the causes of stress.

LOOK FOR CREATIVE SOLUTIONS

- Would joining a group that engages in some physical activity reduce the stress of isolation and inactivity?
- Are there other people in your neighborhood you could walk with?
- Can home chores be rearranged or taken over by others?

CONSIDER OTHER STRESS MANAGEMENT TOOLS

- Exercise regularly.
- Pursue hobbies.
- Talk things over with a friend.
- Cry if that helps you feel better.
- Try yoga, meditation or other muscle-relaxation techniques. The following techniques may be helpful:

Deep breathing: While sitting or lying down, close your eyes and tilt your head forward. Inhale naturally through your nose. Exhale naturally through your nose. As you exhale, without holding your breath, pause and count "one thousand one, one thousand two." Exhale completely. Repeat for several minutes.

Clearing the mind: Give yourself a mental break by focusing your thoughts on a single, peaceful word, thought or image for five to 10 minutes a day. Reduce distractions as much as possible, sit comfortably and begin deep breathing, as described above. Concentrate on your single thought. Stretch and exhale as you complete the exercise.

Tensing and relaxing: Stretch out comfortably on a carpeted or padded floor. Starting with your toes, tense each group of muscles for five to 10 seconds, then release the tension and relax for 10 to 20 seconds. Continue alternating the tensing and relaxing of your muscles, moving up and down your legs; through your back, neck and shoulders; and down your arms. Repeat the process in areas that seem particularly tense.

Stretching: Muscle tension is a physical response to stress. To loosen tight muscles, take a break and try some of these stretches. Remember, it's always a good idea to check with your doctor before starting any new exercises. **If any of the following exercises cause pain, stop them immediately and consult your doctor.**

Back stretch: While sitting on a firm chair, reach out with your hands and bend forward so your upper body rests on your lap. Stretch your arms toward the floor and relax your head and neck. Hold the stretch for a minute, then place your hands on your thighs and press yourself back up to a seated position.

Neck stretch: While looking straight ahead, slowly tilt your head toward one shoulder, then the other. (Do not lift your shoulders or move your head in jerking motions.) Repeat this movement five times.

Shoulder and arm stretch: Lock your hands together by intertwining your fingers. Then stretch your arms over your head, with your palms facing up. Hold this stretch for about 30 seconds, and repeat it five times with rest in between.

Passive back stretch: Lie with your back on the floor, and rest your knees and lower legs above you on a chair so that you're bent at a right angle. As you relax in this position, gently press your lower back against the floor for several minutes. When finished, bring your knees down to the floor to the left or right, and roll over on your side before getting up.

Leg stretch: While standing, place the back of one heel on a low stool or footrest while keeping both legs relatively straight. Slowly lean forward by bending at your hips, reaching for the elevated foot, and keeping your lower back straight. Hold the stretch about 30 seconds, and repeat it several times. Stretch the alternate leg in the same manner. (Do not attempt this stretch if you have balance difficulties.)

Upper body stretch: Stand with your legs shoulder-width apart. Reach over your head with your right arm, and bend to the left at your waist. Hold the stretch 30 seconds, being careful not to twist your right hip forward. Then switch sides and bend the opposite direction.

TRY TO KEEP THINGS IN PERSPECTIVE

- Let go of things that are beyond your control.

- Imagine the worst that could happen in any given situation, the likelihood that it will occur and how you will handle it if it does.

- Consider whether you will even remember this event in a few months or years.

During extremely stressful situations, such as the death of a spouse or close friend, taking time to experience feelings of sadness and loss is an important step toward emotional healing (see *Grief*, p. 291).

ANXIETY

For older adults, anxiety can be a response to helplessness, isolation and insecurity. Some anxiety is normal; it becomes a disorder when physical and emotional symptoms become overwhelming and interfere with daily life.

Some of the physical symptoms of anxiety include trembling, muscle tension, restlessness, fatigue, breathlessness, pounding heart, sweating, cold and clammy hands, dry mouth, dizziness, chills or hot flashes, frequent urination or diarrhea, and nausea.

Emotional symptoms are apprehension, excessive worrying, a feeling that something bad is going to happen, poor concentration, excessive startle response, insomnia, irritability or agitation, and depression.

What you can do

Recognizing and accepting anxiety about certain fears and situations is the first step in reducing symptoms. For example, if you are alone for the first time in your life, it's only natural to feel anxious. Seek out friends, family or a support group, and talk about your concerns. Find ways you can either accept or change your situation. Consider whether excessive caffeine or medications might be making you anxious. One of the best things you can do is to develop positive expectations for the future. As with any stress-related medical concern, finding the cause of the anxiety is important in eliminating the symptoms.

LUMP IN THROAT

The feeling of a lump in the throat is a common symptom of anxiety. The lump makes it difficult to swallow and usually comes and goes, heightened by anxiety and tension. The symptoms seem worse when you concentrate on swallowing.

Several serious diseases can cause swallowing difficulties. In these cases, the symptoms usually develop slowly, begin while eating solid foods, then progressively get worse. This condition — more commonly seen in those over 40 — can result in weight loss. Call your doctor if you develop these symptoms.

Final notes

If you feel you can't cope with a problem, talk to a health care professional, counselor, psychiatrist or a member of the clergy. These steps might be particularly helpful if you can't identify the cause of stress but are having troublesome symptoms.

Seek immediate emergency care if you are thinking about suicide or doing physical harm to others. Call your doctor if you are turning to alcohol or drugs to relieve stress.

Depression

Major depression is a potentially life-threatening physical and mental illness. The classic symptoms are hopelessness and a loss of pleasure in activities that used to be enjoyable. Major depression can be triggered by severe life stresses including the death of a loved one, divorce, serious financial difficulty, chronic illness and chemical dependency — particularly on alcohol. Older adults are often faced with the additional strain of giving up a former residence, moving to a retirement or nursing home, being alone, fighting illness, pain or the loss of a meaningful occupation.

Chronic illness of any sort also can cause depression, as can certain medications, including some used to treat high blood pressure and Parkinson's disease.

Depression can come and go in waves, but the inability to recover from these episodes signals the likelihood of a potential problem requiring some level of professional care. Depression does not have to be something that "just happens."

Despite gains in the past few years, a stigma is unfortunately still attached to undergoing or seeking treatment for mental illness. Some people may avoid acknowledging their depression to avoid this stigma.

Note your symptoms

Common signs of depression include:

- Unintentional weight loss or gain
- Abnormal sleeping patterns
- Fatigue
- Feelings of worthlessness
- Excessive or inappropriate feelings of guilt
- Decreased ability to concentrate
- Recurrent thoughts of death or suicide
- A suicide attempt
- Withdrawal
- Irritability, anxiety, sadness

People with major mood swings — from depression to elation — may be suffering from a different condition known as *bipolar affective disorder*, previously called manic-depressive illness.

Another form of depression is *seasonal affective disorder*, or SAD. SAD is caused by a lack of exposure to sunlight and often occurs during the winter months in people who live in northern regions.

Symptoms can include lethargy, irritability, chronic headaches, increased appetite, weight gain and the need for more sleep. Episodes may last for several weeks.

What you can do

Major depression is a chronic, debilitating illness that can last from weeks to years. A vast majority of people who suffer from depression would benefit from some form of intervention, in the form of medication, psychotherapy (counseling) or both.

Some activities that are helpful in cases of mild depression include:

- Getting regular exercise
- Joining a support group or getting involved in group activities
- Talking to someone about your problems
- Decreasing the use of alcohol or other drugs

Many SAD sufferers benefit from *phototherapy*, a medically supervised therapy that consists of daily exposure to intense full-spectrum lights (the ultraviolet wavelengths are filtered out to protect the skin). Relief usually begins in about a week. A vacation to sunnier climates, like Hawaii or the Caribbean, is a much more pleasant, but short-term, solution.

Seek emergency care if you have serious thoughts of suicide, with or without a specific plan, or if you have made a suicide attempt. If someone you know has threatened suicide, take those threats seriously. Call a crisis hotline or encourage the person to seek help (see *Resources*, p. 360).

GRIEF

Although sadness and grief are normal and an important part of making the transition from one phase of life to another, they can cause depression. No one can tell another person how to grieve, but there are generally recognized stages of grief that many people go through. Knowing these may help you deal with some of your own emotions or offer support to another who is grieving.

Stages of grief

Shock and denial: Not able to believe that the loss has occurred. After a death, the griever may behave as if the dead person is still alive and may "see" or "hear" the person.

Anger: The need to point blame for the loss. Mourners may be angry at a boss for the loss of a job, or at friends, themselves or the deceased after a death.

Depression: Being overwhelmed by the loss and experiencing some or all of the symptoms listed on page 289.

It's important to know that grief is an individual process and that a significant loss causes a wide range of feelings. The grief process can be lengthy or short, and the only measure of "successful" grieving is the griever's eventual acceptance of or ability to cope with the loss. There is no "right" order in which to experience the phases of grief. In fact, some of the stages may not be experienced at all.

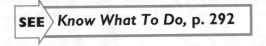
SEE *Know What To Do, p. 292*

Depression
DO THESE APPLY:

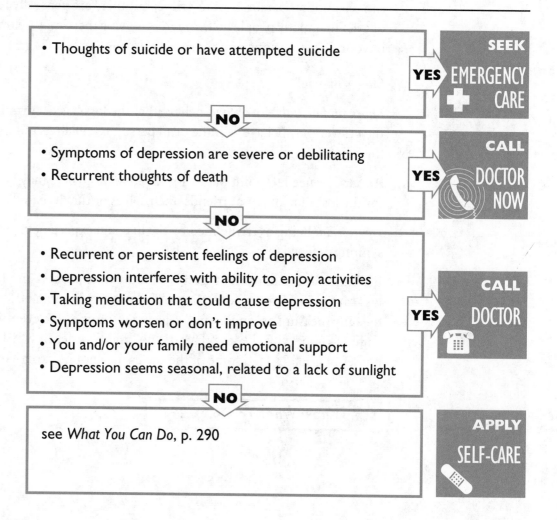

• Thoughts of suicide or have attempted suicide

YES → **SEEK EMERGENCY CARE**

NO

• Symptoms of depression are severe or debilitating
• Recurrent thoughts of death

YES → **CALL DOCTOR NOW**

NO

• Recurrent or persistent feelings of depression
• Depression interferes with ability to enjoy activities
• Taking medication that could cause depression
• Symptoms worsen or don't improve
• You and/or your family need emotional support
• Depression seems seasonal, related to a lack of sunlight

YES → **CALL DOCTOR**

NO

see *What You Can Do*, p. 290

APPLY SELF-CARE

Insomnia

Insomnia is the inability to enjoy adequate or restful sleep. It can be defined as difficulty falling asleep, frequent awakenings during the night or waking too early in the morning.

It is important to establish whether insomnia is *primary* (when no underlying mental or physical conditions cause the problem) or *secondary* (when a physical or mental condition is responsible for the sleep disturbance).

Chronic insomnia (lasting more than a month) may be caused by depression, anxiety disorders, manic disorders, chronic pain syndromes, heart and circulatory disorders, kidney disease or *sleep apnea*, in which breathing is temporarily interrupted by airway obstruction. More than 300 over-the-counter (OTC) and prescription drugs also can contribute to insomnia, including alcohol, caffeine, cardiac medications, nicotine, amphetamines and decongestants (see *Home Pharmacy*, p. 303).

Behaviors that can cause or aggravate insomnia include vigorous exercise or mental exertion before bedtime, chronic use of sleeping pills, staying in bed too long in the morning or napping too much during the day.

What you can do

Practices that promote restful sleep include:

- Exercising on a regular basis (but avoiding exercise within two hours of bedtime)
- Taking a warm bath or drinking warm milk
- A regular bedtime routine that includes relaxing activities such as reading for pleasure
- Reserving the bedroom for sleeping and sex
- Avoiding alcohol and smoking before bedtime
- Drinking caffeine in moderation, and only before noon
- Not napping

You can gain insights into improving your sleep by keeping a diary of your sleep patterns and behaviors.

SEE ▷ *Know What To Do*, p. 294

3

Insomnia
DO THESE APPLY:

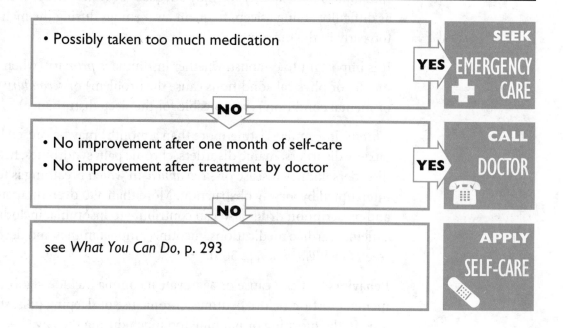

- Possibly taken too much medication

YES ▸ SEEK **EMERGENCY CARE**

NO

- No improvement after one month of self-care
- No improvement after treatment by doctor

YES ▸ CALL **DOCTOR**

NO

see *What You Can Do*, p. 293

APPLY **SELF-CARE**

Medications

4

Using medications

The body's response to medications changes over the years. In later life, the body becomes more sensitive to chemicals and drugs. A dose of medicine that is correct and safe for a young adult often needs to be in a different form or amount for a child or older adult. Age affects the body's ability to absorb, use and eliminate medications. This may cause the medicine's effects to last longer and the level of medication in the bloodstream to go higher than desired. The older adult at age 65 is twice as likely to have unwanted side effects from medicines as someone at age 35, and the 80-year-old is four times more likely to have undesired side effects.

Modern medicines can help keep our lives more active and comfortable. Unfortunately, medications are often overused in the older population. If you are over the age of 65, you are likely to be taking at least four medications. All medicines (prescription and nonprescription) have the risk of interacting and producing undesired results. Nearly one in seven hospitalizations of older adults is due to problems with medications.

OTC and prescribed drugs

All medications must be cautiously and wisely used. *Over-the-counter* (OTC) drugs — those that do not require a prescription — can have as many side effects as prescription drugs. In fact, many of today's OTC drugs are medications that were once available only by prescription. One of the most common OTC drugs, aspirin, is a very effective and useful medicine that can affect the body's temperature system; relieve pain; decrease inflammation; alter blood clotting; and help decrease the risk of heart attack, stroke and cancers in the digestive system; but it can also irritate the stomach lining and affect kidney function. Because of its widespread use, aspirin is often mistakenly thought to be harmless.

Some of today's medicines are based on historical herbal and natural preparations that can affect the body. **All medications, both OTC and prescribed, as well as herbal or "home remedies" and high doses of vitamins and health tonics can affect the body's response and alter the action of other drugs you take.**

FOLLOW DIRECTIONS

- **Ask your doctor or pharmacist about how to take your medicines.** Find out how much, how often and when. It is important to know which can be taken together and which should be taken with food.

- **Ask your doctor how long you may need to take a particular drug.** If more is needed, have your prescription refilled before running out of the medication. It is important not to miss doses.

- **Ask your doctor or pharmacist about the medicine.** Know why you are taking it, what you can expect from it and how soon, what side effects you should report, what you should do if you miss a dose, and when you need to check back.

- **Establish a routine and particular location for your medications.** Unless young children are around, set out all of your medicines for the week using a special medication holder, egg carton or cupcake pan, especially if you have trouble remembering whether you've taken your daily doses. Or, use a calendar and mark off when you have taken your medicines. Take your medicines at a time of day that is easy to remember, like mealtimes or bedtime, or set a timer to remind you. If you still have trouble remembering, a family member, friend or visiting nurse can assist you in setting up a system and give you a reminder call.

- **If you have difficulty with your medication schedule, talk to your doctor.** There may be a way to simplify the schedule or find alternative medicines.

- **Never abruptly stop a prescribed medication without first consulting your doctor.** Some medicines must be tapered off slowly to be safe; some of your other medicines may need to be adjusted when one is stopped.

What you can do

- Tell all of your doctors and pharmacists about all of the medicines you are taking (OTC and prescription), to prevent a reaction between drugs. Having all of your prescriptions filled at the same pharmacy is a good idea.

- Bring a written list of all of your medicines or all medicine bottles to your doctor appointments (see *Personal Medications Record*, p. 364).

- Read labels of all medicines carefully for correct usage and potential side effects.

- Take the correct dosage as prescribed — no more and no less.

- Consult your doctor and pharmacist before taking *any* OTC drug, particularly if you are taking an *MAO* (monoamine oxidase) inhibitor or if you have a serious chronic condition such as asthma, diabetes, epilepsy, glaucoma, enlarged prostate, dementia, high blood pressure or heart disease.

- Never share or trade prescription drugs with anyone. The impact and side effects of drugs vary from person to person and can be unpredictable.

- Store all medications out of the reach of children.

- Throw out medications when they reach their expiration date.

- Ask your doctor if there are other treatment options that may not include drugs, or if a less expensive but equally effective generic form of the drug is available.

- When starting a new medicine, ask your doctor if there are sample packages. If a sample is available, try the new medicine for a few days to see if you have any intolerable side effects before having the prescription filled. Once a prescription has been filled, the medication cannot be returned.

A properly stocked home medicine cabinet can help you be prepared for common illnesses and minor emergencies and can help you avoid unnecessary trips to the doctor and pharmacy. Be sure to go through your medicine cabinet — or wherever you store your medications — at least yearly, checking the labels for expired dates and carefully disposing of those medications (see *First-Aid Supplies*, p. 306).

Also see *Personal Medications Record*, p. 364.

MEDICATIONS THAT CAN CAUSE PROBLEMS WITH CERTAIN HEALTH CONCERNS

In addition to notifying your doctors and pharmacists about all the medications you take — to guard against any possible drug interactions — it's important to tell them about other medical conditions you have, even if these conditions seem unrelated to your current concern. Some prescription or over-the-counter (OTC) medications commonly taken for one condition can have adverse effects on your health if you have certain other medical conditions. The chart below lists some common health concerns and some medications that should be discussed with your doctor.

If this health concern applies to you . . .	These medications should be discussed with your doctor . . .
Congestive Heart Failure	Some eye drops used to treat glaucoma (such as timolol, Betagan C); beta blockers used to treat certain heart and blood pressure conditions (such as Inderal, Tenormin, Corgard, Lopressor); calcium channel blockers that are used to treat angina and certain types of arrhythmias (such as verapamil, nifedipine, diltiazem); and certain antacids that contain calcium, aluminum or sodium (such as Rolaids, Tums, Mylanta or Bromo-Seltzer)
Dementia	Most antihistamines (contained in many cold, allergy and sleeping pills); antidepressants or antipsychotics (such as Elavil or doxepin); gastrointestinal antispasmodics (such as dicyclomine, Bentyl, Pro-Banthine); and narcotic pain killers (such as Demerol, codeine) or any medications that impair memory or judgment
Depression	Beta blockers (such as Inderal, Tenormin, Corgard, Lopressor); certain drugs to treat high blood pressure (such as reserpine, deserpidine); and Indomethacin, a nonsteroidal anti-inflammatory and analgesic
Diabetes	Some beta blockers (such as Inderal, Tenormin, Corgard, Lopressor); corticosteroids (such as prednisone, betamethasone); laxatives that contain large amounts of dextrose (sugar); most antihistamines and decongestants; and Vasodilan, a medication commonly given for senility

Continued on next page

If this health concern applies to you . . .	These medications should be discussed with your doctor . . .
Enlarged Prostate	Some eye drops used to treat glaucoma (such as timolol, Betagan C); beta blockers used to treat certain heart and blood pressure conditions (such as Inderal, Tenormin, Corgard, Lopressor); calcium channel blockers that are used to treat angina and certain types of arrhythmias (such as verapamil, nifedipine, diltiazem); gastrointestinal antispasmodics (such as Dicyclomine, Bentyl, Pro-Banthine); certain antidepressants (such as Elavil, doxepin, imipramine); and any drugs containing atropine (an ingredient in many cold pills)
Gastric Ulcers	NSAIDs (such as aspirin, ibuprofen); many cold pills that have aspirin or ibuprofen as an ingredient; niacin supplements (which are used to treat vitamin B_3 deficiency); and corticosteroids (such as prednisone, betamethasone)
Glaucoma	Most antihistamines (contained in many cold, allergy and sleeping pills); antidepressants or antipsychotics (such as Elavil or doxepin); gastrointestinal antispasmodics (such as Dicyclomine, Bentyl, Pro-Banthine); and many antidyskinetics that are used to treat Parkinson's disease (such as Cogentin, procyclidine)
Impotence	Many drugs used to treat high blood pressure: beta blockers (such as Inderal, Tenormin, Corgard, Lopressor), reserpine, Aldomet and Catapres; narcotics (such as codeine, Darvon, Percocet); barbiturates (such as phenobarbital); and medications used to treat ulcers (such as Tagamet)
Incontinence	Diuretics (such as Lasix, hydrochlorothiazide); antihistamines (contained in many cold, allergy and sleeping pills); sleeping pills and tranquilizers (such as benzodiazepines, Valium); narcotics (such as Darvon, Percocet); and gastrointestinal antispasmodics (such as dicyclomine, Bentyl, Pro-Banthine)
Kidney Failure	Certain medications that are excreted primarily by the kidneys (such as aspirin, ibuprofen); medications used to treat congestive heart failure, high blood pressure or scleroderma (such as captopril, Vasotec); and potassium and vitamin A supplements

Home pharmacy

NONPRESCRIPTION DRUGS (OTC)

Medication	How It Works	Risks	Comments
Antacids	Relieve heartburn or stomach upset by neutralizing acid	Some can cause constipation, others loosen stools; some brands high in sodium and should be avoided by those on low-salt diets	Avoid long-term use
Antidiarrheals	Relieve diarrhea by thickening stools and/or slowing intestinal spasms	Do not use if you have a fever; prolonged use can lead to constipation and can absorb bacteria that aid digestion	Diarrhea is the body's way of flushing out infection, so use antidiarrheals only when necessary; replace body fluids depleted by diarrhea; drugs with bismuth may darken tongue or stools
Antifungal Preparations	Clear up skin fungal infections, such as athlete's foot	Few risks; preparations with selenium sulfide can burn skin if used excessively	Products with tolnaftate, clotrimazole or miconazole effective for difficult cases, but more expensive
Antihistamines/ Decongestants	Antihistamines dry mucous membranes to relieve runny nose, watery eyes and itching; decongestants shrink swollen membranes; purchase either an antihistamine or a decongestant, rather than a combined medication, to treat specific symptoms	Antihistamines can cause drowsiness; decongestants can cause agitation or insomnia	Both can cause problems for people with certain medical conditions

Continued on next page

 If you have a chronic illness or routinely take prescribed or over-the-counter (OTC) drugs, talk to your doctor or pharmacist before taking any other medications.

NONPRESCRIPTION DRUGS (OTC)

Medication	How It Works	Risks	Comments
Anti-inflammatories (aspirin, ibuprofen, naprosyn) (NSAIDs)	Help relieve swelling and pain in muscles and joints	Ibuprofen can pose danger to those on *anticoagulants* (medicine that prevents or delays the blood from clotting); do not exceed dosage limits; aspirin can irritate stomach, cause bleeding or ulcers; aspirin and ibuprofen should be taken with food to avoid stomach irritation. **NEVER give aspirin to children/teenagers. It can cause Reye's syndrome, a rare but often fatal condition.**	Daily, low dose of aspirin may help prevent heart attack, stroke and risk of cancers of the digestive system; naprosyn (Aleve) similar to ibuprofen in uses and risks
Antiseptics (hydrogen peroxide, pHisoHex)	Clean wounds to prevent infection	Read instructions for careful use	Most are of value for cleansing and are minimally effective at killing germs; soap and water can be just as useful
Cough Suppressants/ Expectorants	Suppressants control the coughing reflex to reduce dry, hacking coughs; expectorants thin mucus to make it easier to expel phlegm	Some should not be taken by people with certain health conditions; can interact with sedatives and some antidepressants; can contain alcohol	Coughs help remove phlegm to clear respiratory tract so suppressing them may be counterproductive; products with guaifenesin are effective expectorants, those with dextromethorphan suppress coughs
H_2 Blockers	Decrease gastric acid production	Interact with some medicines and foods and should not be used in presence of some diseases; read directions carefully	Don't use longer than two weeks without seeing your doctor

 If you have a chronic illness or routinely take prescribed or over-the-counter (OTC) drugs, talk to your doctor or pharmacist before taking any other medications.

NONPRESCRIPTION DRUGS (OTC)

Medication	How It Works	Risks	Comments
Nasal Sprays/Nose Drops	Shrink swollen mucous membranes to encourage free breathing; relieve runny nose and postnasal drip	Should not be used for more than three consecutive days; prolonged use can cause more swelling than before using the spray or drops	Not as effective as oral decongestants; less likely to interact with other drugs; provide temporary relief
Pain/Fever Medications (acetaminophen, aspirin, ibuprofen, naprosyn — see *Anti-inflammatories* on previous page) (NSAIDs)	Reduce fever and pain	Excessive use of acetaminophen can contribute to liver damage in heavy drinkers. **NEVER give aspirin to children/ teenagers. It can cause Reye's syndrome, a rare but often fatal condition.**	Acetaminophen is ineffective against inflammation; milder to stomach than ibuprofen or aspirin; do not exceed dosage limits
Skin Irritation Medications (hydrocortisone cream)	Act as anti-inflammatories to temporarily relieve itching from rashes, insect bites and poison ivy	Excessive use can damage skin; generally safe if used for two weeks or less; should not be used on infected skin or near eyes	Suppress the itch reflex, but do not cure the rash; use only as much as will rub easily into skin
Laxatives	Stimulate intestines to prompt bowel movements during constipation; bulking agents soften stool to ease elimination	Few side effects if taken according to directions; regular use can decrease rectal muscle tone and cause reliance on laxatives	Take laxatives with plenty of water; regular use can interfere with body's absorption of vitamin D and calcium

 If you have a chronic illness or routinely take prescribed or over-the-counter (OTC) drugs, talk to your doctor or pharmacist before taking any other medications.

First-aid supplies

In addition to the over-the-counter (OTC) nonprescription drugs, a well-stocked home medicine cabinet should include some first-aid supplies and a first-aid manual. You can put together the elements of a first-aid kit by gathering the items here, or you can purchase first-aid kits for your home, car, boat or other use at drugstores or through organizations such as the American Red Cross. First-aid manuals are also available at these locations.

Item	Uses
Assorted Band-Aids/ Butterfly Bandages	To cover and protect small scrapes and cuts from dirt and moisture; butterfly bandages can bring edges of cut together
Tweezers	To help remove large dirt particles from wounds, slivers
Ice Bag	To reduce swelling from injuries, can provide relief from headaches; for protection, place a washcloth between bare skin and ice
	Home recipe: freeze a one-quart size resealable bag filled with one cup rubbing alcohol and two cups water (can be used many times); also, a frozen bag of peas works well and conforms to body part
Cotton/Cotton-tipped Swabs	Useful in cleaning out wounds, lifting foreign matter from eyes; do not use inside the ear
Thermometer	To help determine presence of fever; oral or rectal thermometers most common; electronic thermometers or ones used in child's ear are faster and easier to use, but more expensive
Gauze Pads/Adhesive Tape	To fashion large dressings for wounds or scrapes that can't be covered with adhesive bandages
Sharp Scissors	To cut gauze rolls, remove jagged edges of scraped skin

Item	Uses
Heating Pad	To speed up healing process after swelling reduced; may relieve headaches; use on low setting
	Home recipe: Pour a five-pound bag of brown rice into an old pillowcase and tie off end. Place into a microwave oven and heat on high for eight to 10 minutes. Do not heat in conventional oven. Cover affected area with a towel and place the heated rice pack on the towel (always protect skin with towel covering). Heat will last almost 30 minutes, and the brown rice, unlike white rice, can be reheated many times.
Anaphylactic Kit	To treat life-threatening allergic reactions; available by prescription from your doctor

Prevention

5

GETTING AND STAYING HEALTHY

There are many steps you can take to slow the effects of aging and maintain your good health. Excellent places to start include eating a healthy diet; controlling your weight; staying active; avoiding drinking alcohol and smoking; getting necessary checkups, screenings and immunizations; and preventing accidents and injuries.

In addition, most of these healthy behaviors — especially avoiding alcohol and smoking, eating a low-fat diet and exercising — may decrease your risk of cancer (see index for specific topics).

The good news is that it's never too late! By adopting a positive attitude and making healthy behavior choices, you can *dramatically* enhance the rest of your life.

Eating right

Making wise food choices is an important element in a healthy lifestyle for people of all ages, and it is even more important as you get older.

Malnutrition (not consuming enough foods that contain proper nutrients) is a common problem among older adults. One reason is that the body's ability to absorb nutrients declines with age. Taking multiple drugs — as many older adults do — can hamper the body's ability to absorb nutrients and can also diminish your appetite (see *Using Medications*, p. 298). What's more, the tongue loses some of its taste buds as you age, so foods that were once flavorful may taste bland and unappealing; and dental problems may make it more difficult to eat (see *Mouth Concerns*, p. 142). Other factors that may contribute to malnutrition include the expense of buying food or meals, the isolation of eating alone and the effort of fixing meals.

Just as detrimental as not eating *enough* of the right foods is eating *too much*. Excessive body weight stresses the heart, muscles and bones. It increases the likelihood of hernias, hemorrhoids, gallbladder disease and varicose veins. It can aggravate arthritis and other chronic conditions.

A healthy diet — low-fat, low-calorie, high-fiber — combined with regular exercise (see *Staying Active*, p. 316) reduces your risk of numerous health problems such as cancer, heart disease, stroke, osteoporosis and diabetes. Eating right helps you control obesity and other health problems such as elevated blood sugar, blood pressure and cholesterol levels — while improving your energy level, moods and how you feel about your appearance.

HEALTHY WEIGHT

Growing older is not an excuse for gaining extra pounds, according to the new "Dietary Guidelines for Americans," released by the departments of Agriculture and Health and Human Services (1995). This means you should keep your adult weight within a given range for your height, rather than allowing pounds to add up over time.

Use the chart below to evaluate your body weight. The chart applies to men and women of all ages, since the risks associated with excess weight appear to be the same for younger and older adults, men and women alike.

Losing weight safely and keeping it off require gradual, steady changes in eating and exercising habits. A reasonable goal for effective weight loss is **one-half to one pound a week**.

HEALTHY WEIGHT RANGES FOR MEN AND WOMEN

Height	Weight (lbs.)	Height	Weight (lbs.)	Height	Weight (lbs.)
4' 10"	91 – 119	5' 5"	114 – 150	6' 0"	140 – 184
4' 11"	94 – 124	5' 6"	118 – 155	6' 1"	144 – 189
5' 0"	97 – 128	5' 7"	121 – 160	6' 2"	148 – 195
5' 1"	101 – 132	5' 8"	125 – 164	6' 3"	152 – 200
5' 2"	104 – 137	5' 9"	129 – 169	6' 4"	156 – 205
5' 3"	107 – 141	5' 10"	132 – 174	6' 5"	160 – 211
5' 4"	111 – 146	5' 11"	136 – 179	6' 6"	164 – 216

U.S. Department of Agriculture/U.S. Department of Health and Human Services

GOOD CHOLESTEROL/BAD CHOLESTEROL

Cholesterol is a fat-like substance found in the bloodstream. It forms part of our cells and *some* of it is essential. The problem is that many of us have *too much* cholesterol in our blood — the result of genetics or of eating excessive amounts of butter, whole milk, eggs and animal fats, among other things.

Cholesterol has two components: *low-density lipoprotein* (LDL) and *high-density lipoprotein* (HDL). LDL is called "bad" cholesterol because it can cause cholesterol to gather on the walls of your arteries, contributing to heart disease (see *Heart Disease*, p. 159). HDL, the "good" cholesterol, prevents blockage of the arteries by carrying cholesterol out of the coronary artery walls.

In general, your LDL should be below 130 mg/dl (milligrams per deciliter) and your HDL should be above 45 mg/dl. Your total cholesterol should be below 200 mg/dl.

If you exercise and don't smoke, you will be able to lower your LDL while raising your HDL. Also, eat foods with reduced cholesterol or less than one gram of saturated fat per 100 calories.

For tips on cutting down on "bad" fats, see *Fat*, p. 313.

DIET AND NUTRITION

The goal of a healthy diet is to eat a wide range of foods every day from each of the major food groups: the bread, cereal, rice and pasta group; the vegetable group; the fruit group; the milk, yogurt and cheese group; and the meat, poultry, fish, dry beans, eggs and nuts group. Stay away from foods that are high in fat and sugar. They provide calories, but not the nutrients you need.

The Food Guide Pyramid (see Figure 30, p. 313) illustrates the six basic food groups and the daily amounts of various foods you should eat to get all the needed nutrients. Select the bulk of your food from the lower levels of the Pyramid, with emphasis on fruits, vegetables and whole grains (whole-grain rice, pasta and bread, rather than white).

Eat lots of beans (although they are listed near the top of the Pyramid, they are an excellent nonfat source of carbohydrates, fiber, vitamins and protein) and choose milk products that are 1% milk fat or nonfat.

Food Guide Pyramid

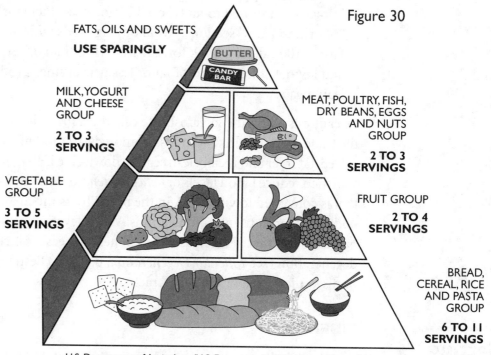

Figure 30

U.S. Department of Agriculture/U.S. Department of Health and Human Services

Cutting back

FAT

While some dietary fat is essential for good health, most people consume too much of it. Excessive dietary fat contributes to aging and certain diseases such as atherosclerosis (see *CHD*, p. 159) and cancer. Evidence is especially strong for the connection between dietary fat and colon cancer (see *Colon Cancer*, p. 199). Foods most strongly associated with increased risk of colon cancer are beef, pork and lamb. Other especially high-fat foods include whole milk, butter, eggs and other animal fats.

To cut back on your fat intake:

- Eat grains and beans or legumes — instead of animal protein — whenever possible. Fish and skinless poultry (such as turkey or chicken) are animal proteins that are lower in fat. When you eat red meat, use leaner cuts.

- Try nonfat dairy products and low-fat cheese.

- Substitute fresh vegetables, graham crackers or low-fat yogurt for fat-laden snacks such as potato chips or cookies.

- Use oils sparingly and choose those lowest in saturated fat and cholesterol: canola, corn, olive, sesame, soybean and sunflower.

- Try steaming, boiling, baking, grilling or braising. Sauté foods in broth, water or wine instead of oil.

- Because food-package claims can be misleading, read their labels carefully for information related to fat (every U.S. food product label now displays a "Nutrition Facts" section). Avoid buying foods with more than three grams of fat per 100 calories. Look for "fat-free" (less than 0.5 gram of fat per serving) and low-fat (three grams of fat or less per serving) products, and lean or extra lean meats.

Be cautious about the fat substitute called *Olestra*, which is marketed under the trade name Olean. Olestra is promoted as a fat that withstands the heat of a deep-fat fryer and is calorie-free. The down side is that, in some cases, it has been shown to reduce blood levels of *beta-carotene* (a nutrient found in many vegetables that is converted to vitamin A in the body) by as much as 60% and robs the body of other nutrients and vitamins. When levels of beta-carotene and other nutrients fall, there is increased risk of heart disease, cancer and macular degeneration (see *Macular Degeneration*, p. 115). Olestra may also cause diarrhea or discomfort in your digestive tract.

FIBER

Getting more

A high-fiber diet — one that includes a variety of whole grains, fruits, beans and vegetables — helps prevent constipation (see *Constipation*, p. 188), certain cancers, diverticulitis (see *Diverticulosis*, p. 198) and other illnesses. In addition, it lowers cholesterol and reduces your risk of heart disease.

You can begin getting more fiber in your diet by making some simple changes. Try bran cereals instead of low-fiber, sugary cereals; fresh or dried fruit instead of fruit juice; brown rice instead of white rice; whole-wheat bread in place of white bread; and beans instead of meat. It will probably take your body a little time to get used to more fiber, so start with just a few additions, then gradually add more every week until you've established a high-fiber diet.

SALT

Using less

As taste buds dull with age, your ability to taste salt (*sodium*) decreases. You may be tempted to add more salt to your foods, but try to resist the urge. Excess sodium can raise your blood pressure and increase your risk of stroke, heart attack or kidney failure.

Try to keep your daily intake of sodium under 2,400 milligrams a day. Read food labels carefully and select low-sodium (140 milligrams of sodium or less per serving) or very-low-sodium (35 milligrams of sodium or less per serving) products.

All packaged spice mixes (taco, gravy, dressing, stew, spaghetti sauce) are extremely high in sodium, so experiment with making your own spice blends or purchasing no-salt blends. Season foods with herbs and other spices such as basil, oregano, tarragon, ginger, mint, nutmeg and cinnamon — rather than salt.

SUGAR

Keeping a balance

Your ability to digest large amounts of sugar rapidly decreases as you get older, which means your blood sugar climbs higher after eating sugar than when you were younger. While it's not necessary to avoid sugar completely, it's wise to eat sweets in moderation.

It is not uncommon for older adults to develop *diabetes* (an elevation of blood sugar caused by inadequate amounts of insulin in the body), so alert your doctor if you notice any of the symptoms (see *Diabetes*, p. 201).

VITAMINS AND HERBAL SUPPLEMENTS

 If you're eating a well-balanced diet that includes fresh fruits and vegetables, meat and dairy products, taking vitamin and mineral supplements is usually not necessary. If you have trouble eating a well-balanced diet, however, taking multivitamins may be helpful. Your doctor can advise you on appropriate and safe dosages. Also, if you have osteoporosis (see *Osteoporosis*, p. 216) or are at high risk for the disease, ask your doctor about calcium and vitamin D supplements.

Herbal supplements sold in health food stores are very popular these days for everything from treating the flu to helping you lose weight. Unfortunately, there is limited scientific proof that herbal supplements can actually help you. What's more, they are not currently required to be evaluated for safety and effectiveness, so taking them may be risky. At the very minimum, don't take them for serious diseases such as cancer, heart disease and arthritis. Also, keep your doctor informed about any supplements you're taking to avoid interactions with other medications (see *Using Medications*, p. 298).

 If you have a chronic illness or routinely take prescribed or over-the-counter (OTC) drugs, talk to your doctor or pharmacist before taking any other medications.

Staying active

Many people tend to become less physically active as they age — so it becomes more and more important to make a decided effort to get enough exercise. In general, older adults benefit from regular exercise as much as younger people. Age doesn't have to be an automatic limitation, and it's never too late to begin. In fact, most people find that — as they exercise and become more physically fit — they feel better and have more energy.

Regular exercise can lower your blood pressure, prevent constipation and improve sleep. It can reduce your risk of serious illnesses (and their complications) such as diabetes (see *Diabetes*, p. 201), coronary heart disease (see *Heart Disease*, p. 159) and cancer; improve the conditioning of your heart; control your weight; reduce stress levels; increase your chances of cutting down or stopping smoking (see *Smoking Cessation*, p. 319); and make you less likely to experience shortness of breath or fatigue. Exercise is a vital component of good health — whatever your age.

CHOOSING AN EXERCISE PROGRAM

"No pain, no gain" is a common misconception about exercising. Other misconceptions are that you have to be athletic to benefit from exercising, and that exercising takes a lot of time.

On the contrary, you don't have to run marathons or swim miles to enjoy significant benefits from regular physical activity. What's more, many forms of exercise don't require any special athletic abilities.

The Surgeon General advises adults to exercise 30 minutes on most, if not all, days of the week. Regular, brisk and sustained exercises such as walking, jogging, cycling and swimming are excellent ways to improve the efficiency of your heart and lungs and burn a significant amount of calories. Informal exercise — such as using the stairs instead of the elevator, playing golf, bowling, strolling with friends, doing housework or gardening — offer health benefits to a lesser but still important degree, including increasing your flexibility and muscle strength. In addition, light exercise can be fun and pleasurable, and it can provide opportunities for socializing.

The key to a successful exercise program is choosing an activity — or activities — that you will enjoy on a regular basis for months and years to come. It's also important to consider your physical capabilities. If you have heart or lung problems, start with slow walking, or stretching in place. If you suffer from arthritis, you'll want to choose an activity that doesn't cause further pain (swimming is an excellent choice). If you have problems with your balance, exercise while seated.

Consult your doctor before starting any exercise program. If you've had a heart attack, surgery, joint problems or other chronic or acute illnesses, your doctor can help you choose a program that is safe, effective and right for you. If you have temporary or permanent physical limitations, a physical therapist can recommend modified exercises that suit your situation.

Before getting started, also make sure you have athletic shoes that provide cushioning, heel and ankle support and stability. Some athletic shoes are designed for specific activities such as running, aerobics and walking. Cross-training shoes combine characteristics of many types of athletic shoes and can be used for multiple activities.

Well-rounded exercise

A well-rounded exercise program includes:

- **A warm-up period and stretching exercises.** Cold muscles injure easily, so it's essential to warm up before stretching. Just do your regular exercise activity at an *easy* pace for five to 10 minutes. Next, begin slowly stretching specific muscle groups — shoulders, back, hips, thighs, calves and ankles — to help your muscles limber up and prevent stiffness. Stretch slowly and avoid bouncing and jerking movements.

- **Aerobic (endurance) exercises** (brisk walking, jogging, cycling, swimming, dancing, cross-country skiing or jumping rope). Aerobic exercises raise and sustain your heart rate for a period of time, burn calories and strengthen your heart and lungs. Whichever exercises you choose, they should be sustained for at least 12 to 15 minutes for you to receive cardiovascular benefits. Also, you should be able to talk or laugh without difficulty while you exercise — even during the most strenuous parts. If you can't, slow down.

- **Strengthening exercises** (push-ups, sit-ups, pull-ups or working with barbells, elastic bands or weight machines). These exercises strengthen your abdominal and back muscles (decreasing the chance of back injury) and the muscles around knee joints (protecting the knees from injuries).

- **A cool down (recovery) period.** Slow down gradually, then exercise at a relaxed pace for at least five minutes. Never stand still after vigorous exercise. In cold weather, warm up and cool down indoors.

STARTING SLOWLY AND OVERCOMING SETBACKS

The most common cause of injury is exercising too aggressively, too soon. Instead, start out gradually and slowly increase the time and intensity of your exercise program. This will give your muscles and joints time to adjust to exercising. Also, a gradual start will increase the likelihood that you will stick with your program until it becomes routine.

If you skip exercising for a day or two, don't get discouraged. Just get back into your routine as soon as you can. If the exercise you've chosen is too strenuous or causes injuries, slow down or switch to something else. If you can keep up your exercise program for the first month, it will most likely become a regular habit you look forward to and enjoy.

Smoking cessation

Each year, approximately 430,000 Americans die as a result of using tobacco, and many of them are older adults.

Cigarettes, pipe tobacco, cigars, snuff and chewing tobacco all contain *nicotine*, a highly addictive and unhealthy substance. Using tobacco increases your risk of developing numerous illnesses such as coronary heart disease (CHD), strokes, emphysema, chronic bronchitis, pneumonia, atherosclerosis, lung cancer and a variety of other cancers. (Although chewing tobacco may not threaten the respiratory system, it can still cause a number of health problems, including cancer of the mouth.)

Smoking tobacco can worsen symptoms of asthma and allergies and, even if *you* don't smoke, evidence shows that inhaling *secondhand smoke* (smoke from others who are smoking) can still make you ill. In addition, smoking is one of the leading causes of accidental death due to fires among older adults (see *Fires*, p. 330).

It's never too late

The more you have smoked over your lifetime, the more likely you are to develop smoking-related illnesses. However, it's *never* too late to stop smoking and enjoy positive health benefits. Within 12 hours of your last cigarette, your body begins to repair the damage to your heart and lungs. Your risk of lung cancer starts to decline about one year after you kick the habit, and by the time you've been a nonsmoker for 10 or 15 years, your risk of cancer is about the same as for people who have never smoked. Kicking the habit may not be easy — but it's definitely worth the effort.

KICKING THE HABIT — FOREVER

The first step in giving up tobacco products is to resolve to become — and remain — a non-user. The next step is to find ways to replace the mental and physical pleasures of nicotine with other less harmful substitutes — a process that takes planning, preparation, perseverance and moral support.

Preparing to quit smoking

- Begin "getting in shape" for quitting by incorporating regular physical activity into your lifestyle (see *Staying Active*, p. 316), adopting a healthy diet (see *Eating Right*, p. 310), and practicing relaxation skills (see *Stress*, p. 284). These lifestyle improvements can provide pleasurable sensations similar to the ones you're getting from nicotine.

- Choose a "partner" who's readily available to give support and encouragement. (It's most effective if this person does not use tobacco.) Tell other friends and family members you are quitting, and ask for their support.

- Consider quitting with someone else. You can offer each other support and help each other through difficult times.

- Start cutting back on tobacco gradually, and set a date for quitting completely (in a month or six weeks).

Once you quit smoking

- Have your car, carpets and upholstery cleaned as soon as you quit smoking; then make your car and home nonsmoking environments for any friends or family members who still use tobacco.

- Brush your teeth as soon as you wake up in the morning and right after meals so you have a fresh taste in your mouth.

- If you associate coffee with smoking, drink tea or another beverage instead. Or have coffee while doing an activity that keeps your hands busy, so you can minimize the urge to reach for a "smoke."

- Keep low-calorie snacks, sugarless gum or toothpicks on hand.

- Sit in nonsmoking sections of restaurants. Plan other activities in nonsmoking environments such as shopping centers and movie theaters.

- Congratulate and reward yourself frequently for quitting.

Handling setbacks

If you backslide on occasion (by having a cigarette or two), recognize the lapse as a small setback. Just get rid of any tobacco you may have bought, figure out the reason for the lapse, and make plans for how you're going to better handle the situation next time. That might involve getting out of the house for a walk, taking a shower or calling your "partner" or another supportive friend.

Getting help

While some people are able to quit using tobacco without any formal help, others need assistance — and it's readily available. For example:

- Nicotine patches and nicotine gum help some people minimize withdrawal symptoms after they've stopped smoking. Talk to your doctor if you're interested in either of these approaches.

  - The nicotine patch is designed to help people wean themselves off nicotine and minimize withdrawal symptoms in the process. The patch is most effective when combined with counseling programs that provide ongoing psychological support.

  - Nicotine gum provides a temporary substitute for nicotine inhaled by smoking and is most successful when used by heavily addicted smokers who are motivated to quit.

- Other resources include smoking cessation workshops and support groups. For information about programs in your area, contact your local chapter of the American Cancer Society or the American Lung Association (see *Resources*, p. 360).

Use of alcohol

Drinking alcohol in moderation — a glass of wine or a beer with dinner, for example — is usually nothing to be concerned about. However, remember that your body may react differently to alcohol than when you were younger, and your tolerance for alcohol may be reduced.

Alcohol abuse among older adults is a serious problem that needs prompt attention. Until recently, older problem drinkers tended to be overlooked by both health professionals and the general public due to perceived low numbers. This is because chronic problem drinkers — who abuse alcohol off and on for most of their lives — often die before becoming older adults. Also, older adults — who may be retired or have fewer social contacts — often hide their drinking problems, and medical professionals, family members and friends may not see the signals. Alcohol abuse can occur at any age, even if the problem doesn't materialize until the later years of life.

Heavy drinkers experience an increase in health risks, including *cirrhosis* (a chronic disease of the liver); obesity; high blood pressure; cancer of the esophagus, throat and mouth, as well as breast cancer in women; and traffic accidents or accidents at home.

Some alcoholics develop a form of *dementia* (memory problems) or *asterixes* (tremor or jerky movements), and alcoholism may cause or accelerate osteoporosis (see *Osteoporosis*, p. 216). Among older adults, one of the most frequent problems brought on by excessive use of alcohol is depression, which can have a negative impact on *all* areas of a person's life (see *Depression*, p. 289).

OVERCOMING ALCOHOLISM

The good news is that many people successfully overcome alcoholism. The first essential step is to acknowledge that you — or your spouse, child, coworker or friend — have a problem with alcohol and that continuing to drink can cause serious, if not deadly, consequences. (One of the heartbreaking symptoms of the disease is that the alcoholic often doesn't realize — or denies — there is a problem.)

The next step is to get help. (Individuals with a dependency or addiction to alcohol are rarely able to stop drinking permanently on their own.) A few of the most successful and well-known resources that are available in most communities include:

Resources

- Alcoholics Anonymous (AA), which uses a self-help group approach to help the alcoholic fully understand the seriousness of the problem, and begin — and stick with — a recovery program.
- Al-Anon, a program for family and friends of alcoholics.
- Alateen, a program similar to Al-Anon but specifically for teens and children in families where a drinking problem exists.

Other resources include alcohol treatment programs, your health care professional, public health departments, mental health agencies or — if one is available to you — an employee assistance program.

Also see *Appendix*, p. 360, for a list of national resources.

Catching problems early

It is a fact that some medical tests are unnecessary, costly and overprescribed. Yet others can play an important role in increasing your longevity and quality of life, while saving thousands — or even hundreds of thousands — of dollars in the long run by catching potentially serious problems early.

Screening guidelines

Here are a few of the preventive tests that are recommended for **healthy adults over 50**. If you have a serious medical condition or other high-risk factors, consult your doctor about other necessary tests, or more frequent tests.

Exam	Who Needs It	How Often
Complete Physical	All adults	Every one to three years until age 75, then yearly
Blood Pressure Measurement	All adults	Every two years for healthy adults, or every visit
Cholesterol Screening (to detect high blood cholesterol levels, which may lead to atherosclerosis)	All adults, most important for middle-aged men, anyone with history of heart disease, or smokers	Every five years
Pap Smear (to detect cervical cancer)	All women beginning at age 18 or at onset of sexual activity	Annually if there is a history of STDs or multiple sex partners, or every three years after two normal annual exams; after age 65, check with your doctor for frequency
Mammogram	All women beginning at age 40. It is not recommended that women under 40 have routine screening by mammogram unless there is a family history of premenopausal breast cancer in mother or sister	Every year

Exam	Who Needs It	How Often
Professional Breast Exam	All women during routine checkup; beginning annually at age 40, or at age 35 if a family history of premenopausal breast cancer in mother or sister	Every year (a monthly self-exam is also recommended*)
Sigmoidoscopy (to detect colorectal cancer)	Adults 50 years and over	Every three to five years
Fecal Occult Blood Testing (stool test for early detection of colorectal cancer)	Adults 50 years and over	Every year
Digital Rectal Exam (to detect prostate cancer)	All men over age 40	Every year
Glaucoma Screen	Everyone over age 40, African-Americans beginning at age 20	Every two years or on doctor's advice
Glucose	All adults age 45 or older.	If tested normal once, repeated at three-year intervals or on doctor's advice
Electrocardiogram or EKG (to detect coronary heart disease)	Not recommended for routine screening of people without symptoms	Selectively on doctor's advice
Exercise Stress Test (to screen for heart disease)	Not recommended as routine screening of people without symptoms. Men over 40 who have two or more major risk factors for heart disease (high cholesterol, high blood pressure, smoking, diabetes, family history of early onset of heart disease)	Selectively on doctor's advice

Continued on next page

* see *Breast Self-Exam*, p. 253

Exam	Who Needs It	How Often
Chest X-ray	Not recommended as routine screening of people without symptoms	Selectively on doctor's advice
Common Lab Tests (CBC, urinalysis, thyroid, liver, kidney, syphilis, tuberculin)	Not recommended as routine screening of people without symptoms	Selectively on doctor's advice
Osteoporosis Screening	Not recommended as routine screening of people without symptoms. May be recommended to assist with decisions on whether to start hormone replacement therapy	Selectively on doctor's advice

Immunization schedule

A thorough immunization plan is an important lifetime health investment that protects you against a host of life-threatening diseases such as smallpox, cholera and polio — and it continues to be a very important part of life as you get older.

Immunizations you need after age 65 include:

- A *pneumococcal vaccine* (one time only, in most cases) to decrease the likelihood of getting pneumonia and reduce the severity of the disease if you do get it.

- An *influenza vaccination* (given annually) to protect you against the flu — an illness that can be very serious and even life-threatening among older adults.

- A *tetanus diphtheria (Td) booster* every 10 years for all ages of adults (everyone needs to have completed a primary series of three shots), or every five years if you get a dirty wound, to fend off tetanus (also known as *lockjaw*).

Develop a schedule with your doctor to make sure you stay current on your immunizations, and keep your own record of vaccines at home.

Safety

Injuries due to falls and fires are one of the leading causes of accidental death among older adults. While the frequency of accidents doesn't necessarily increase with age, the number of accidents leading to injury and death do. This is because your body becomes less able to withstand injury as you grow older.

By planning ahead, you can considerably reduce your risk of most accidents. The following information provides some pointers.

FALLS

Each year, about one-third of adults over age 65 suffer falls, and 10% to 15% of them are significantly injured. A serious fall can cause you to limit your level of activity — due to injuries and the fear of falling again — so it pays to take extreme care to avoid falling in the first place.

Falls among older adults frequently result from slowed reaction time, lack of conditioning, poor vision or hearing, diseases such as osteoporosis that weaken the bones (see *Osteoporosis*, p. 216), or dizziness that can result from several causes, including medication (see *Dizziness/Fainting*, p. 79; *Using Medications*, p. 298; *Home Pharmacy*, p. 303).

Prevention

- **Keep your body as strong as possible** by eating right (see *Eating Right*, p. 310), exercising regularly (see *Staying Active*, p. 316) and taking steps to avoid or reduce the progression of osteoporosis. Your eyes and ears contribute to balance, so have them checked regularly (see index for specific topics).

- **Carefully inspect your home**, asking yourself: "Where are the places I'm likely to fall, and what can I do to reduce my risks?" and "What is my physical condition, and what are the compensations I can make?" Your list might include putting non-skid tape in the bathtub, adding handrails along staircases, getting rid of throw rugs that may slide under you, padding sharp corners or improving lighting.

- **Avoid excessive alcohol consumption.** As you grow older, you become more sensitive to alcohol and other drugs so your reflexes may be impaired by much less alcohol than when you were younger (see *Use Of Alcohol*, p. 322).

- **Make a habit of getting up slowly.** A normal drop in your blood pressure when you stand up — caused by your heart not being able to speed up as quickly as it used to (see *Heart Disease*, p. 159) — can result in dizziness that contributes to falls.

- **Don't stand on a stool or chair** to reach items stored up high. Have someone help you get them down — then move them to a spot within easy reach.

- **Use a cane or walker** if you have problems with balance.

> For information about other precautions — such as getting a personal response system for your home or wearing a medical-alert bracelet — see *Being Prepared*, p. 12.

TRAFFIC SAFETY

Automobile accidents cause a significant number of deaths among older adults and are frequently the result of slowed reaction time and impaired vision or hearing. However, practicing a few precautions can help you maximize your safety.

Prevention

Driving an automobile

- Enroll in a safe-driver training course to refresh your driving skills.
- Schedule yearly eye examinations. Ask your ophthalmologist whether you have experienced any vision changes that will have an impact on your driving abilities.
- If you wear glasses or a hearing aid, use them when driving, if appropriate.
- If you don't have to be on the road during rush hour, don't. If you know your vision is worse after dark, avoid driving at night.
- Keep a car window open a bit so you can hear sirens and other warning signals more easily. When using your car radio, keep the volume down low.
- Don't drive if any of your medications impair your driving ability.
- Take frequent breaks on long drives to rest your eyes and stretch your muscles.
- Wear your seat belt while in all motor vehicles and place children in proper car seats.

As a pedestrian

- Wear light-colored and/or reflective clothing when walking after sundown.

- When looking to the left and right before entering an intersection, use extra caution if your vision or hearing is impaired. Walk with a friend if possible.

- Stand on the sidewalk when waiting to cross a street — never in the street.

FIRES

The death rate due to fires is highest among older adults. Common causes of fires include unsafe use of cigarettes; malfunctioning smoke detectors and fire extinguishers; problems with fireplaces, electrical outlets or space heaters; and accidents in the kitchen.

Prevention

- If you smoke, make every effort to kick the habit. Research shows your risk from fires will be immediately reduced by one-third.

- Obtain fire extinguishers for your residence and learn how to use them. Also, install smoke detectors and keep the batteries fresh. Check these safety items every few months to make sure they're in working order.

- Keep your fireplace clean and make sure the screen is closed when you're burning a fire. Never leave a fire unattended.

- Don't overload electrical outlets, which can cause wires to overheat.

- Use space heaters carefully. Keep paper, furniture, curtains and combustible liquids away from the heater.

- In the kitchen, keep curtains, paper towels and wall hangings away from the stove, and make sure burners are turned off when not in use. Also, keep your burners and oven grease-free and be particularly cautious if you are deep-frying; the grease can cause a flare-up of flames that results in a larger fire.

Planning escape routes

All the prevention in the world can't absolutely guarantee that a fire won't occur, so make plans — in advance — for how you will get out of your residence if a fire occurs. Carefully plan at least two escape routes out of every room and make sure those routes are free of hazards.

CRIME

Unfortunately, older adults do fall prey to thieves and other petty criminals — but there's plenty you can do to avoid potentially dangerous situations. The goal is to make it difficult for the crime to occur in the first place — before you become a victim.

Prevention

At home

- Make sure all doors and windows have locks that are in good order.

- Install a peephole if you don't already have one, and use it. Never open the door to strangers or let them know you're alone.

- Keep the exterior of your home well lit, and bushes and trees trimmed to ensure good visibility.

- Don't give any information to strangers over the phone, and hang up on obscene or other nuisance phone calls.

- When you go on a trip, take steps to make your house or apartment look "lived in" while you're away. Stop delivery of mail and newspapers, or arrange for a neighbor or friend to pick up deliveries. Leave some shades up and/or lights on (or use an automatic timer), and arrange for someone to care for the yard.

- Have your Social Security checks deposited directly into your bank account; theft of Social Security checks is a prime source of crime against older adults.

- Get acquainted with your neighbors. Watch out for one another.

- Consider getting a dog. Even a little one can deter unwanted visitors while providing companionship.

- Attend a crime prevention program.

Away from home

- Avoid carrying large amounts of money or expensive personal items (don't wear flashy jewelry, for example) when out in public.

- Never carry a deadly weapon; it can be used against you. Instead, carry a whistle you can easily access and blow to scare away muggers, or carry a cane or umbrella you can use to defend yourself if necessary.

- Stay in well-lit, busy areas at night. If you have "the feeling" you're in danger, trust your instincts. Do whatever seems necessary to restore your sense of safety.

- Walk and act like you know where you're going.

• When you walk or drive, go with a friend or friends. There *really* is safety in numbers.

Finally, if your prevention methods are unsuccessful and you are accosted, don't resist: hand over your purse or wallet without hesitating. Purse and wallet snatchers are usually more interested in your money or possessions than in hurting you.

SCAMS

• No matter what your age, it *always* pays to be an informed consumer and stay alert to possible "scams."

• Never give out information — especially your credit card number — to anyone over the phone unless you placed the call. Ask for requests for confidential information in writing.

• Purchase home improvement services from respected, well-established companies. Ask for references.

• Carefully read and fully understand documents before you sign them. Have a trusted friend or family member provide assistance if necessary.

• Be cautious of "good causes" and "hard luck stories." Select the causes you wish to support and only donate an amount that feels comfortable to you.

• Keep in mind that investment opportunities that sound too good to be true probably are.

• Don't let yourself be pressured by anyone demonstrating a product or service in your home. You're under no obligation to buy.

• Evaluate insurance offers — especially unsolicited ones — very carefully. Call a trusted relative or financial advisor if you have any questions.

• If you feel at all unsure about a purchase, trust your feelings and don't sign anything until you're sure. Instead, buy yourself some time by saying: "Give me everything in writing. I want to review this with my attorney."

ABUSE

Elder abuse (mistreatment of older adults) can occur in assisted living centers, nursing homes, and even in your own home — by people you hire to care for you. Sadly, even family members can be abusive.

The important thing to remember is that every person — regardless of age — has the legal right to be protected from assault, abuse and harassment. The goals are to prevent abuse from occurring whenever possible, recognize an abusive situation when you find yourself in one, and get help as quickly as possible.

Prevention

Use caution when selecting care or other services to be delivered in the home or some other setting; quality can vary dramatically. Find out if staff members are trained and well-qualified, if cleanliness and safety are maintained at all times, how supervision of staff members is handled, and what your course of action is if you're not satisfied with the care. Ask for references and check them before you contract for any services. Encourage your caregiver (especially a family member) to take needed breaks and care properly for themselves (see *Care For The Caregiver*, p. 354).

Recognizing abusive behavior

It's safe to assume you are being abused if you are:

- Hit, slapped, pushed, shoved or in any way intentionally harmed or injured
- Verbally harassed, continually insulted, belittled, criticized or made to feel inadequate or bad
- Neglected or placed in a situation that is unsafe or unhealthy

What you can do

Immediately report any abusive behavior to the abuser's supervisor or sponsoring agency, friends and family, or the police. Be prepared to explain exactly what happened, the time and date of the incident(s), the name of the person who hurt you and anyone who saw it happen, and the kind of injury or discomfort.

Many older adults don't speak up when they find themselves in an abusive situation because they're embarrassed, afraid of being hurt even more, feel like no one cares, or think no one will do anything to help. Try to remember, instead, that the person who is abusing you is breaking the law (even if it is a family member), and that speaking up may prevent others from being abused by the same person or situation. What's more — **you deserve to be treated with respect and kindness.**

Managing illness

6

MANAGING YOUR ILLNESS

Regardless of your age, many illnesses can be prevented — or their progress slowed — by taking good care of yourself. Aging doesn't have to equate with illness. For example, exercise, weight control, being a nonsmoker and eating a healthy diet can lower your risk of certain types of heart disease, cancer and arthritis (see index for specific topics), conditions once thought to be unavoidable. Physical and mental exercises help keep the body and mind fit no matter what your age.

While many illnesses can be prevented or slowed, others are beyond your control. Genetics may play a role in increasing your risk of some diseases, such as certain forms of cancer. Other illnesses may be traced to actions taken earlier in life, when causes and risk factors for a condition were not yet known, or to the lack of a healthy lifestyle. Other conditions, such as Parkinson's disease, rheumatoid arthritis and ulcerative colitis, seem to appear at random, without any means to prevent them.

The good news is that you can still take control at some level. Whether you experience a temporary setback or are diagnosed with a chronic disease, the power to prevent illness or cope with it when it does occur is basically in *your* hands. Making choices that preserve and improve your quality of life helps to reassert your independence, rejuvenate you emotionally and enhance your sense of well-being.

In this section you'll learn how to take charge by understanding your attitudes about your health, setting realistic goals for your health and the medical care you receive, practicing good techniques for preventing acute illnesses and managing chronic conditions, and making changes that significantly affect your situation for the better.

You're in charge

For starters, follow the steps to *primary prevention* (see *Steps To Primary Prevention*, p. 339). These lifestyle choices can help you avoid injury and many *acute illnesses* (illnesses that can generally be treated and cured) associated with aging, as well as improve your overall health.

It is important to remember that even with acute and chronic illnesses, you can live a productive life. Your attitude and adaptability can help you make the most out of your situation. If your mobility has been affected by arthritis, for example, you may feel depressed, isolated and threatened by a loss of independence. These feelings, although understandable, do not have to dictate your situation. You can make the choice to begin an exercise program to improve your agility; you can investigate manipulation aids designed to help with household chores; you can take advantage of community services that assist with meal preparation and special transportation needs. Making choices like these does not mean you've lost your independence — it means you have exercised it.

It's never too late

Self-care, prevention and a healthy lifestyle are important throughout your lifetime, and it's never too late to start taking steps toward improving your situation. Studies repeatedly show that older adults who engage in exercise often regain or exceed the strength they had in their earlier years. The lung damage caused by years of smoking is slowed and eventually reversed by giving up smoking, even late in life. Cutting back on the fat in your diet can reduce your cholesterol levels, which can lessen the risk or progression of heart disease and stroke. Managing stress, limiting salt intake, exercising and quitting smoking help to control high blood pressure (see *Hypertension*, p. 168).

STEPS TO TAKING CHARGE

• Practice healthy lifestyle behaviors (see *Prevention*, p. 309).

• Learn all you can about your condition or illness:

 - Ask questions (particularly of your doctor or health care team).

 - Call a professional nurse telephone line or a national hotline.

 - Contact a community agency or national organization that deals with your condition or situation (see *Resources*, p. 360). These groups have a number of clearly written materials that can be sent to you.

• Actively participate in your care plan:

 - Consider yourself a partner with your doctor and health care team.

 - Encourage those in your family who help with your care to join your "team."

 - Don't assume your doctor knows how you feel. Take the initiative to communicate your assessment of your health status.

(see *A Self-Care Approach*, p. 4)

PRIMARY PREVENTION

Most people develop one or more acute illnesses during their lifetime (see *Acute Illness*, p. 340). Primary prevention means avoiding or postponing the occurrence of sudden acute illnesses and injuries, as well as the onset of chronic conditions. The following chart shows some general guidelines that promote health while reducing the risk of an acute illness or injury.

To reduce the risk of an acute illness or injury

STEPS TO PRIMARY PREVENTION

Eat a balanced diet low in fat and salt. Limiting fat and salt intake can reduce your risk of heart disease and high blood pressure, for example. A balanced diet also helps control weight, an essential element in the prevention of many diseases (see *Eating Right*, p. 310). Use alcohol moderately (one to two drinks a day or less) or not at all (see *Use Of Alcohol*, p. 322).

Develop and maintain a program of regular exercise, including aerobic exercise to strengthen your heart. Regular exercise conditions your heart and lungs, and keeps you fit (see *Staying Active*, p. 316).

Make every effort to stop smoking and avoid inhaling the smoke of others (see *Smoking Cessation*, p. 319). Cigarette smoke can lead to lung cancer and emphysema, and it makes you more susceptible to pneumonia and bronchitis (see *Respiratory Concerns*, p. 146).

Adhere to a schedule of regular screenings and vaccinations (see *Screening Guidelines*, p. 324; *Immunization Schedule*, p. 327). Many illnesses can be detected early with routine screenings such as mammograms and Pap smears. A pneumonia vaccination and annual flu shots will limit your risk of contracting these illnesses.

Take steps to ensure your personal safety (see *Safety*, p. 328). Use your seat belt, install handrails in your shower to prevent falls, make your home secure and take other actions to decrease the likelihood of injury.

ACUTE VS. CHRONIC ILLNESS

Understanding the differences between acute and chronic illness will help you make wiser decisions about maintaining good health and preventing its decline.

Acute illness involves the sudden onset of an illness or injury. The progression and treatment for the condition are often predictable, and a complete recovery — or a return to good health — is usually possible. An acute illness might be pneumonia (see *Pneumonia*, p. 155) or a peptic ulcer (see *Peptic Ulcer*, p. 175). Your chances of avoiding or recovering faster from illness greatly increase with prevention — vaccinating against diseases, eating a healthy diet, being a nonsmoker and exercising regularly all keep the immune system strong to fight off illness and infection.

May be lifelong

Chronic illness is a condition that, once you have it, will likely continue for the remainder of your life. The disease's progression and treatment vary somewhat from person to person, making certain stages of the condition unpredictable, while other stages are more foreseeable. The challenge facing someone with a chronic illness is not how to return to full health, but how to slow or stabilize progression and deal with the consequences of a lifelong condition.

Chronic illnesses include conditions such as coronary heart disease (CHD), arthritis, diabetes, emphysema, stroke, osteoporosis and hypertension (see index for specific topics). Once you have a chronic illness, *self-management* is key. Self-management refers to steps you can take to slow the progress of your disease and cope with its impacts (see *Steps To Self-Management*, p. 346).

The success of prevention and self-management hinges on your willingness to become an active partner in your health care, your confidence in your ability to make changes, and your commitment to taking charge of your life.

Making healthy decisions

Remarkably, how healthy you see yourself, combined with your ability to develop good decision-making skills, are two of the most crucial aspects in effectively managing a chronic illness or condition.

The more aspects of your situation you believe you can control, the better you feel; the better you feel, the more incentive you have to take control. It's a cycle that becomes self-fulfilling, and can spiral in either a positive or negative direction based on your choices.

In spite of the challenges, ups and downs and disappointments that may accompany chronic conditions, you have ongoing opportunities to call a lot of the shots. And the better prepared you are for these opportunities, the better your levels of health and quality of life can be.

UNDERSTANDING HOW AND WHY YOU MAKE CERTAIN CHOICES

To self-manage any illness, understanding yourself as well as understanding the disease are important and central to having a positive effect on your situation. This helps you better recognize those things you can do something about, versus those you just need to accept, work with or work around.

For example, do you believe you can make a difference in your health, or do you think things are pretty much out of your hands? Do you feel you and your doctor are on the same team, or are you anxious and distrustful about your medical care? Are healthy lifestyle changes important to you, or do you tend to discount them? Your answers to these and many similar questions that crop up in the course of your illness reflect your attitudes and have a significant impact on your decision process.

Different types of patients

Your attitude or outlook clearly plays a role in your health care decisions and the way you connect with the medical system. The following information may provide you with insight into how and why you make decisions about your health the way you do.

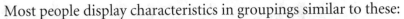

Most people display characteristics in groupings similar to these:

- Many older adults are proactive, are involved in their own health care and tend to adopt healthy lifestyle habits (such as eating a well-balanced diet and exercising). They trust their doctors.

- Some people regret some of the unhealthy habits they established when they were younger (such as wishing they had eaten better). Because these aspects of their lifestyle are so ingrained, they are the least likely to change (and begin a balanced diet now). They see their doctors regularly, prefer specialists and are the most likely of the four types listed here to try new over-the-counter (OTC) drugs.

- Others tend to describe themselves as rarely sick. They take medicine only when they have to and, unlike the previous group, *don't* like to try new over-the-counter (OTC) drugs.

- And still others have very little faith in the medical system. Their worries center on their health insurance and whether their doctors are well-informed about how different medicines interact in older adults.

In other words, if you are a proactive patient diagnosed with some aspect of heart disease, you may have fewer challenges trying to follow a low-fat diet than individuals in the other three categories, simply because healthy habits (to some extent) are already part of your lifestyle.

It is beneficial to take stock of your attitudes about medical care as well as your confidence in managing your health. Knowing the level of difficulty you are likely to face (given your particular set of attitudes), can help you more readily accept yourself, and may prevent you from giving up on a lifestyle change that can greatly benefit your chronic condition.

Different stages of decision making

The process of choice and change has stages. Again, understanding where you are in the process helps you make the best decisions for change, given your situation, your attitudes and your condition.

One common aspect of chronic-disease management is learning to adapt your behavior, sometimes on a daily basis. You may be incorporating lifestyle changes (making your diet more nutritious, exercising, kicking the smoking habit), or you may be learning to adhere to your doctor's treatment plan (in the case of diabetes, self-managing glucose testing and taking your medication as directed). If you move through all five of the following stages, you will arrive at a more effective level of handling your condition.

1. **Hesitation:** In the very beginning you will not be thinking about making changes. You may not even want to read or talk about ways you can manage your disease. In the case of diabetes, you may underestimate the benefits of changing your diet, and overestimate the amount of effort it will take.

2. **Consideration:** At the next level you are seriously thinking about changing your behavior sometime in the next six months. The pros and the cons are much more equal in your mind, although you may still believe the reasons not to change outweigh the benefits. For example, you may plan to begin eating more nutritious, well-balanced meals in the next six months because it will make it easier for you to control your diabetes, but for now the meal planning and preparation seem like too much work.

3. **Preparation:** By the time you begin preparing to make changes, you are in the third stage. In fact, you may have already attempted some small steps (cutting back on the fat in your diet, eating more fresh fruits and vegetables). You now believe there is greater benefit to making changes than not. This is the time to ask your doctor or health care team for help in setting realistic goals and learning specific skills.

4. **Action:** When you progress to the fourth stage, which usually lasts about six months, you are accomplishing significant changes, but you are also the most vulnerable to slipping back into your old behaviors or habits. Ask your doctor or health care team for specific activities that will keep you focused on your goal, and don't be shy about seeking praise and support (see *Resources*, p. 360, for a list of various support groups).

5. **Maintenance:** After approximately six months of carrying out an action plan, you will have achieved the level of maintenance. The goal now is to keep doing what you're doing. Ask for support to prevent backsliding into old behaviors. Acquiring techniques that prompt or encourage you to follow through on certain actions is most helpful (post your exercise schedule, join a health club, treat yourself to new workout clothes, exercise with a friend, remind yourself how good you feel when you exercise).

It is important to note that you may "recycle" back through previous stages on your way to the new behavior. In fact, you may experience "two steps forward and one step back" several times before you achieve your goal. Be patient with yourself, seek the help you need to succeed, and refocus on the behavior you want to acquire.

6

Self-managing chronic illness

The role of any good manager is to be responsible for decisions and see that these decisions are carried out. Managing your health is no different.

You're not alone

Keep in mind that self-managing does not mean going it alone. An essential part of your decision process is connecting with a variety of skilled sources for information, guidance and support. Your health care team (primary care physician, specialists, physical therapist, nutritionist, etc.) is your major source. Think of your doctor as your partner and the other health care professionals as your consultants providing advice and services. Together, you will manage the day-to-day course of your illness — with you in charge.

Setting realistic goals

EFFECTIVE TECHNIQUES

Managing a chronic illness is never as simple as deciding what you want to do and just doing it. If you fail to set *realistic* goals (keep in mind that a chronic illness may mean giving up some options), or haven't learned certain skills needed to reach your goals, you may decide there's no way you can improve the situation. Setbacks will become overwhelming, and the situation will probably get worse.

- **Understand why you feel the way you do:** All chronic health problems share certain traits including fatigue or loss of energy, sleep problems (pain and difficulty breathing are two causes), some physical disability, depression (worrying about the future, loss of some independence, feeling helpless), and lowered self-esteem (due to most of the points just mentioned).

- **Learn as much as you can:** Your chronic condition will have its own set of trends or stages. It's important to educate yourself about these so you know what to generally expect and can prepare for the best ways to manage and adapt to the situation. Some of the most successful self-managers are described as thinking of their illness as a path — sometimes it's rough, sometimes flat; sometimes you can go fast, other times slow; sometimes it takes several different approaches to navigate the turns.

- **Practice problem-solving skills:** You will be faced with daily opportunities to make choices (see *Making Healthy Decisions*, p. 341). The process can become unmanageable unless you break it down into steps. As with any new skill, you'll find that this approach becomes more effective with practice, until you eventually adopt it as routine.

Problem-solving steps

- **Decide what you want to realistically accomplish.** (For example, you've recently been diagnosed with emphysema and want to learn some exercises to aid your breathing.)

- **Look for multiple ways to reach your goal or solve your problem.** (You can ask your doctor for instruction; you can call the American Lung Association for information and resources within your community; you can obtain a list of exercises to teach yourself at home; you can join a support group or class at a local hospital that offers classes and regular exercise sessions.)

- **Select an option and try it, keeping in mind your chance for success is greatest where your interest is highest.** (Because you'd rather exercise in the comfort of your own home and you don't drive, you choose a booklet to read about exercises you can do on your own.)

- **Check your results.** (After a week, you don't notice that breathing is any easier, and you're not sure you're doing the exercises correctly. You start to wonder if this was a good idea.)

- **Substitute another idea or approach if the first one doesn't work.** (You locate a breathing-exercise class for individuals with chronic lung conditions. It's nearby and also offers transportation, so you decide to participate and reevaluate your situation after a few sessions.)

- **Reward yourself.** (You congratulate yourself with a bouquet of flowers for having the determination to step out of your comfort zone.)

You may find that the situation, for now, is unchangeable or unsolvable. That's important to know, and it's all right. Don't dwell on what you can't do, but start looking for another goal you can accomplish. Seek out a support group that deals with the same condition or issues you are facing.

Using self-management skills

The decision to self-manage your chronic condition is a wise health care choice because of the benefits to you. You will enjoy the greatest benefits if your goals are to keep your daily functioning (work, chores, recreational and social activities) and your well-being (mental health, pain, perception of health status) at optimal levels, given your situation. By using self-management techniques to slow or prevent the progress of your current condition, your chances of limiting other illnesses and improving your overall health are very good.

STEPS TO SELF-MANAGEMENT

Develop and maintain exercise and nutrition programs. Even after the onset of atherosclerosis (see *CHD*, p. 159), a low-fat diet is important to minimize future heart problems. Eating right also helps avoid complications of diabetes (see *Diabetes*, p. 201). Weight control can help lessen the symptoms of arthritis (see *Arthritis*, p. 209).

Monitor your symptoms. Do you feel better, worse or the same? How does a certain treatment affect you? Regular monitoring and reporting back to your doctor will help detect subtle changes in your condition so steps may be taken to lessen the impact of your symptoms or find alternative treatments.

Take the initiative to contact your doctor when you believe you need medical attention and keep your scheduled visits. In addition, routine screenings, immunizations and checkups are as important as ever.

Follow your treatment plan and minimize any side effects. Failure to comply with your doctor's instructions can have a serious impact on controlling your condition. However, if a treatment or medication is affecting you in an unexpected or adverse way, speak up. Often your doctor can adjust your care plan to be more suitable to your needs. Be sure your doctor and pharmacist know about any other prescriptions and over-the-counter (OTC) medications you may be using (see *Personal Medications Record*, p. 364).

Work and communicate effectively with your doctor and/or health care team (see *A Self-care Approach*, p. 4). Share information, ask questions and express your needs.

Find out about and use community and other support resources. Find ways to compensate for changes in your lifestyle. Learn how others are handling similar situations (see *Resources*, p. 360). Don't try to go it alone!

Planning for the future

7

Action plan for independence

If you're like most people, you genuinely value your independence. You enjoy the freedom of making your own decisions and going where you want, when you want.

As people grow older, there is sometimes a fear that this independence must be surrendered. The good news is that — with planning and a positive, realistic outlook — it is possible for many people to maintain a level of independence throughout their entire life.

A key factor in preserving this freedom is planning. By anticipating the way your life may change — and adapting — you can most likely avoid hasty decisions that may be dictated by circumstance, and make choices better suited to your personal preferences.

Important questions

Use the following list to think about the future and how you can keep the independence you enjoy.

WHERE DO YOU WANT TO LIVE?

Are you happy where you are now? Are family, friends and activities accessible? Are the weather and climate acceptable to you?

If you're pondering a move to a different city, you may want to plan it at a time in your retirement when you feel comfortable making new friends and adapting to new surroundings. You may also want to make a trial visit for an extended period before coming to a final decision.

WHAT SIZE OF HOME CAN YOU MAINTAIN?

Older adults often decide to sell homes with large lawns and a lot of upkeep — and opt for smaller places. Those who live in the country may move into nearby towns where services are closer. City dwellers may want a smaller apartment, or one that's closer to friends or activities. Also, changes in your health may create temporary or long-term requirements for changes in your living environment.

WHAT ARE YOUR FINANCIAL RESOURCES?

Take a candid look at your resources. What are you able to afford, and how can you enjoy the lifestyle that you want with the funds that are available to you? Develop a monthly budget based on your resources. If you're worried about your resources, look into governmental programs that may be available to you. Don't be embarrassed about tapping these resources — that's why they exist. Remember, too, that many of the most enjoyable activities don't require money: chatting with a good friend, curling up with a great book from the library, taking a stroll through the park, or gardening on a sunny afternoon.

ASK THE "WHAT IF?" QUESTIONS

Sometimes, it's helpful to consider some of the possible changes and then think of solutions before you actually need them. For example:

* **What if I could no longer drive my car?** Is there a local taxi company? What about buses? Is there a special shuttle service for older adults? Is it possible to walk to key services and activities? How comfortable would I be relying on friends for errands? What about shopping by phone?

* **What if I need help with housework or yard work?** Can I make things simpler — by closing off several rooms, or by doing less yard work? Could I hire live-in help? Would a smaller place be easier to maintain? Is there equipment that would make things easier?

* **What if I need ongoing assistance?** What is available in the area? Do my friends have people helping them who seem competent? What services are available through local health care organizations, churches or social service groups?

* **If I were to become seriously ill, what kind of care would I want?** Several important tools — a Living Will and Durable Power of Attorney for Health Care — help you convey the kind of care you want even if you're too ill to communicate. These are explained more fully on page 356.

* **What if my spouse/partner were to die?** The simple fact is that if you're married or in a long-term relationship, one person will likely outlive the other. It can be very reassuring to talk honestly with your husband, wife or partner about how one of you will cope without the other. Although this topic may be uncomfortable, talking about it often leads to deeply intimate and satisfying discussions.

7

The point of anticipating these possible situations is to think positively about solutions and how you can cope, long before an emergency or major change occurs.

WHAT ASSISTANCE IS AVAILABLE IN YOUR AREA?

Do a little fact-finding to see which programs and services are available to you. Some good resources for information are senior centers, the local Area Agency on Aging, home health agencies, United Way, hospital geriatric departments, libraries, the local Visiting Nurse Association and religious organizations.

You'll soon discover a wide range of services that may include adult day care, assistance with shopping, employment and volunteer opportunities, home health aides, homemakers and chore services, housing assistance, legal services, mental health services, respite care for the caregiver and retirement planning (see *Appendix*, p. 360, for national resources).

Plans and outlook

SHARE YOUR THOUGHTS WITH FAMILY AND FRIENDS

Chances are your children or close friends would like to hear your ideas and plans. Although it sometimes takes courage, most children welcome hearing a parent say, "I've been thinking about the future, and here are some changes that I plan to make as I grow older."

By sharing with people who are important to you, you can benefit from their ideas and suggestions as well as give them the opportunity to help you fulfill your plans.

BE POSITIVE, AND ENJOY THIS SPECIAL SEASON OF LIFE

Thankfully, our culture is re-defining what it means to grow older. No longer is aging thought of as a long list of surrenders — giving up various things long enjoyed. Instead, it's seen for what it really is: a time of reflection, of living as actively and fully as possible, and of drawing on the richness, experience and wisdom of a long-lived life.

Tapping your resources

A wide variety of services is available to help you maintain your independence. Think about the obstacles that could make your life more difficult and less enjoyable, then ask yourself what you need help with; how often the help is required (ongoing, hourly, daily or just one time); or if these obstacles are something you can solve by yourself with the right equipment or help.

Problem solving

For example, an obstacle might be: "I want to stay in my home, but I don't have the flexibility and strength for the housekeeping that I once did." Ask yourself these questions:

- What needs to be done and why?
- How often does it need to be done?
- If there is a cost, how can it be paid for?

Then, think about solutions, which might include:

- Special cleaning tools that minimize the need for bending
- Closing off one room so it doesn't need to be cleaned
- Having bedding and towels cleaned by a laundry service
- Hiring a window-cleaning service for the outside windows
- Hiring someone to help inside your home on a regular basis

Older adults sometimes find themselves needing assistance with housing and house maintenance, daily grooming, medical care, and staying active and in touch with friends.

Community services

You can take satisfaction in knowing that any problem you're likely to face has already been successfully solved by someone else. Services that are in place in a number of communities include:

Personal emergency response systems. These types of systems let you immediately signal the local hospital, ambulance or emergency response system if you fall or need instant medical attention (see *Being Prepared*, p. 12).

Telephone reassurance programs. Volunteers phone you regularly to make sure you're well, remind you to take medications or offer support in other ways.

Friendly visits. Some organizations such as churches or local social service agencies will send people to visit, chat, play cards or keep you company.

Chore services. These companies offer a modern-day equivalent of the "handyman" for yard work, general home maintenance or minor household repairs.

Meals services. These programs deliver nutritious meals right to your home, often for a very modest fee or donation.

Companion services. A variety of these services is available that help keep your home running smoothly, with housekeeping, essential shopping and meal preparation.

Home health aides. They can supply all the help provided by companion services, as well as assist with administering oral medication as prescribed, dressing and bathing.

Skilled home care. Qualified health care providers bring even more expertise right to your home with help in medication management, specialized treatments and nutritional counseling. Home care providers can oversee other people providing services in your home, and make recommendations for other assistance that might be needed.

Respite services. These people "fill-in" to provide care while the regular caregiver(s) takes time away.

Hospices. These special programs provide care to people who are dying, often in their homes. They help deliver medical care that reduces pain and makes life more acceptable, rather than providing intensive medical services. The hospice team might include a doctor, nurse, social worker, member of the clergy and volunteers.

CARE FOR THE CAREGIVER

Caring for a friend or loved one can be an opportunity to show your concern, but realize that it is also a big commitment. Don't overdo — and remember the emotional toll that giving care can take on you.

If you are considering being a caregiver, think about:

Physical ability and stamina. Don't promise to do tasks that are beyond your own strength or energy level.

Time management. Remember, you have your own life, too. Make a commitment that allows you the time you need for your life and its demands.

Emotional impact. Providing care, especially for someone in your own family, can bring up a number of emotionally charged issues such as resentment or past family conflicts. Be aware that this often occurs, and seek help if it becomes an issue.

What you can do

- Join a support group and share stories, tips and ideas with others providing care.

- Schedule breaks in the routine (*respite care*) to get some well-deserved time away. This is vital since the likelihood of verbal or physical abuse increases as the caregiver becomes more depleted and resentful, and feels there is no option for relief. Over-extended caregivers may find themselves acting in a way they could never imagine possible in ordinary circumstances.

- Scale down other demands on your time, if possible.

- Help the person in need tap their resources. A loving family member should realize that, in addition to doing tasks personally, an equally beneficial service is looking for professional resources and lining up other help.

- Become a creative problem solver. Look for new, fresh ways to get the assistance needed for both you and the person you're caring for.

- Watch out for guilt. Don't demand perfection of yourself, and don't be motivated by guilt. If you've committed to something that you're not able to do, admit it honestly and help find other resources for getting the job done.

Important documents

No one likes to think about the possibility of being so ill or seriously injured that they can't communicate with a doctor directly about the kind of care they want. Unfortunately, that can happen. However, there are steps you can take to make sure your care is carried out in the way that you would choose if you are unable to make your wishes about medical treatment known.

When you make your preferences known now, you benefit from making decisions at a time when you can thoughtfully consider them. Plus, you take stress away from loved ones and family members, should they ever have to make medical decisions on your behalf in an emergency or end-of-life situation.

Decide in advance

The two documents discussed below deal with medical situations where you are unable to communicate directly about the kind of care you want. They are sometimes referred to as *Advance Medical Directives*, because they set out your wishes in advance of you actually needing them.

The Directive to Physicians (Living Will) is a written statement in which you specify what type of care you want if you are terminally ill and dying, or if you are permanently unconscious. It helps guide the actions of your doctor, family members and others making decisions about your care.

The Durable Power of Attorney for Health Care is a legally binding document in which you give someone else the authority to make health care decisions for you if you're not able to make them yourself. If you do not have this document, the law specifies who will make decisions on your behalf. In some states this would be your spouse, adult children, parents or siblings (in that order).

It is not necessary to consult an attorney to complete these documents, although some people feel more comfortable having worked with their lawyer on these issues. Bear in mind that these documents may vary from state to state, so if you have moved or reside at more than one location, make sure that your documents are recognized in all places where you spend long periods of time.

Complete the forms and make sure that they are signed, dated, notarized and witnessed if required.

When you've decided

Once you've finished them:

- Talk with the person to whom you've given durable power of attorney for your health care so they know their role in advance.

- Discuss your desires about care with this person, so they are best able to make decisions that reflect your preferences and plans.

- Give your doctor a copy of these documents.

- If you have a chart at a hospital, ask that a copy of these documents be added to your file, or bring a copy with you when you go to the hospital.

- Keep copies near other important or legal papers, so someone looking through your belongings can easily find them.

The Directive to Physicians and Durable Power of Attorney for Health Care are very important in an era when medical technology can artificially prolong life for weeks, months and even years.

You can always make changes

Most hospitals can provide you with pre-written and fill-in-the-blank forms for these documents. If you are using a pre-written form, realize that you have the right to change any of the language in the form. For example, the standardized form might say: "I consider artificially administered nutrition and hydration to be forms of life-sustaining treatment and direct that under my directions they be withheld or withdrawn the same as other forms of treatment." If you don't agree with this statement, you could cross it out entirely, or modify it by allowing hydration to be administered, or any other change you desire.

Bear in mind that the Directive to Physicians is focused on situations when a person has incurable injury, disease or illness certified to be terminal by two doctors, and medical measures would only prolong the dying process. As you are able to communicate with your doctor, you'll be the one making the decisions about your own care.

One last point: Know that you can change, revise and update these forms as often as you like. Just make sure that all the key people have the most current copy.

Appendix

Resources

Many of these associations can refer you to local chapters that provide services in your community, as well as provide educational material and information on local support groups. Most of the numbers are toll-free.

NATIONAL ASSOCIATIONS RELATED TO SPECIFIC CONDITIONS

Al-Anon Family Group Headquarters
1600 Corporate Landing Pkwy
Virginia Beach, VA 23458
1-757-563-1600
web site: http://www.al-anon-alateen.org

Alcoholics Anonymous
475 Riverside Dr, 11th Floor
New York, NY 10115
1-212-870-3400

Alzheimer's Association
919 N Michigan Ave, Suite 1000
Chicago, IL 60611-1676
1-800-272-3900
web site: http://www.alz.org

American Cancer Society
1599 Clifton Rd
Atlanta, GA 30329-4251
1-800-227-2345
web site: http://www.cancer.org

American Council for Headache Education
875 Kings Highway, Suite 200
Woodbury, NJ 08096
for membership information:
1-800-255-2243

American Council of the Blind
1155 15th St NW, Suite 720
Washington, DC 20005
1-202-467-5081 or 1-800-424-8666
web site: http://www.acb.org

American Diabetes Association
1660 Duke St
Alexandria, VA 22314
1-800-232-3472
web site: http://www.diabetes.org

American Foundation for Urologic Disease
300 West Pratt St, Suite 401
Baltimore, MD 21201
1-800-242-2383

American Heart Association
7272 Greenville Ave
Dallas, TX 75231-4599
1-800-242-8721
web site: http://www.amhrt.org

American Kidney Fund
6110 Executive Blvd, Suite 1010
Rockville, MD 20852
1-800-638-8299
web site: http://www.akfinc.org

American Lung Association
1740 Broadway
New York, NY 10019-4374
1-800-586-4872

National Parkinson Foundation, Inc.
1501 NW 9th Ave (Bob Hope Road)
Miami, FL 33136
1-800-327-4545
web site: http://www.parkinson.org

Arthritis Foundation
P O Box 7669
Atlanta, GA 30357
1-800-283-7800

**The Lighthouse National Center
for Vision and Aging**
111 East 59th St
New York, NY 10022
1-800-334-5497
web site: http://www.lighthouse.org

**National Alliance of Breast Cancer
Organizations**
9 East 37th St, 10th Floor
New York, NY 10016
1-212-719-0154

National Association for Continence
P O Box 8310
Spartanburg, SC 29305-8310
1-800-252-3337
web site: http://www.nafc.org

**National Heart, Lung and Blood
Institute**
9000 Rockville Pike
Bethesda, MD 20892
1-301-496-4000
web site: http://www.nhlbi.nih.gov

National Hospice Organization
1901 N Moore St, Suite 901
Arlington, VA 22209
1-800-658-8898

National Mental Health Association
1021 Prince St
Alexandria, VA 22314-2971
1-800-969-6642
web site: http://www.nmha.org

National Osteoporosis Foundation
1150 17th St NW, Suite 500
Washington, DC 20037-4603
1-800-223-9994
web site: http://www.nof.org

National Safety Council
1121 Spring Lake Dr
Itasca, IL 60143-3201
1-800-621-7619
web site: http://www.nsc.org/nsc

National Women's Health Network
514 10th St NW, Suite 400
Washington, DC 20004
for membership information:
1-202-347-1140

**Self-Help for Hard of Hearing
People, Inc.**
7910 Woodmont Ave, Suite 1200
Bethesda, MD 20814
1-301-657-2248
web site: http://www.shhh.org

The Thyroid Foundation of America, Inc.
Ruth Sleeper Hall, RSL 350
40 Parkman St
Boston, MA 02114-2698
1-800-832-8321

United Ostomy Association
36 Executive Park, Suite 120
Irvine, CA 92714-6744
1-800-826-0826
web site: http://www.uoa.org

ADDITIONAL RESOURCES FOR OLDER ADULTS AND CAREGIVERS

These organizations have information about resources that may be available to you, depending on your situation.

American Association of Homes and Services for the Aging
901 E St NW, Suite 500
Washington, DC 20004-2011
1-202-783-2242
web site: http://www.aahsa.org

American Association of Retired Persons (AARP)
601 E Street NW
Washington, DC 20049
1-800-424-3410
web site: http://www.aarp.org
(sponsors various community service programs and offers many free publications that deal with a variety of subjects related to older adult consumers)

American Red Cross
1621 N. Kent St
Arlington, VA 22209
1-703-248-4222 or 1-800-HELP-NOW
website: http://www.redcross.org

Children of Aging Parents
1609 Woodbourne Rd, Suite 302A
Levittown, PA 19057
1-800-227-7294

National Association of State Units on Aging (NASUA)
1225 I Street NW, Suite 725
Washington, DC 20005
1-202-898-2578
(call for your local Area Agencies on Aging, which can give you information on a variety of services in your area including housing, Medicaid, Medicare, transportation, etc.)

National Council of Senior Citizens
8403 Colesville Rd, Suite 1200
Silver Spring, MD 20910-3314
1-301-578-8800
web site: http://www.ncscinc.org
(offers a variety of benefits to members and supports housing programs, a senior-aide program, a nursing home information service and a department of consumer affairs)

United Way of America
701 N Fairfax St
Alexandria, VA 22314
1-703-836-7100
web site: http://www.unitedway.org

INFORMATION LINES

These information lines can provide you with current information over the phone, and many can send you written material. In some cases, you can be connected to local services. Most of these numbers are toll-free.

American Cancer Society's Cancer Response System
1-800-227-2345
web site: http://www.cancer.org

American Speech-Language-Hearing Association
1-800-638-8255
web site: http://www.asha.org

Asthma and Allergy Foundation of America
1-800-727-8462
web site: http://www.aafa.org

Cancer Information Service, National Cancer Institute
1-800-422-6237
web site: http://www.nci.nih.gov

Eldercare Locator
1-800-677-1116
web site: http://www.n4a.org

FDA Consumer Information Line
1-800-332-1088
web site: http://vm.cfsan.fda.gov

Hospice Helpline
1-800-658-8898

International Theos Foundation
1-412-471-7779 (information on local support groups for widows/widowers)

National Council on Alcoholism and Drug Dependence Hope Line
1-800-622-2255
web site: http://www.ncadd.org

National Drug Information Treatment and Routing Service
1-800-662-4357

National Eye Care Project Helpline
1-800-222-3937

National Hearing Aid Helpline
1-800-521-5247

National Herpes Hotline
1-919-361-8488

National HIV/AIDS Hotline, Centers for Disease Control and Prevention
1-800-342-2437

National Kidney Foundation Information Center
1-800-622-9010
web site: http://www.kidney.org

National STD Hotline, Centers for Disease Control and Prevention
1-800-227-8922
web site: http://209.193.161.12

National Stroke Association
1-800-787-6537
e-mail: info@stroke.org
web site: http://www.stroke.org

Smoking, Tobacco and Health Information Line, Centers for Disease Control and Prevention
1-800-232-1311

PERSONAL MEDICATIONS RECORD

Name _____

Date _____

A chart like this one can help you inform your doctors and pharmacists about all the medicines you're currently taking — both prescription and over-the-counter (OTC) — in order to avoid dangerous drug interactions and other problems. Simply photocopy this page, complete the record, and take it with you whenever you have a doctor's appointment or a prescription filled. It's also a good idea to regularly update this record every time you stop taking a medication or add a new one, and to give a recent copy to a close family member or trusted friend in case of an emergency (see *Being Prepared*, p. 12).

Name of medication/ prescription number	What it's for	Dosage: Amounts/times	Special directions	Notes (when you began taking, any side effects, etc.)

Drug allergies or other problem medications:

Index